A People's History of the United States
Volume I

Also by Howard Zinn

La Guardia in Congress

The Southern Mystique

SNCC: The New Abolitionists

New Deal Thought (editor)

Vietnam: The Logic of Withdrawal

Disobedience and Democracy

The Politics of History

The Pentagon Papers: Critical Essays
    (editor, with Noam Chomsky)

Postwar America

Justice in Everyday Life

Declarations of Independence:
    Cross-Examining American Ideology

Failure to Quit: Reflections of an Optimistic Historian

You Can't Be Neutral on a Moving Train

A People's History of the United States: The Wall Charts

A People's History of the United States:
    1492–Present, Revised and Updated Edition

A People's History of the United States

Volume I: American Beginnings to Reconstruction

Teaching Edition

Howard Zinn

Teaching materials by
Kathy Emery

THE NEW PRESS

NEW YORK
LONDON

© 1980, 1995, 1997, 2003 by Howard Zinn. Teaching materials © 1997 by Katherine Emery.
All rights reserved. No part of this book may be reproduced, in any form,
without written permission from the publisher.

Published in the United States by The New Press, New York, 2003
Distributed by W.W. Norton & Company, Inc., New York

ISBN 1-56584-724-5
CIP data available

The New Press was established in 1990 as a not-for-profit alternative to the large,
commercial publishing houses currently dominating the book publishing industry.
The New Press operates in the public interest rather than for private gain, and is committed
to publishing, in innovative ways, works of educational, cultural, and community value
that are often deemed insufficiently profitable.

The New Press
38 Greene Street, 4th floor
New York, NY 10013
www.thenewpress.com

In the United Kingdom:
6 Salem Road
London W2 4BU

Composition by dix!

Printed in the United States of America

10 9 8 7 6 5 4 3 2 1

To Noah
and his generation

Rise like lions after slumber
In unvanquishable number!
Shake your chains to earth, like dew
Which in sleep had fallen on you—
Ye are many, they are few!

PERCY BYSSHE SHELLEY

Why do you stand
    they were asked, and
        Why do you walk?

Because of the children, they said, and
    because of the heart, and
    because of the bread.

DANIEL BERRIGAN

Contents

Acknowledgments

To André Schiffrin and Ellen Reeves of the New Press, for imagining and undertaking this special edition.

To Kathy Emery, for her heroic work in enriching the book for high school students.

To my two original editors, for their incalculable help: Cynthia Merman of Harper & Row, and Roslyn Zinn.

To Rick Balkin, my literary agent, for provoking me to do the original "People's History."

To Hugh Van Dusen of HarperCollins, for wonderful help and support throughout the history of this book.

To *Akwesasne Notes*, Mohawk Nation, for the passage from Ila Abernathy's poem.

To Dodd, Mead, & Company, for the passage from "We Wear the Mask," from *The Complete Poems of Paul Laurence Dunbar*.

To Harper & Row, for "Incident," from *On These I Stand* by Countee Cullen. Copyright 1925 by Harper & Row, Publishers, Inc.; renewed 1953 by Ida M. Cullen.

Acknowledgments

To Alfred A. Knopf, Inc., for the passage from "I, Too," from *Selected Poems of Langston Hughes*.

To *The New Trail*, 1953 yearbook of the Phoenix Indian School, Phoenix, Arizona, for the poem "It Is Not!"

To Random House, Inc., for the passage from Langston Hughes's "Lenox Avenue Mural," from *The Panther and the Lash: Poems of Our Time*.

To Esta Seaton, for her poem "Her Life," which first appeared in *The Ethnic American Woman* by Edith Blicksilver, Kendall/Hunt Publishing Company, 1978.

To Warner Bros., for the excerpt from "Brother, Can You Spare a Dime?" Lyrics by Jay Gorney, music by E. Y. Harburg. © 1932 Warner Bros. Inc. Copyright Renewed. All rights reserved. Used by permission.

Introduction

Kathy Emery

In every year of my twenty years of teaching, I have been responsible
for teaching an American history survey course. This meant having to
deal with the issue of boring textbooks. When I chose to become a
teacher, I promised myself that, if nothing else, I would not bore my students. So I needed to discover a way in which my students could enjoy
learning. To accomplish this task, I began to expose my students to several points of view and then teach them the skills to pick and choose
among the different views. I wanted them to develop opinions about history that they cared about. For me, this involved teaching a process of
moral evaluation as well as rational analysis and explication of data. At
first, I used Blum's *The National Experience* for its detail.[1] But it was still
only one point of view and did not allow for the range of debate I was
looking for. So I began assigning a different textbook to each student.
This was an improvement over using only one interpretation of the past,
since the standard textbooks of American history differ somewhat in
their interpretations of events and selection of data.[2]

But after several years of experimentation with different textbooks, I
still was not satisfied with the results. The range of difference was still too
small to provoke the desired degree of controversy and thus interest in
the material. I tried to expand the interpretive continuum with Grob and
Billias's *Interpretations of American History*.[3] But I had to spend too much
time in the classroom dissecting each article so the students could understand the arguments and data. I was never able to make it to the twenti-

eth century by the end of the school year. Though I kept experimenting with a variety of secondary sources as supplements to the textbook, always looking for the perfect fit, it was only when I discovered Howard Zinn's *A People's History of the United States* that I found the solution to the problem I had posed to myself so many years earlier.

Zinn provides what no other textbook does: the human impact, the human cost of decisions made by politicians and businessmen. With other texts, I had been asking my students to evaluate these decisions as a way to develop critical thinking. But such an exercise was only partially successful—students could not challenge generalizations made in standard texts without a significant range of data at their disposal, and they needed this full range if they were to think for themselves, to have opinions that they cared about. With the data that Zinn provides, however, the range of interpretations is wide enough for students to really have a choice in what they believe and, then, in what they know.

How to Read This Book

Every teacher needs to develop his or her own style and method. But no style or method can be created in a vacuum. I have provided methodological suggestions from which you may pick and choose. At the end of each chapter there are "study guide" questions, and at the end of the book there are four appendices. Appendix A includes suggestions for teaching a group paragraph, a suggested system of assessment (i.e. giving grades), a commentary on the uses and abuses of extra credit, the role of geography in a history class, useful approaches to using the debate format in teaching content and critical thinking, and techniques for class discussion. Appendix B provides a specific example of how standard American history textbooks differ. Appendix C provides a highly selective and annotated list of additional resources. Zinn allows the teacher to help students raise questions that require further research. Appendix D is an idiosyncratic but intriguing introduction to Bloom's taxonomy.

The questions at the end of each chapter are of several kinds—some simply ask the reader to extract detail,[4] while others demand that students do more than accumulate knowledge and gain comprehension. They ask students to analyze the text, select relevant data, synthesize that data into an answer, and then evaluate the answer. The higher order questions provoke the most interesting discussions since they demand that students begin to attach meaning to the data and detail.[5]

In the years I have been using history to teach critical thinking, I have discovered that moving back and forth between the concrete and the abstract (inherent in both deductive and inductive thinking) is a skill that needs to be explicitly taught. A few students are "naturals," but most need to be shown how it is done and they need a great deal of practice doing it. Constantly asking students to define the terms[6] of their questions and statements is a crucial first step in developing this kind of thinking. Many of the questions after each chapter therefore ask the reader to define the terms Zinn uses or certain terms the historical actors used. Questions requiring analysis and synthesis require that the terms of the question be fully understood.

To illustrate this point let me examine one of the questions from the chapter on Reconstruction. I ask "After the Civil War, was the South reduced to colonial status?" Before a student even begins to look for an answer to this question, several of the terms need to be understood in a very concrete way, in particular the word "colonial." Depending on how one defines "colonial," the answer could be yes or it could be no. If the teacher and student share the same definition of "colonial" then the teacher is more likely to approve of the student's answer. To explicitly define the essential terms of a question avoids misunderstanding and ensures a greater likelihood of success by the student.

A teacher might use the above question for discussion in class, as a topic for a group paragraph, or as written homework. Regardless of the actual form of an assignment, the process of completing it needs to be taught (repeatedly and consistently throughout the year). Break the question down into its discrete terms. For example, "the South" —identify the states to which the question refers; "after the Civil War"—identify the time period during which the South's "status" is being assessed. Then tackle the thornier problem of defining "colonial." For this, a dictionary can be useful. But use historical precedents in tandem with the dictionary. The American states used to be English colonies. What was their status in relation to England? (A politically dependent territory used as a source of raw materials and a market for manufactured goods?). *Merriam Webster's Collegiate Dictionary* provides several choices of definitions for the word "colony." Which one best fits the historical context?

★ a body of people living in a new territory but retaining ties with the parent state

⋆ a group of people institutionalized away from others
⋆ a dependent area or people controlled, dominated, or
    exploited by a parent state?

Once the terms are defined so their applicability to a specified group of historical data is clear, students previously unable to complete the question on their own will now be able to do so.

There are a few questions I have asked herein to which Zinn does not provide the answer. For example, after Chapter 9 in question 26, I ask, "Was the Georgia legislature successful in expelling its black members?" The text indicates that the legislature made the attempt. We don't know if the attempt was, in fact, successful. This is what students sometimes call a "trick" question. But if one's goal is to empower students, this kind of question teaches students to read carefully.

Another skill introduced and reinforced by some of the chapter questions is that of being able to categorize data, for the purposes of then synthesizing it and evaluating economic, political, social, and cultural factors. Most standard texts keep discussion at the political level, and most students are thus not used to thinking in terms of economic and social causes and consequences. But an important component of critical thinking is establishing relationships.[7] Zinn's data and explanations provide a wonderful opportunity to teach students how to develop a socioeconomic analysis of political events. Zinn hopes that the development of such thinking about the past will lead to such thinking about the present. It does.

Notes

1. Blum, J., et al., *The National Experience*, Harcourt Brace Jovanovich, New York.

2. One of the most successful assignments emerged when I asked students to investigate what happened during Bacon's Rebellion (1676). See Appendix B for a bibliography of the textbooks I used, page references to passages covering the events surrounding Bacon's Rebellion, and the questions I used to provoke debate.

3. Grob, G., and Billias, G. A., *Interpretations of American History*, The Free Press, New York.

4. I use the word "detail" instead of "evidence" or "fact" very consciously. The distinction between an "interpretation" and a "fact" is a slippery one. To avoid having constantly to deal with what was fact and what was not in the classroom, I made distinctions with my students only in terms of levels of detail. I required them to support a topic sentence (a generalization) with the next level of detail, some of which could be considered fact while other kinds of detail were not considered fact but still qualified as evidence. This proved over the years to be a very practical choice of diction.

5. I borrowed these categories of questions from Bloom's taxonomy. Please refer to Appendix D for more details on the nature of the taxonomy.

6. "Define your terms" was a mantra I repeated often so my students would internalize it. Effective communication depends on the participants sharing the same definition of key terms. To ensure those definitions are shared, they need to be made explicit at the beginning of any argument or thesis presentation. A common mistake in developing an argument is changing the definitions of the terms in medias res; hence the need to make this process explicit.

7. Refer to Chapter 10 in John Dewey's *Democracy and Education* for an explanation of why "establishing relationships" is important.

A People's History of the United States
Volume I

Chapter 1

Columbus, the Indians, and Human Progress

Arawak men and women, naked, tawny, and full of wonder, emerged from their villages onto the island's beaches and swam out to get a closer look at the strange big boat. When Columbus and his sailors came ashore, carrying swords, speaking oddly, the Arawaks ran to greet them, brought them food, water, gifts. He later wrote of this in his log:

> They...brought us parrots and balls of cotton and spears and many other things, which they exchanged for the glass beads and hawks' bells. They willingly traded everything they owned.... They were well-built, with good bodies and handsome features.... They do not bear arms, and do not know them, for I showed them a sword, they took it by the edge and cut themselves out of ignorance. They have no iron. Their spears are made of cane.... They would make fine servants.... With fifty men we could subjugate them all and make them do whatever we want.

These Arawaks of the Bahama Islands were much like Indians on the mainland, who were remarkable (European observers were to say again and again) for their hospitality, their belief in sharing. These traits did not stand out in Renaissance Europe, dominated as it was by the religion of popes, the government of kings, the frenzy for money that marked Western civilization and its first messenger to the Americas, Christopher Columbus.

Columbus wrote:

3

As soon as I arrived in the Indies, on the first Indies, on the first Island which I found, I took some of the natives by force in order that they might learn and might give me information of whatever there is in these parts.

The information that Columbus wanted most was: Where is the gold? He had persuaded the king and queen of Spain to finance an expedition to the lands, the wealth, he expected would be on the other side of the Atlantic—the Indies and Asia, gold and spices. For, like other informed people of his time, he knew the world was round and that he could sail west in order to get to the Far East.

Spain was recently unified, one of the new modern nation-states, like France, England, and Portugal. Spain's population, mostly poor peasants, worked for the nobility, who were 2 percent of the population and owned 95 percent of the land. Spain had tied itself to the Catholic Church, expelled all the Jews, driven out the Moors. Like other states of the modern world, Spain sought gold, which was becoming the new mark of wealth, more useful than land because it could buy anything.

There was gold in Asia, it was thought, and certainly silks and spices, for Marco Polo and others had brought back marvelous things from their overland expeditions centuries before. Now that the Turks had conquered Constantinople and the eastern Mediterranean, and controlled the land routes to Asia, a sea route was needed. Portuguese sailors were working their way around the southern tip of Africa. Spain decided to gamble on a long sail across an unknown ocean.

In return for bringing back gold and spices, Ferdinand and Isabella promised Columbus 10 percent of the profits, governorship over new-found lands, and the fame that would go with a new title: Admiral of the Ocean Sea. He was a merchant's clerk from the Italian city of Genoa, part-time weaver (the son of a skilled weaver), and expert sailor. He set out with three sailing ships; the largest of which was the *Santa María*, perhaps one hundred feet long, and with thirty-nine crew members.

Columbus would never have made it to Asia, which was thousands of miles farther away than he had calculated, imagining a smaller world. He would have been doomed by that great expanse of sea. But he was lucky. One-fourth of the way there he came upon an unknown, uncharted land that lay between Europe and Asia—the Americas. It was early October 1492, thirty-three days since he and his crew had left the Canary Islands, off the Atlantic coast of Africa. Now they saw branches and sticks floating

4

in the water. They saw flocks of birds. These were signs of land. Then, on October 12, a sailor called Rodrigo saw the early morning moon shining on white sands, and cried out. It was an island in the Bahamas, the Caribbean sea. The first man to sight land was supposed to get a yearly pension of ten thousand maravedis for life, but Rodrigo never got it. Columbus claimed he had seen a light the evening before. He got the reward.

So, approaching land, they were met by the Arawak Indians, who swam out to greet them. The Arawaks lived in village communes, had a developed agriculture of corn, yams, cassava. They could spin and weave, but they had no horses or work animals. They had no iron, but they wore tiny gold ornaments in their ears.

This was to have enormous consequences: it led Columbus to take some of them aboard ship as prisoners because he insisted that they guide him to the source of the gold. He then sailed to what is now Cuba, then to Hispaniola (the island that today consists of Haiti and the Dominican Republic). There, bits of visible gold in the rivers, and a gold mask presented to Columbus by a local Indian chief, led to wild visions of gold fields.

On Hispaniola, out of timbers from the *Santa María*, which had run aground, Columbus built a fort, the first European military base in the Western Hemisphere. He called it Navidad (Christmas) and left thirty-nine crew members there, with instructions to find and store the gold. He took more Indian prisoners and put them aboard his two remaining ships. At one part of the island he got into a fight with Indians who refused to trade as many bows and arrows as he and his men wanted. Two Arawaks were run through with swords and bled to death. Then the *Niña* and the *Pinta* set sail for the Azores and Spain. When the weather turned cold, the Indian prisoners began to die.

Columbus's report to the royal court in Madrid was extravagant. He insisted he had reached Asia (it was Cuba) and an island off the coast of China (Hispaniola). His descriptions were part fact, part fiction:

> Hispaniola is a miracle. Mountains and hills, plains and pastures, are both fertile and beautiful...the harbors are unbelievably good and there are many wide rivers of which the majority contain gold.... There are many spices, and great mines of gold and other metals....

The Indians, Columbus reported, "are so naive and so free with their possessions that no one who has not witnessed them would believe it.

When you ask for something they have, they never say no. To the contrary, they offer to share with anyone...." He concluded his report by asking for a little help from their Majesties, and in return he would bring them from his next voyage "as much gold as they need...and as many slaves as they ask." He was full of religious talk: "Thus the eternal God, our Lord, gives victory to those who follow His way over apparent impossibilities."

Because of Columbus's exaggerated report and promises, his second expedition was given seventeen ships and more than twelve hundred men. The aim was clear: slaves and gold. They went from island to island in the Caribbean, taking Indians as captives. But as word spread of the Europeans' intent they found more and more empty villages. On Haiti, they found that the sailors left behind at Fort Navidad had been killed in a battle with the Indians, after they had roamed the island in gangs looking for gold, taking women and children as slaves for sex and labor.

Now, from his base on Haiti, Columbus sent expedition after expedition into the interior. They found no gold fields, but had to fill up the ships returning to Spain with some kind of dividend. In the year 1495, they went on a great slave raid, rounded up fifteen hundred Arawak men, women, and children, put them in pens guarded by Spaniards and dogs, then picked the five hundred best specimens to load onto ships. Of those five hundred, two hundred died en route. The rest arrived alive in Spain and were put up for sale by the archdeacon of the town, who reported that, although the slaves were "naked as the day they were born," they showed "no more embarrassment than animals." Columbus later wrote: "Let us in the name of the Holy Trinity go on sending all the slaves that can be sold."

But too many of the slaves died in captivity. And so Columbus, desperate to pay back dividends to those who had invested, had to make good his promise to fill the ships with gold. In the province of Cicao on Haiti, where he and his men imagined huge gold fields to exist, they ordered all persons fourteen years or older to collect a certain quantity of gold every three months. When they brought it, they were given copper tokens to hang around their necks. Indians found without a copper token had their hands cut off and bled to death.

The Indians had been given an impossible task. The only gold around was bits of dust garnered from the streams. So they fled, were hunted down with dogs, and were killed.

Trying to put together an army of resistance, the Arawaks faced Spaniards who had armor, muskets, swords, and horses. When the Spaniards took prisoners, they hanged them or burned them to death.

Among the Arawaks, mass suicides began, with cassava poison. Infants were killed to "save" them from the Spaniards. In two years, through murder, mutilation, or suicide, half of the two hundred fifty thousand Indians on Haiti were dead.

When it became clear that there was no gold left, the Indians were taken as slave labor on huge estates, known later as *encomiendas*. They were worked at a ferocious pace, and died by the thousands. By the year 1515, there were perhaps fifty thousand Indians left. By 1550, there were five hundred. A report of the year 1650 shows none of the original Arawaks or their descendants left on the island.

The chief source—and, on many matters, the only source—of information about what happened on the islands after Columbus came is Bartolomé de las Casas, who, as a young priest, participated in the conquest of Cuba. For a time he owned a plantation on which Indian slaves worked, but he gave that up and became a vehement critic of Spanish cruelty. Las Casas transcribed Columbus's journal and, in his fifties, began a multivolume *History of the Indies*.

Women in Indian society were treated so well as to startle the Spaniards. Las Casas describes sex relations:

> Marriage laws are nonexistent: men and women alike choose their mates and leave them as they please, without offense, jealousy or anger. They multiply in great abundance; pregnant women work to the last minute and give birth almost painlessly; up the next day, they bathe in the river and are as clean and healthy as before giving birth. If they tire of their men, they give themselves abortions with herbs that force stillbirths, covering their shameful parts with leaves or cotton cloth; although on the whole, Indian men and women look upon total nakedness with as much casualness as we look upon a man's head or at his hands.

The Indians, Las Casas says, "put no value on gold and other precious things. They lack all manner of commerce, neither buying nor selling, and rely exclusively on their natural environment for maintenance. They are extremely generous with their possessions and by the same token covet the possessions of their friends and expect the same degree of liberality...."

Las Casas tells about the treatment of the Indians by the Spaniards.

> Endless testimonies...prove the mild and pacific temperament of the natives.... But our work was to exasperate, ravage, kill, mangle and destroy; small wonder, then, if they tried to kill one of us now and then.... The admiral, it is true, was blind as those who came after him,

and he was so anxious to please the King that he committed irreparable crimes against the Indians....

Total control led to total cruelty. The Spaniards "thought nothing of knifing Indians by tens and twenties and of cutting slices off them to test the sharpness of their blades." Las Casas tells how "two of these so-called Christians met two Indian boys one day, each carrying a parrot; they took the parrots and for fun beheaded the boys."

While the native men were sent many miles away to the mines, their wives remained to work the soil, forced into the excruciating job of digging and making thousands of hills for cassava plants.

> Thus husbands and wives were together only once every eight or ten months and when they met they were so exhausted and depressed on both sides...they ceased to procreate. As for the newly born, they died early because their mothers, overworked and famished, had no milk to nurse them, and for this reason, while I was in Cuba, 7,000 children died in three months. Some mothers even drowned their babies from sheer desperation.... In this way, husbands died in the mines, wives died at work, and children died from lack of milk...and in a short time this land which was so great, so powerful and fertile...was depopulated.... My eyes have seen these acts so foreign to human nature, and now I tremble as I write....

When he arrived on Hispaniola in 1508, Las Casas says, "there were 60,000 people living on this island, including the Indians; so that from 1494 to 1508, over three million people had perished from war, slavery, and the mines. Who in future generations will believe this?"

Thus began the history, five hundred years ago, of the European invasion of the Indian settlements in the Americas, a history of conquest, slavery, and death. But in the history books given to children in the United States, for generation after generation, it all starts with heroic adventure—there is no bloodshed—and Columbus Day is a celebration. Only in recent years do we see droplets of change.

Past the elementary and high schools, there have been only occasional hints of something else. Samuel Eliot Morison, the Harvard historian, was the most distinguished writer on Columbus, the author of a multivolume biography, and was himself a sailor who retraced Columbus's route across the Atlantic. In his popular book *Christopher Columbus, Mariner*, written in 1954, he tells about the enslavement and the killing: "The cruel policy initiated by Columbus and pursued by his successors resulted in complete genocide."

That is on one page, buried halfway into the telling of a grand romance. In the book's last paragraph, Morison sums up his view of Columbus:

He had his faults and his defects, but they were largely the defects of the qualities that made him great—his indomitable will, his superb faith in God and in his own mission as the Christ-bearer to lands beyond the seas, his stubborn persistence despite neglect, poverty and discouragement. But there was no flaw, no dark side to the most outstanding and essential of all his qualities—his seamanship.

One can lie outright about the past. Or one can omit facts which might lead to unacceptable conclusions. Morison does neither. He refuses to lie about Columbus. He does not omit the story of mass murder; indeed he describes it with the harshest word one can use: genocide.

But he does something else. He mentions the truth quickly and goes on to other things more important to him. Outright lying or quiet omission takes the risk of discovery, which, when made, might arouse the reader to rebel against the writer. To state the facts, however, and then to bury them in a mass of other information is to say to the reader with a certain infectious calm: yes, mass murder took place, but it's not that important—it should weigh very little in our final judgments; it should affect very little what we do in the world.

It is true that the historian cannot avoid emphasis of some facts and not of others. This is as natural to him as to the mapmaker, who, in order to produce a usable drawing for practical purposes, must first flatten and distort the shape of the earth, then choose out of the bewildering mass of geographic information those things needed for the purpose of this or that particular map.

My argument cannot be against selection, simplification, or emphasis, which are inevitable for both cartographers and historians. But the mapmaker's distortion is a technical necessity for a common purpose shared by all people who need maps. The historian's distortion is more than technical, it is ideological; it is released into a world of contending interests, where any chosen emphasis supports (whether the historian means to or not) some kind of interest, whether economic or political or racial or national or sexual.

Furthermore, this ideological interest is not openly expressed in the way a mapmaker's technical interest is obvious ("This is a Mercator projection for long-range navigation—for short-range, you'd better use a different projection"). No, it is presented as if all readers of history had a common interest that historians serve to the best of their ability.

To emphasize the heroism of Columbus and his successors as navigators and discoverers, and to deemphasize their genocide, is not a technical necessity but an ideological choice. It serves—unwittingly—to justify what was done.

My point is not that we must, in telling history, accuse, judge, condemn Columbus *in absentia*. It is too late for that; it would be a useless scholarly exercise in morality. But the easy acceptance of atrocities as a deplorable but necessary price to pay for progress (Hiroshima and Vietnam, to save Western civilization; Kronstadt and Hungary, to save socialism; nuclear proliferation, to save us all)—that is still with us. One reason these atrocities are still with us is that we have learned to bury them in a mass of other facts, as radioactive wastes are buried in containers in the earth.

The treatment of heroes (Columbus) and their victims (the Arawaks)—the quiet acceptance of conquest and murder in the name of progress—is only one aspect of a certain approach to history, in which the past is told from the point of view of governments, conquerors, diplomats, leaders. It is as if they, like Columbus, deserve universal acceptance, as if they—the Founding Fathers, Jackson, Lincoln, Wilson, Roosevelt, Kennedy, the leading members of Congress, the famous justices of the Supreme Court—represent the nation as a whole. The pretense is that there really is such a thing as "the United States," subject to occasional conflicts and quarrels, but fundamentally a community of people with common interests. It is as if there really is a "national interest" represented in the Constitution, in territorial expansion, in the laws passed by Congress, the decisions of the courts, the development of capitalism, the culture of education, and the mass media.

"History is the memory of states," wrote Henry Kissinger in his first book, *A World Restored*, in which he proceeded to tell the history of nineteenth-century Europe from the viewpoint of the leaders of Austria and England, ignoring the millions who suffered from those statesmen's policies. From his standpoint, the "peace" that Europe had before the French Revolution was "restored" by the diplomacy of a few national leaders. But for factory workers in England, farmers in France, people of color in Asia and Africa, women and children everywhere except in the upper classes, it was a world of conquest, violence, hunger, and exploitation—a world not restored but disintegrated.

My viewpoint, in telling the history of the United States, is different: that we must not accept the memory of states as our own. Nations are not communities and never have been. The history of any country, presented as the history of a family, conceals fierce conflicts of interest (sometimes exploding, most often repressed) between conquerors and conquered, masters and slaves, capitalists and workers, dominators and dominated in race and sex. And in such a world of conflict, a world of victims and executioners, it is the job of thinking people, as Albert Camus suggested, not to be on the side of the executioners.

Thus, in that inevitable taking of sides which comes from selection and emphasis in history, I prefer to try to tell the story of the discovery of America from the viewpoint of the Arawaks, of the Constitution from the standpoint of the slaves, of Andrew Jackson as seen by the Cherokees, of the Civil War as seen by the New York Irish, of the Mexican War as seen by the deserting soldiers of Scott's army, of the rise of industrialism as seen by the young women in the Lowell textile mills, of the Spanish-American War as seen by the Cubans, the conquest of the Philippines as seen by black soldiers on Luzon, the Gilded Age as seen by southern farmers, the First World War as seen by socialists, the Second World War as seen by pacifists, the New Deal as seen by blacks in Harlem, the postwar American empire as seen by peons in Latin America. And so on, to the limited extent that any one person, however he or she strains, can "see" history from the standpoint of others.

My point is not to grieve for the victims and denounce the executioners. Those tears, that anger, cast into the past, deplete our moral energy for the present. And the lines are not always clear. In the long run, the oppressor is also a victim. In the short run (and so far, human history has consisted only of short runs), the victims, themselves desperate and tainted with the culture that oppresses them, often turn on other victims.

Still, understanding the complexities, this book will be skeptical of governments and their attempts, through politics and culture, to ensnare ordinary people in a giant web of nationhood pretending to a common interest. I will try not to overlook the cruelties that victims inflict on one another as they are jammed together in the boxcars of the system. I don't want to romanticize them. But I do remember (in rough paraphrase) a statement I once read: "The cry of the poor is not always just, but if you don't listen to it, you will never know what justice is."

I don't want to invent victories for people's movements. But to think that history writing must aim simply to recapitulate the failures that dominate the past is to make historians collaborators in an endless cycle of defeat. If history is to be creative, to anticipate a possible future without denying the past, it should, I believe, emphasize new possibilities by disclosing those hidden episodes of the past when, even if in brief flashes, people showed their ability to resist, to join together, occasionally to win. I am supposing, or perhaps only hoping, that our future may be found in the past's fugitive moments of compassion rather than in its solid centuries of warfare.

That, being as blunt as I can, is my approach to the history of the United States. The reader may as well know that before going on.

What Columbus did to the Arawaks of the Bahamas, Cortés did to the Aztecs of Mexico, Pizarro to the Incas of Peru, and the English settlers of Virginia and Massachusetts to the Powhatans and the Pequots.

It seems there was a frenzy in the early capitalist states of Europe for gold, for slaves, for products of the soil, to pay the bondholders and stockholders of the expeditions, to finance the monarchical bureaucracies rising in Western Europe, to spur the growth of the new money economy rising out of feudalism, to participate in what Karl Marx would later call "the primitive accumulation of capital." These were the violent beginnings of an intricate system of technology, business, politics, and culture that would dominate the world for the next five centuries.

Jamestown, Virginia, the first permanent English setlement in the Americas, was set up inside the territory of an Indian confederacy, led by the chief, Powhatan. Powhatan watched the English settle on his people's land, but did not attack, maintaining a posture of coolness. When the English were going through their "starving time" in the winter of 1610, some of them ran off to join the Indians, where they would at least be fed. When the summer came, the governor of the colony sent a messenger to ask Powhatan to return the runaways, whereupon Powhatan, according to the English account, replied with "noe other than prowde and disdaynefull Answers." Some soldiers were therefore sent out "to take Revendge." They fell upon an Indian settlement, killed fifteen or sixteen Indians, burned the houses, cut down the corn growing around the village, took the queen of the tribe and her children into boats, then ended up throwing the children overboard "and shoteinge owtt their Braynes in the water." The queen was later taken off and stabbed to death.

Twelve years later, the Indians, alarmed as the English settlements kept growing in numbers, apparently decided to try to wipe them out for good. They went on a rampage and massacred 347 men, women, and children. From then on it was total war.

Not able to enslave the Indians, and not able to live with them, the English decided to exterminate them. According to historian Edmund Morgan, "Within two or three years of the massacre the English had avenged the deaths of that day many times over."

In that first year of the white man in Virginia, 1607, Powhatan had addressed a plea to John Smith that turned out prophetic. How authentic it is may be in doubt, but it is so much like so many Indian statements that it may be taken as, if not the rough letter of that first plea, the exact spirit of it:

> I have seen two generations of my people die.... I know the difference between peace and war better than any man in my country. Why will you take by force what you may have quietly by love? Why will you destroy us who supply you with food? What can you get by war? Why are you jealous of us? We are unarmed, and willing to give you what you ask, if you come in a friendly manner, and not so simple as not to know that it is much better to eat good meat, sleep comfortably, live quietly with my wives and children, laugh and be merry with the English, and trade for their copper and hatchets, than to run away from them, and to lie cold in the woods, feed on acorns, roots and such trash, and be so hunted that I can neither eat nor sleep.

When the Pilgrims came to New England, they too were coming not to vacant land but to territory inhabited by tribes of Indians.

The Pequot Indians occupied what is now southern Connecticut and Rhode Island. The Puritans wanted them out of the way; they wanted their land. So, the war with the Pequots began. Massacres took place on both sides. The English developed a tactic of warfare used earlier by Cortés and later, in the twentieth century, even more systematically: deliberate attacks on noncombatants for the purpose of terrorizing the enemy.

So the English set fire to the wigwams of villages. William Bradford, in his *History of the Plymouth Plantation* written at the time, describes John Mason's raid on the Pequot village:

> Those that scaped the fire were slaine with the sword; some hewed to peeces, others rune throw with their rapiers, so as they were quickly dispatchte, and very few escaped. It was conceived they thus destroyed about 400 at this time. It was a fearful sight to see them thus frying in the fyer.

A footnote in Virgil Vogel's book *This Land Was Ours* (1972) says: "The official figure on the number of Pequots now in Connecticut is twenty-one persons."

For a while, the English tried softer tactics. But ultimately, it was back to annihilation. The Indian population of ten million that lived north of Mexico when Columbus came would ultimately be reduced to less than a million. Huge numbers of Indians would die from diseases introduced by the whites.

Behind the English invasion of North America, behind their massacre of Indians, their deception, their brutality, was that special powerful drive born in civilizations based on private property. It was a morally ambiguous drive; the need for space, for land, was a real human need. But in conditions of scarcity, in a barbarous epoch of history ruled by competition, this human need was transformed into the murder of whole peoples.

Was all this bloodshed and deceit—from Columbus to Cortés, Pizarro, the Puritans—a necessity for the human race to progress from savagery to civilization?

If there *are* necessary sacrifices to be made for human progress, is it not essential to hold to the principle that those to be sacrificed must make the decision themselves? We can all decide to give up something of ours, but do we have the right to throw into the pyre the children of others, or even our own children, for a progress that is not nearly as clear or present as sickness or health, life or death?

Beyond all that, how certain are we that what was destroyed was inferior? Who were these people who came out on the beach and swam to bring presents to Columbus and his crew, who watched Cortés and Pizarro ride through their countryside, who peered out of the forests at the first white settlers of Virginia and Massachusetts?

Columbus called them Indians, because he miscalculated the size of the earth. In this book we too call them Indians, with some reluctance, because it happens too often that people are saddled with names given them by their conquerors.

Widely dispersed over the great land mass of the Americas, they numbered approximately seventy-five million people by the time Columbus came, perhaps twenty-five million in North America. Responding to the different environments of soil and climate, they developed hundreds of different tribal cultures, perhaps two thousand different languages. They perfected the art of agriculture and figured out how to grow maize (corn), which cannot grow by itself and must be planted, cultivated, fertilized, harvested, husked, and shelled. They ingeniously developed a variety of other vegetables and fruits, as well as peanuts and chocolate and tobacco and rubber.

On their own, the Indians were engaged in the great agricultural revolution that other peoples in Asia, Europe, and Africa were going through about the same time.

While many of the tribes remained nomadic hunters and food gatherers in wandering, egalitarian communes, others began to live in more settled communities where there was more food, larger populations, more divisions of labor among men and women, more surplus to feed chiefs and priests, more leisure time for artistic and social work, for building houses.

From the Adirondacks to the Great Lakes, in what is now Pennsylvania and upper New York, lived the most powerful of the northeastern tribes, the League of the Iroquois. In the villages of the Iroquois, land was owned in common and worked in common. Hunting was done together, and the catch was divided among the members of the village.

Women were important and respected in Iroquois society. The women tended the crops and took general charge of village affairs while the men were always hunting or fishing. As Gary B. Nash notes in his fascinating study of early America, *Red, White, and Black*, "Thus power was shared between the sexes and the European idea of male dominancy and female subordination in all things was conspicuously absent in Iroquois society."

Children in Iroquois society, while taught the cultural heritage of their people and solidarity with the tribe, were also taught to be independent, not to submit to overbearing authority.

All of this was in sharp contrast to European values as brought over by the first colonists, a society of rich and poor, controlled by priests, by governors, by male heads of families. Gary Nash describes Iroquois culture:

No laws and ordinances, sheriffs and constables, judges and juries, or courts or jails—the apparatus of authority in European societies— were to be found in the northeast woodlands prior to European arrival. Yet boundaries of acceptable behavior were firmly set. Though priding themselves on the autonomous individual, the Iroquois maintained a strict sense of right and wrong.... He who stole another's food or acted invalourously in war was "shamed" by his people and ostracized from their company until he had atoned for his actions and demonstrated to their satisfaction that he had morally purified himself.

Not only the Iroquois but other Indian tribes behaved the same way.

So, Columbus and his successors were not coming into an empty wilderness, but into a world which in some places was as densely populated as Europe itself, where the culture was complex, where human relations were more egalitarian than in Europe, and where the relations among men, women, children, and nature were more beautifully worked out than perhaps any place in the world.

They were people without a written language, but with their own laws, their poetry, their history kept in memory and passed on, in an oral vocabulary more complex than Europe's, accompanied by song, dance, and ceremonial drama. They paid careful attention to the development of personality, intensity of will, independence and flexibility, passion and potency, to their partnership with one another and with nature.

John Collier, an American scholar who lived among Indians in the 1920s and 1930s in the American Southwest, said of their spirit: "Could we make it our own, there would be an eternally inexhaustible earth and a forever lasting peace."

Perhaps there is some romantic mythology in that. But even allowing for the imperfection of myths, it is enough to make us question, for that time and ours, the excuse of progress in the annihilation of races, and the telling of history from the standpoint of the conquerors and leaders of Western civilization.

Exercises

1. Before reading the chapter: Write down all that you think you know about Columbus, including myth as well as reality. Examples: Columbus sailed in 1492; people believed the earth was round; Columbus sailed on three ships.

    While or after reading the chapter: Write down passages in the text that either support or contradict each item generated by the assignment above, then identify those events and actions discussed in the text that had not been part of your thinking about Columbus originally.

2. After reading the first chapter, choose two adjectives that describe Columbus, two that describe the Spanish, two that describe the English, two for the Arawaks, and two for the Powhatans. You may use the same adjective for more than one group. *Do not feel confined to using only the adjectives listed.*

CRUEL	NAIVE	HONEST	GREEDY
GENEROUS	KIND	BRAVE	IGNORANT
CIVILIZED	ADVENTUROUS	PRIMITIVE	INFERIOR
PRACTICAL	INTELLIGENT	HEROIC	THOUGHTFUL
ARROGANT	LAZY	DEDICATED	

For each of the adjectives you choose:

    a. Write down the definition that best describes the applicable group.

    b. Write ten short sentences using the selected adjectives—one adjective for each sentence. For example:

      ★ The Spanish were generous.

      ★ Columbus was brave.

      ★ The Arawaks were generous.

    c. Then look for details/facts in the text that you think illustrate the definitions of the selected adjectives.

Important: In defining a word, you cannot use any part of that word in the definition. Furthermore, useful definitions for this exercise will be ones that do not employ the opposite of the word. An example of a useless definition would be: primitive = not civilized. The problem here is what does "civilized" mean? Not primitive? If you have a dictionary that gives you such circular definitions, go find a more detailed dictionary or use a thesaurus.

3. Choose an infinitive to finish each of the sentences below.

    a. Use a dictionary to define the infinitive.

    b. Look for details/facts in the text that you think illustrate the definitions.

    The purpose of Columbus's voyage(s) was...

    The result of Columbus's voyage(s) was...

Some options: to civilize, to explore, to exploit, to conquer, to establish trade, to discover, to Christianize, to destroy, to convert, to destroy...

4. Write down the five most important things Zinn says about Columbus (include page numbers). Write down the two most important things he says about the writing of history.

Compare your list with a classmate(s). Why are your lists different? What are the criteria you each used in making your choices? [This is a real brainteaser.]

5. Was Columbus responsible for the behavior of his men?

    a. Identify what the soldiers' behaviors were.

    b. For each act, identify what Columbus could or could not have done to alter that behavior.

6. Compare Columbus's log entries with Las Casas's journal entries.

    a. Identify differences and similarities (e.g., how each describes the Arawaks).

    b. Identify topics the other did not discuss.

    c. What accounts for the differences? the similarities (their personalities, their goals, their job functions, their status in relation to the other Spaniards)?

7. Write a two-page story of Columbus that you would want read to a third-grade class at the point when the students are first being introduced to Columbus.

8. For each of the suggested phrases below that completes the sentence, identify the passage(s) in the book that either supports or challenges each assertion. Identify irrelevant phrases with NP (no passage applies). When choosing a relevant passage, note its page number and whether the passage supports, challenges, or doesn't apply.

    Zinn thinks that Morison....

    a. omits the truth.

    b. believes that all readers share a common interest.

    c. writes the kind of history that allows atrocities to continue to be committed.

    d. is critical of Columbus.

    e. idealizes Columbus.

    f. is as accurate as a mapmaker.

g. allows his opinions of Columbus to select out only the positive.

h. buries the negative facts with positive facts.

i. omits the bloodshed.

9. If communities share common interests, did Columbus and Las Casas belong to the same community? If so, what are their common interests ? (What was Columbus in the Caribbean for? Las Casas?) If not, what interests separate them into different communities? Did Las Casas have more in common with the Arawaks than he did with Columbus?

10. Zinn argues (p. 10) that most history texts pretend that there is such a thing as "The United States"—a community of people with common interests.

    a. What are the "communities" that Zinn identifies? What "interests" do you think these groups have in common? What "interests" do they not share? What "interests" of one group might be in opposition to an "interest" of another group?

    b. Identify the community that you belong to, your community's interests, and other communities that share your interests, as well as those communities that do not share or oppose your interests (possibilities: students, teachers, administrators, male, female, young, old, ethnic and racial identities, neighborhood, city, suburb). Do the policies of the United States government favor some communities over others?

11. Brainstorming from details:

    a. Choose a detailed description of an event from the text.

    b. Then write down a series of questions that knowledge of the event may enable one to answer.

    c. Choose two of the questions and answer them.

Example

    a. *detailed description of an event from the text:* on page 5, Columbus "got into a fight with Indians who refused to trade as many bows and arrows as he and his men wanted. Two [Indians] were run through with swords and bled to death."

b. *a series of questions that knowledge of the above event may enable one to answer:* What does the above event reveal about Columbus's personality? about the purpose of the voyage? about Spanish culture? about Arawak culture? about the comparative military strength of the Spanish and Arawaks?

c. *answers to two of the questions above:* The Spanish had military superiority—swords versus bows and arrows. Columbus wanted to dictate the terms of trade.

12. Hollywood Movies: Fact or Fiction? Much controversy has surrounded the making of the films *Mississippi Burning* and *JFK*. Many critics complain that when Americans see these films, they will believe falsely that the events and circumstances dramatized in these films accurately represent what happened during the periods in question. And for unstated reasons, this is wrong. The Left has criticized *Mississippi Burning* for leaving the impression that the FBI was honestly trying to help the civil rights advocates when "in fact" the FBI was aiding the KKK. Most of the mainstream media excoriated *JFK* for implying that John Kennedy's assassination was engineered by Lyndon Johnson. Several questions are begged by this criticism. Do fictional movies (as opposed to documentaries) have a responsibility to reflect history accurately? Or do they have poetic license with reality, as art claims to have, in order to make a point about universal truth? But, more to the point with regard to Columbus, is "history" accurate? If films are supposed to convey "accurate" history, who decides what is the official version of the past? In order to explore this issue in more depth:

    a. Watch a movie made about Columbus.

    b. Compare the content of the movie with Zinn's chapter about Columbus in addition to any other historical sources you may wish to consult (the more the better).

Possible points comparison: reasons for the voyage, Columbus's first perceptions of the native inhabitants, Spanish treatment of the native inhabitants, success of the voyage(s), failures of the voyage(s), degree of Columbus's navigational skills, Columbus's leadership skills, the nature of the reception of Columbus by the native inhabitants, the portrayal of native inhabitants.

c. Respond to any of the questions raised in the introduction to this assignment above. For example:

- ★ Is the movie historically accurate?
- ★ Is the movie good art?
- ★ Does the movie have a thesis?
- ★ Does it address a universal truth?
- ★ What is the difference between history and art?
- ★ Is the difference merely one of style?

Chapter 2

Drawing the Color Line

There is not a country in world history in which racism has been more important, for so long a time, as the United States. And the problem of "the color line," as W. E. B. Du Bois put it, is still with us. So it is more than a purely historical question to ask: How did it start?—and an even more urgent question: How might it end? Or, to put it differently: Is it possible for whites and blacks to live together without hatred?

If history can help answer these questions, then the beginnings of slavery in North America—a continent where we can trace the coming of the first whites and the first blacks—might supply at least a few clues.

In the English colonies, slavery developed quickly into a regular institution, into the normal labor relation of blacks to whites. With it developed that special racial feeling—whether hatred, or contempt, or pity, or patronization—that accompanied the inferior position of blacks in America for the next 350 years: that combination of inferior status and derogatory thought we call racism.

Everything in the experience of the first white settlers acted as a pressure for the enslavement of blacks.

The Virginians of 1619 were desperate for labor, to grow enough food to stay alive. Among them were survivors from the winter of 1609–10, the "starving time," when, crazed for want of food, they roamed the woods for nuts and berries, dug up graves to eat the corpses, and died in batches until five hundred colonists were reduced to sixty.

They needed labor, to grow corn for subsistence, to grow tobacco for export. They had just learned from the Indians how to grow tobacco, and in 1617 they sent off the first cargo to England. Finding that, like all pleasurable drugs tainted with moral disapproval, it brought a high price, the planters, despite their high religious talk, were not going to ask questions about something so profitable.

They couldn't force Indians to work for them, as Columbus had done. They were outnumbered, and while, with superior firearms, they could massacre Indians, they would face massacre in return. They could not capture them and keep them enslaved; the Indians were tough, resourceful, defiant, and at home in these woods, as the transplanted Englishmen were not.

There may have been a kind of frustrated rage at their own ineptitude, at the Indian superiority at taking care of themselves, that made the Virginians especially ready to become the masters of slaves. Edmund Morgan imagines their mood as he writes in his book *American Slavery, American Freedom*:

> If you were a colonist, you knew that your technology was superior to the Indians'. You knew that you were civilized, and they were savages.... But your superior technology had proved insufficient to extract anything. The Indians, keeping to themselves, laughed at your superior methods and lived from the land more abundantly and with less labor than you did.... And when your own people started deserting in order to live with them, it was too much.... So you killed the Indians, tortured them, burned their villages, burned their cornfields. It proved your superiority, in spite of your failures. And you gave similar treatment to any of your own people who succumbed to their savage ways of life. But you still did not grow much corn.

Black slaves were the answer. And it was natural to consider imported blacks as slaves, even if the institution of slavery would not be regularized and legalized for several decades. Because, by 1619, a million blacks had already been brought from Africa to South America and the Caribbean, to the Portuguese and Spanish colonies, to work as slaves. Fifty years before Columbus, the Portuguese took ten African blacks to Lisbon: this was the start of a regular trade in slaves. African blacks had been stamped as slave labor for a hundred years. So it would have been strange if those twenty blacks, who had been forcibly transported to Jamestown and sold as objects to settlers anxious for a steadfast source of labor, were considered as anything but slaves.

Their helplessness made enslavement easier. The Indians were on their own land. The whites were in their own European culture. The blacks had been torn from their land and culture, forced into a situation where the heritage of language, dress, custom, and family relations was bit by bit obliterated except for the remnants that blacks could hold on to by sheer, extraordinary persistence.

Was their culture inferior—and so subject to easy destruction? The African civilization was as advanced in its own way as that of Europe. In certain ways, it was more admirable; but it also included cruelties, hierarchical privilege, and the readiness to sacrifice human lives for religion or profit. It was a civilization of one hundred million people, using iron implements and skilled in farming. It had large urban centers and remarkable achievements in weaving, ceramics, and sculpture.

European travelers in the sixteenth century were impressed with the African kingdoms of Timbuktu and Mali, already stable and organized at a time when European states were just beginning to develop into modern nations.

Africa had a kind of feudalism, like Europe, based on agriculture, with hierarchies of lords and vassals. But African feudalism did not come, as did Europe's, out of the slave societies of Greece and Rome, which had destroyed ancient tribal life. In Africa, tribal life was still powerful, and some of its better features—a communal spirit, more kindness in law and punishment—still existed. And because the lords did not have the weapons that European lords had, they could not command obedience as easily.

In England, even as late as 1740, a child could be hanged for stealing a rag of cotton. But in the Congo, communal life persisted, the idea of private property was a strange one, and thefts were punished with fines or various degrees of servitude. A Congolese leader, told of the Portuguese legal codes, asked a Portuguese once, teasingly: "What is the penalty in Portugal for anyone who puts his feet on the ground?"

Slavery existed in the African states, and it was sometimes used by Europeans to justify their own slave trade. But, as Basil Davidson points out in *The African Slave Trade*, the "slaves" of Africa were more like the serfs of Europe—in other words, like most of the population of Europe. It was a harsh servitude, but they had rights that the slaves brought to America did not have, and they were "altogether different from the human cattle of the slave ships and the American plantations."

African slavery lacked two elements that made American slavery the most cruel form of slavery in history: the frenzy for limitless profit that comes from capitalistic agriculture; the reduction of the slave to less than human status by the use of racial hatred, with that relentless clarity based on color, where white was master, black was slave.

In fact, it was because they came from a settled culture, of tribal customs and family ties, of communal life and traditional ritual, that African blacks found themselves especially helpless when removed from this. They were captured in the interior (frequently by blacks caught up in the slave trade themselves), sold on the coast, then shoved into pens with blacks of other tribes, often speaking different languages.

The conditions of capture and sale were crushing affirmations to the black African of his helplessness in the face of superior force. The marches to the coast, sometimes for a thousand miles, with people shackled around the neck, under whip and gun, were death marches, in which two of every five blacks died. On the coast, they were kept in cages until they were picked and sold.

Then they were packed aboard the slave ships, in spaces not much bigger than coffins, chained together in the dark, wet slime of the ship's bottom, choking in the stench of their own excrement.

On one occasion, hearing a great noise from belowdecks where the blacks were chained together, the sailors opened the hatches and found the slaves in different stages of suffocation, many dead, some having killed others in desperate attempts to breathe. Slaves often jumped overboard to drown rather than continue their suffering. To one observer a slave deck was "so covered with blood and mucus that it resembled a slaughterhouse."

Under these conditions, perhaps one of every three blacks transported overseas died, but the huge profits (often double the investment on one trip) made it worthwhile for the slave trader, and so the blacks were packed into the holds like fish.

First the Dutch, then the English, dominated the slave trade. (By 1795 Liverpool had more than a hundred ships carrying slaves and accounted for half of all the European slave trade.) Some Americans in New England entered the business, and in 1637 the first American slave ship, the *Desire*, sailed from Marblehead, Massachusetts. Its holds were partitioned into racks, two feet by six feet, with leg irons and bars.

By 1800, ten to fifteen million blacks had been transported as slaves to the Americas, representing perhaps one-third of those originally seized in Africa. It is roughly estimated that Africa lost fifty million human beings to death and slavery in those centuries we call the beginnings of modern Western civilization, at the hands of slave traders and plantation owners in western Europe and America, the countries deemed the most advanced in the world.

With all of this—the desperation of the Jamestown settlers for labor, the impossibility of using Indians and the difficulty of using whites, the availability of blacks offered in greater and greater numbers by profit-seeking dealers in human flesh, and with such blacks possible to control because they had just gone through an ordeal that, if it did not kill them, must have left them in a state of psychic and physical helplessness—is it any wonder that such blacks were ripe for enslavement?

And under these conditions, even if some blacks might have been considered servants, would blacks be treated the same as white servants?

The evidence, from the court records of colonial Virginia, shows that in 1630 a white man named Hugh Davis was ordered "to be soundly whipt...for abusing himself...by defiling his body in lying with a Negro." Ten years later, six servants and "a negro of Mr. Reynolds" started to run away. While the whites received lighter sentences, "Emanuel the Negro to receive thirty stripes and to be burnt in the cheek with the letter *R*, and to work in shackle one year or more as his master shall see cause."

This unequal treatment, this developing combination of contempt and oppression, feeling and action, which we call "racism"—was this the result of a "natural" antipathy of white against black? If racism can't be shown to be natural, then it is the result of certain conditions, and we are impelled to eliminate those conditions.

All the conditions for blacks and whites in seventeenth-century America were powerfully directed toward antagonism and mistreatment. Under such conditions even the slightest display of humanity between the races might be considered evidence of a basic human drive toward community.

In spite of preconceptions about blackness, which in the English language suggested something "foul...sinister" (*Oxford English Dictionary*), in spite of the special subordination of blacks in the Americas in the seventeenth century, there is evidence that where whites and blacks found themselves with common problems, common work, a common enemy in their master, they behaved toward one another as equals.

The swift growth of plantation slavery is easily traceable to something other than natural racial repugnance: the number of arriving whites, whether free or indentured servants (under four- to seven-year contracts), was not enough to meet the need of the plantations. By 1700, in Virginia, there were 6,000 slaves, one-twelfth of the population. By 1763, there were 170,000 slaves, about half the population.

From the beginning, the imported black men and women resisted their enslavement, under the most difficult conditions, under pain of mutilation and death. Only occasionally was there an organized insurrection. More often they showed their refusal to submit by running away. Even more often, they engaged in sabotage, slowdowns, and subtle forms of resistance which asserted, if only to themselves and their brothers and sisters, their dignity as human beings.

A Virginia statute of 1669 referred to "the obstinacy of many of them," and in 1680 the Assembly took note of slave meetings "under the pretense of feasts and brawls" which they considered of "dangerous consequence." In 1687, in the colony's Northern Neck, a plot was discovered in which slaves planned to kill all the whites in the area and escape during a mass funeral.

Slaves recently from Africa, still holding on to the heritage of their communal society, would run away in groups and try to establish villages of runaways out in the wilderness, on the frontier. Slaves born in America, on the other hand, were more likely to run off alone, and, with the skills they had learned on the plantation, try to pass as free men.

In the colonial papers of England, a 1729 report from the lieutenant governor of Virginia to the British Board of Trade tells how "a number of Negroes, about fifteen...formed a design to withdraw from their Master and to fix themselves in the fastnesses of the neighboring Mountains. They had found means to get into their possession some Arms and Ammunition, and they took along with them some Provisions, their Cloths, bedding and working Tools.... Tho' this attempt has happily been defeated, it ought nevertheless to awaken us into some effectual measures...."

In 1710, warning the Virginia Assembly, Governor Alexander Spotswood said:

> ...freedom wears a cap which can without a tongue, call together all those who long to shake off the fetters of slavery and as such an Insurrection would surely be attended with most dreadful consequences so I think we cannot be too early in providing against it, both by putting our selves in a better posture of defence and by making a law to prevent the consultations of those Negroes.

Indeed, considering the harshness of punishment for running away, that so many blacks did run away must be a sign of a powerful rebelliousness. All through the 1700s, the Virginia slave code read:

If the slave is apprehended…it shall…be lawful for the county court, to order such punishment for the said slave, either by dismembering, or in any other way…as they in their discretion shall think fit, for the reclaiming any such incorrigible slave, and terrifying others from the like practices.…

Fear of slave revolt seems to have been a permanent fact of plantation life. William Byrd, a wealthy Virginia slaveholder, wrote in 1736:

We have already at least 10,000 men of these descendants of Ham, fit to bear arms, and these numbers increase every day, as well by birth as by importation. And in case there should arise a man of desperate fortune, he might with more advantage than Cataline kindle a servile war…and tinge our rivers wide as they are with blood.

It was an intricate and powerful system of control that the slave owners developed to maintain their labor supply and their way of life, a system both subtle and crude, involving every device that social orders employ for keeping power and wealth where they are.

The system was psychological and physical at the same time. The slaves were taught discipline, were impressed again and again with the idea of their own inferiority to "know their place," to see blackness as a sign of subordination, to be awed by the power of the master, to merge their interest with the master's, destroying their own individual needs. To accomplish this there was the discipline of hard labor, the breakup of the slave family, the lulling effects of religion (which sometimes led to "great mischief," as one slaveholder reported), the creation of disunity among slaves by separating them into field slaves and more privileged house slaves, and finally the power of law and the immediate power of the overseer to invoke whipping, burning, mutilation, and death.

Still, rebellions took place—not many, but enough to create constant fear among white planters.

A letter to London from South Carolina in 1720 reports:

I am now to acquaint you that very lately we have had a very wicked and barbarous plot of the designe of the negroes rising with a designe to destroy all the white people in the country and then to take Charles Town in full body but it pleased God it was discovered and many of them taken prisoners and some burnt and some hang'd and some banish'd.

Herbert Aptheker, who did detailed research on slave resistance in North America for his book *American Negro Slave Revolts*, found about 250 instances where a minimum of ten slaves joined in a revolt or conspiracy.

From time to time, whites were involved in the slave resistance. As early as 1663, indentured white servants and black slaves in Gloucester County, Virginia, formed a conspiracy to rebel and gain their freedom. The plot was betrayed, and ended with executions.

In New York in 1741, there were ten thousand whites in the city and two thousand black slaves. It had been a hard winter and the poor—slave and free—had suffered greatly. When mysterious fires broke out, blacks and whites were accused of conspiring together. Mass hysteria developed against the accused. After a trial full of lurid accusations by informers, and forced confessions, two white men and two white women were executed, eighteen slaves were hanged, and thirteen slaves were burned alive.

Only one fear was greater than the fear of black rebellion in the new American colonies. That was the fear that discontented whites would join black slaves to overthrow the existing order. In the early years of slavery, especially, before racism as a way of thinking was firmly ingrained, while white indentured servants were often treated as badly as black slaves, there was a possibility of cooperation.

And so, measures were taken. About the same time that slave codes, involving discipline and punishment, were passed by the Virginia Assembly, Edmund Morgan writes:

> Virginia's ruling class, having proclaimed that all white men were superior to black, went on to offer their social (but white) inferiors a number of benefits previously denied them. In 1705 a law was passed requiring masters to provide white servants whose indenture time was up with ten bushels of corn, thirty shillings, and a gun, while women servants were to get 15 bushels of corn and forty shillings. Also, the newly freed servants were to get 50 acres of land.

Morgan concludes: "Once the small planter felt less exploited by taxation and began to prosper a little, he became less turbulent, less dangerous, more respectable. He could begin to see his big neighbor not as an extortionist but as a powerful protector of their common interests."

We see now a complex web of historical threads to ensnare blacks for slavery in America: the desperation of starving settlers, the special helplessness of the displaced African, the powerful incentive of profit for slave trader and planter, the temptation of superior status for poor whites, the elaborate controls against escape and rebellion, the legal and social punishment of black and white collaboration.

The point is that the elements of this web are historical, not "natural."

This does not mean that they are easily disentangled and dismantled. It means only that there is a possibility for something else, under historical conditions not yet realized. And one of these conditions would be the elimination of that class exploitation which has made poor whites desperate for small gifts of status, and has prevented that unity of black and white necessary for joint rebellion and reconstruction.

Around 1700, the Virginia House of Burgesses declared:

> The Christian Servants in this country for the most part consists of the Worser Sort of the people of Europe. And since...such numbers of Irish and other Nations have been brought in of which a great many have been soldiers in the late wars that according to our present Circumstances we can hardly governe them and if they were fitted with Armes and had the Opertunity of meeting together by Musters we have just reason to fears they may rise upon us.

It was a kind of class consciousness, a class fear. There were things happening in early Virginia, and in the other colonies, to warrant it.

Exercises

1. Why did Virginians massacre Indians instead of enslaving them?

2. How does the answer to the above question explain the choice to import black slaves?

3. Why were Africans vulnerable to enslavement?

4. Page 27: "...where whites and blacks found themselves with common problems, common work, a common enemy in their master, they behaved toward one another as equals."

   What were the "problems" that blacks and whites shared? What was the "work" that blacks and whites did? Was it the same? Did they work together? How did the "master" treat his indentured servant? How did the "master" treat his slave? To what degree was the treatment the same?

5. How do we know that slaves resisted their enslavement?

6. How do we know that indentured servants resisted their indentured condition?

7. How did the Virginia ruling class begin to drive a wedge between the white indentured servants and enslaved blacks?

8. Below are three versions of one essential question. Choose ONE of the three to answer.

   a. Zinn argues that racism is not natural but a product of human choice and historical circumstances. Given the forces that created racism, what choices need to be made to undo it?

   b. What were the historical forces that caused white plantation owners to choose black slaves as their labor source? Was it a "decision" to make a profit, or were Englishmen forced to do it? Would the Powhatans have accepted wages to labor in the fields of the plantation owners? Does that constitute a historical force?

   c. Zinn argues that racism is not natural. Does he mean that it is caused by human decisions or historical forces? Explain your answer by first defining the difference between historical forces and human decision. What is a "historical force"? Do such forces compel humans to make decisions they would otherwise not have made?

9. At what point in the chronology of American history is the topic of slavery covered in traditional American history texts? At what point is it covered in Zinn's text? How might you explain the difference in placement? (What are the purposes of including slavery in the traditional texts? What are the purposes for Zinn?)

Chapter 3

Persons of Mean
and Vile Condition

In 1676, seventy years after Virginia was founded, a hundred years before
it supplied leadership for the American Revolution, that colony faced a
rebellion of white frontiersmen, joined by slaves and servants, a rebellion
so threatening that the governor had to flee the burning capital of
Jamestown and England decided to send a thousand soldiers across the
Atlantic, hoping to maintain order among forty thousand colonists. This
was Bacon's Rebellion. After the uprising was suppressed, its leader,
Nathaniel Bacon, dead and his associates hanged, was described in a Royal
Commission report:

> He seduced the Vulgar and most ignorant people to believe (two thirds
> of each county being of that Sort) Soe that their whole hearts and hopes
> were set now upon Bacon. Next he charges the Governour as negligent
> and wicked, treacherous and incapable, the Lawes and Taxes as unjust
> and oppressive and cryes up absolute necessity of redress.

Bacon's Rebellion began with conflict over how to deal with the Indians, who were close by, on the western frontier, constantly threatening.
Whites who had been ignored when huge land grants around Jamestown
were given away had gone west to find land, and there they encountered
Indians. Were those frontier Virginians resentful that the politicos and
landed aristocrats who controlled the colony's government in Jamestown
first pushed them westward into Indian territory and then seemed indeci-
sive in fighting the Indians? That might explain the character of their
rebellion, not easily classifiable as either antiaristocrat or anti-Indian,
because it was both.

And the governor, William Berkeley, and his Jamestown crowd—
were they more conciliatory to the Indians (they wooed certain of them as
spies and allies) now that they had monopolized the land in the East, could
use frontier whites as a buffer, and needed peace? The desperation of the
government in suppressing the rebellion seemed to have a double motive:
developing an Indian policy that would divide Indians in order to control
them, and teaching the poor whites of Virginia that rebellion did not
pay—by a show of superior force, by calling for troops from England
itself, by mass hanging.

Times were hard in 1676. "There was genuine distress, genuine
poverty.... All contemporary sources speak of the great mass of people as
living in severe economic straits," writes Wilcomb Washburn, who, using
British colonial records, has done an exhaustive study of Bacon's Rebellion.

Bacon himself had a good bit of land and was probably more enthusiastic about killing Indians than about redressing the grievances of the poor.
But he became a symbol of mass resentment against the Virginia establishment and was elected in the spring of 1676 to the House of Burgesses.
When he insisted on organizing armed detachments to fight the Indians,
outside official control, Berkeley proclaimed him a rebel and had him captured, whereupon two thousand Virginians marched into Jamestown to
support him. Berkeley let Bacon go, in return for an apology, but Bacon
went off, gathered his militia, and began raiding the Indians.

Bacon's "Declaration of the People" of July 1676 shows a mixture of
populist resentment against the rich and frontier hatred of the Indians. It
indicted the Berkeley administration for unjust taxes, for putting favorites
in high positions, for monopolizing the beaver trade, and for not protect-
ing the western farmers from the Indians.

But in the fall, Bacon, aged twenty-nine, fell sick and died, because of,
as a contemporary put it, "swarmes of Vermyn that bred in his body."

The rebellion didn't last long after that. A ship armed with thirty
guns, cruising the York River, became the base for securing order, and its
captain, Thomas Grantham, used force and deception to disarm the last
rebel forces. Coming upon the chief garrison of the rebellion, he found
four hundred armed Englishmen and Negroes, a mixture of freemen, servants, and slaves. He promised to pardon everyone, to give freedom to
slaves and servants, but when they got into the boat, he trained his big guns
on them, disarmed them, and eventually delivered the slaves and servants
to their masters. The remaining garrisons were overcome one by one.
Twenty-three rebel leaders were hanged.

It was a complex chain of oppression in Virginia. The Indians were plundered by white frontiersmen, who were taxed and controlled by the Jamestown elite. And the whole colony was being exploited by England, which bought the colonists' tobacco at prices it dictated and made one hundred thousand pounds a year for the king.

From the testimony of the governor himself, the rebellion against him had the overwhelming support of the Virginia population. A member of his council reported that the defection was "almost general" and laid it to "the Lewd dispositions of some Persons of desperate Fortunes" who had "the Vaine hopes of taireing the Countrey wholley out of his Majesty's handes into their owne." Another member of the Governor's Council, Richard Lee, noted that Bacon's Rebellion had started over Indian policy. But the "zealous inclination of the multitude" to support Bacon was due, he said, to "hopes of levelling."

"Leveling" meant equalizing the wealth. Leveling was to be behind countless actions of poor whites against the rich in all the English colonies, in the century and a half before the Revolution.

The servants who joined Bacon's Rebellion were part of a large underclass of miserably poor whites who came to the North American colonies from European cities whose governments were anxious to be rid of them. In England, the development of commerce and capitalism in the 1500s and 1600s, the enclosing of land for the production of wool, filled the cities with vagrant poor, and from the reign of Elizabeth on, laws were passed to punish them, imprison them in workhouses, or exile them.

In the 1600s and 1700s, by forced exile, by lures, promises, and lies, by kidnapping, by their urgent need to escape the living conditions of the home country, poor people wanting to go to America became commodities of profit for merchants, traders, ship captains, and eventually their masters in America.

After signing the indenture, in which the immigrants agreed to pay their cost of passage by working for a master for five or seven years, they were often imprisoned until the ship sailed, to make sure they did not run away. In the year 1619, the Virginia House of Burgesses, born that year as the first representative assembly in America (it was also the year of the first importation of black slaves), provided for the recording and enforcing of contracts between servants and masters. As in any contract between unequal powers, the parties appeared on paper as equals, but enforcement was far easier for master than for servant.

The voyage to America lasted eight, ten, or twelve weeks, and the servants were packed into ships with the same fanatic concern for profits that marked the slave ships. If the weather was bad, and the trip took too long, they ran out of food. Gottlieb Mittelberger, a musician, traveling from Germany to America around 1750, wrote about his voyage:

> During the journey the ship is full of pitiful signs of distress—smells, fumes, horrors, vomiting, various kinds of sea sickness, fever, dysentery, headaches, heat, constipation, boils, scurvy, cancer, mouth-rot, and similar afflictions, all of them caused by the age and the high salted state of the food, especially of the meat, as well as by the very bad and filthy water.... Add to all that shortage of food, hunger, thirst, frost, heat, dampness, fear, misery, vexation, and lamentation as well as other troubles.... On board our ship, on a day on which we had a great storm, a woman about to give birth and unable to deliver under the circumstances, was pushed through one of the portholes into the sea....

Indentured servants were bought and sold like slaves. An announcement in the *Virginia Gazette*, March 28, 1771, read:

> "Just arrived at Leedstown, the Ship Justitia, with about one Hundred Healthy Servants, Men Women & Boys.... The Sale will commence on Tuesday the 2nd of April."

Against the rosy accounts of better living standards in the Americas one must place many others, like one immigrant's letter from America: "Whoever is well off in Europe better remain there. Here is misery and distress, same as everywhere, and for certain persons and conditions incomparably more than in Europe."

Beatings and whippings were common. Servant women were raped. In Virginia in the 1660s, a master was convicted of raping two women servants. He also was known to beat his own wife and children; he had whipped and chained another servant until he died. The master was berated by the court, but specifically cleared on the rape charge, despite overwhelming evidence.

The master tried to control completely the sexual lives of the servants. It was in his economic interest to keep women servants from marrying or from having sexual relations, because childbearing would interfere with work. Benjamin Franklin, writing as "Poor Richard" in 1736, gave advice to his readers: "Let thy maidservant be faithful, strong, and homely."

Sometimes servants organized rebellions, but one did not find on the mainland the kind of large-scale conspiracies of servants that existed, for instance, on Barbados in the West Indies.

Despite the rarity of servants' rebellions, the threat was always there, and masters were fearful. After Bacon's Rebellion, two companies of English soldiers remained in Virginia to guard against future trouble, and their presence was defended in a report to the Lords of Trade and Plantation saying: "Virginia is at present poor and more populous than ever. There is great apprehension of a rising among the servants, owing to their great necessities and want of clothes; they may plunder the storehouses and ships."

Escape was easier than rebellion. "Numerous instances of mass desertions by white servants took place in the Southern colonies," reports Richard Morris (*Government and Labor in Early America*), on the basis of an inspection of colonial newspapers in the 1700s. "The atmosphere of seventeenth-century Virginia," he says, "was charged with plots and rumors of combinations of servants to run away."

The mechanism of control was formidable. Strangers had to show passports or certificates to prove they were freemen. Agreements among the colonies provided for the extradition of fugitive servants (these became the basis of the clause in the U.S. Constitution that persons "held to Service or Labor in one State...escaping into another... shall be delivered up...").

Sometimes, servants went on strike. One Maryland master complained to the Provincial Court in 1663 that his servants did "peremptorily and positively refuse to goe and doe their ordinary labor." The servants responded that they were fed only "Beanes and Bread" and they were "soe weake, wee are not able to perform the imploym'ts hee puts us uppon." They were given thirty lashes by the court.

More than half the colonists who came to the North American shores in the colonial period came as servants. They were mostly English in the seventeenth century, Irish and German in the eighteenth century. More and more, slaves replaced them, as they ran away to freedom or finished their time, but as late as 1755, white servants made up 10 percent of the population of Maryland.

What happened to these servants after they became free? There are cheerful accounts in which they rise to prosperity, becoming landowners and important figures. But Abbot Smith, after a careful study (*Colonists in Bondage*), concludes that colonial society "was not democratic and certainly not equalitarian; it was dominated by men who had money enough to make others work for them." And: "Few of these men were descended from indentured servants, and practically none had themselves been of this class."

It seems quite clear that class lines hardened through the colonial period; the distinction between rich and poor became sharper. By 1700 there were fifty rich families in Virginia, with wealth equivalent to fifty thousand pounds (a huge sum in those days), who lived off the labor of black slaves and white servants, owned the plantations, sat on the governor's council, served as local magistrates. In Maryland, the settlers were ruled by a proprietor whose right of total control over the colony had been granted by the English king. Between 1650 and 1689 there were five revolts against the proprietor.

Carl Bridenbaugh's study of colonial cities, *Cities in the Wilderness*, reveals a clear-cut class system. He finds: "The leaders of early Boston were gentlemen of considerable wealth who, in association with the clergy, eagerly sought to preserve in America the social arrangements of the Mother Country."

At the very start of the Massachusetts Bay Colony in 1630, the governor, John Winthrop, had declared the philosophy of the rulers: "in all times some must be rich, some poore, some highe and eminent in power and dignitie; others meane and in subjection."

Rich merchants erected mansions; persons "of Qualitie" traveled in coaches or sedan chairs, had their portraits painted, wore periwigs, and filled themselves with rich food and Madeira. A petition came from the town of Deerfield in 1678 to the Massachusetts General Court: "You may be pleased to know that the very principle and best of the land; the best for soile; the best for situation; as laying in ye center and midle of the town: and as to quantity, nere half, belongs unto eight or nine proprietors...."

New York in the colonial period was like a feudal kingdom. The Dutch had set up a patroonship system along the Hudson River, with enormous landed estates, where the barons controlled completely the lives of their tenants. In 1689, many of the grievances of the poor were mixed up in the farmers' revolt of Jacob Leisler and his group. Leisler was hanged, and the parceling out of huge estates continued. Under Governor Benjamin Fletcher, three-fourths of the land in New York was granted to about thirty people. He gave a friend a half million acres for a token annual payment of thirty shillings.

In 1700, New York City church wardens had asked for funds from the common council because "the Crys of the poor and Impotent for want of Relief are Extreamly Grevious." In the 1730s, demand began to grow for institutions to contain the "many Beggarly people daily suffered to wander about the Streets."

A letter to Peter Zenger's New York *Journal* in 1737 described the poor street urchin of New York as "an Object in Human Shape, half starv'd with Cold, with Cloathes out at the Elbows, Knees through the Breeches, Hair standing on end.... From the age about four to Fourteen they spend their Days in the Streets...then they are put out as Apprentices, perhaps four, five, or six years...."

The colonies grew fast in the 1700s. English settlers were joined by Scotch-Irish and German immigrants. Black slaves were pouring in; they were 8 percent of the population in 1690; 21 percent in 1770. The population of the colonies was 250,000 in 1700; 1,600,000 by 1760. Agriculture was growing. Small manufacturing was developing. Shipping and trading were expanding. The big cities—Boston, New York, Philadelphia, and Charleston—were doubling and tripling in size.

Through all that growth, the upper class was getting most of the benefits and monopolized political power. In Boston, by 1770, the top 1 percent of property owners owned 44 percent of the wealth.

Everywhere the poor were struggling to stay alive, simply to keep from freezing in cold weather. All the cities built poorhouses in the 1730s, not just for old people, widows, cripples, and orphans, but for unemployed, war veterans, new immigrants. In New York, at midcentury, the city almshouse, built for one hundred poor, was housing over four hundred. A Philadelphia citizen wrote in 1748: "It is remarkable what an increase of the number of Beggars there is about this town this winter." In 1757, Boston officials spoke of "a great Number of Poor...who can scarcely procure from day to day daily Bread for themselves & Families."

The colonies, it seems, were societies of contending classes—a fact obscured by the emphasis, in traditional histories, on the external struggle against England, the unity of colonists in the Revolution. The country therefore was not "born free" but born slave and free, servant and master, tenant and landlord, poor and rich. As a result, the political authorities were opposed "frequently, vociferously, and sometimes violently," according to Gary Nash. "Outbreaks of disorder punctuated the last quarter of the seventeenth century, toppling established governments in Massachusetts, New York, Maryland, Virginia, and North Carolina."

Free white workers were better off than slaves or servants, but they still resented unfair treatment by the wealthier classes. A severe food shortage in Boston in 1713 brought a warning from town selectmen to the General Assembly of Massachusetts, saying that the "threatening scarcity of provisions" had led to such "extravagant prices that the necessities of the poor in the approaching winter must needs be very pressing." Andrew Belcher, a wealthy merchant, was exporting grain to the Caribbean because the profit was greater there. On May 19, two hundred people rioted on the Boston Common. They attacked Belcher's ships, broke into his warehouses looking for corn, and shot the lieutenant governor when he tried to interfere.

In the 1730s, in Boston, people protesting the high prices established by merchants demolished the public market in Dock Square while (as a conservative writer complained) "murmuring against the Government & the rich people." No one was arrested, after the demonstrators warned that arrests would bring "Five Hundred Men in Solemn League and Covenent" who would destroy other markets set up for the benefit of rich merchants.

Bostonians rioted also against impressment, in which men were drafted for naval service. They surrounded the house of the governor, beat up the sheriff, locked up a deputy sheriff, and stormed the townhouse where the General Court sat. The militia did not respond when called to put them down, and the governor fled. The crowd was condemned by a merchants' group as a "Riotous Tumultuous Assembly of Foreign Seamen, Servants, Negroes, and Other Persons of Mean and Vile Condition."

In New Jersey in the 1740s and 1750s, poor farmers occupying land, over which they and the landowners had rival claims, rioted when rents were demanded of them. In 1745, Samuel Baldwin, who had long lived on his land and who held an Indian title to it, was arrested for nonpayment of rent to the proprietor and taken to the Newark jail. A contemporary described what happened then: "The People in general, supposing the Design of the Proprietors was to ruin them...went to the Prison, opened the Door, took out Baldwin."

Through this period, England was fighting a series of wars (Queen Anne's War in the early 1700s, King George's War in the 1730s). Some merchants made fortunes from these wars, but for most people they meant higher taxes, unemployment, poverty. An anonymous pamphleteer in Massachusetts, writing angrily after King George's War, described the situation: "Poverty and Discontent appear in every Face (except the Countenances of the Rich) and dwell upon every Tongue." He spoke of a few men, fed by "Lust of Power, Lust of Fame, Lust of Money," who got rich during the war. "No Wonder such Men can build Ships, Houses, buy Farms, set up their Coaches, Chariots, live very splendidly, purchase

Fame, Posts of Honour." He called them "Birds of prey...Enemies to all Communities—wherever they live."

The forced service of seamen led to a riot against impressment in Boston in 1747. Then crowds turned against Thomas Hutchinson, a rich merchant and colonial official who had backed the governor in putting down the riot, and who also designed a currency plan for Massachusetts which seemed to discriminate against the poor. Hutchinson's house burned down, mysteriously, and a crowd gathered in the street, cursing Hutchinson and shouting, "Let it burn!"

By the years of the Revolutionary crisis, the 1760s, the wealthy elite that controlled the British colonies on the American mainland had 150 years of experience, had learned certain things about how to rule. They had various fears, but also had developed tactics to deal with what they feared.

With the problem of Indian hostility and the danger of slave revolts, the colonial elite had to consider the class anger of poor whites—servants, tenants, the city poor, the propertyless, the taxpayer, the soldier and sailor. As the colonies passed their hundredth year and went into the middle of the 1700s, as the gap between rich and poor widened, as violence and the threat of violence increased, the problem of control became more serious.

What if these different despised groups—the Indians, the slaves, the poor whites—should combine? Even before there were so many blacks, in the seventeenth century, there was, as Abbot Smith puts it, "a lively fear that servants would join with Negroes or Indians to overcome the small number of masters."

Bacon's Rebellion was instructive: to conciliate a diminishing Indian population at the expense of infuriating a coalition of white frontiersmen was very risky. Better to make war on the Indian, gain the support of the white, divert possible class conflict by turning poor whites against Indians for the security of the elite.

Might blacks and Indians combine against the white enemy? In the Carolinas, whites were outnumbered by black slaves and nearby Indian tribes; in the 1750s, twenty-five thousand whites faced forty thousand black slaves, with sixty thousand Creek, Cherokee, Choctaw, and Chickasaw Indians in the area.

The white rulers of the Carolinas seemed to be conscious of the need for a policy, as one of them put it, "to make Indians & Negros a checque upon each other lest by their Vastly Superior Numbers we should be crushed by one or the other." And so laws were passed prohibiting free blacks from traveling in Indian country. Treaties with Indian tribes contained clauses requiring the return of fugitive slaves. Governor Lyttle-town of South Carolina wrote in 1738: "It has always been the policy of this government to create an aversion in them [Indians] to Negroes."

Blacks ran away to Indian villages, and the Creeks and Cherokees harbored runaway slaves by the hundreds. Many of these were amalgamated into the Indian tribes, married, produced children. But the combination of harsh slave codes and bribes to the Indians to help put down black rebels kept things under control.

It was the potential combination of poor whites and blacks that caused the most fear among the wealthy white planters. If there had been the natural racial repugnance that some theorists have assumed, control would have been easier. But sexual attraction was powerful, across racial lines. In 1743, a grand jury in Charleston, South Carolina, denounced "The Too Common Practice of Criminal Conversation with Negro and other Slave Wenches in this Province."

What made Bacon's Rebellion especially fearsome for the rulers of Virginia was that black slaves and white servants joined forces. All through those early years, black and white slaves and servants ran away together, as shown both by the laws passed to stop this and the records of the courts. A letter from the southern colonies in 1682 complained of "no white men to superintend our negroes, or repress an insurrection of negroes...." A report to the English government in 1721 said that in South Carolina "black slaves have lately attempted and were very near succeeding in a new revolution...and therefore, it may be necessary... to propose some new law for encouraging the entertainment of more white servants in the future."

This fear may help explain why Parliament, in 1717, made transportation to the New World a legal punishment for crime. After that, tens of thousands of convicts could be sent to Virginia, Maryland, and other colonies.

Racism was becoming more and more practical. Edmund Morgan, on the basis of his careful study of slavery in Virginia, sees racism not as "natural" to black-white difference, but something coming out of class scorn, a realistic device for control. "If freemen with disappointed hopes should make common cause with slaves of desperate hope, the results might be worse than anything Bacon had done. The answer to the problem, obvious if unspoken and only gradually recognized, was racism, to separate dangerous free whites from dangerous black slaves by a screen of racial contempt."

There was still another control which became handy as the colonies grew, and which had crucial consequences for the continued rule of the elite throughout American history. Along with the very rich and the very poor, there developed a white middle class of small planters, independent farmers, city artisans, who, given small rewards for joining forces with merchants and planters, would be a solid buffer against black slaves, frontier Indians, and very poor whites.

While it was the rich who ruled Boston, there were political jobs available for the moderately well-off, as "cullers of staves," "measurer of Coal Baskets," "Fence Viewer." Aubrey Land found in Maryland a class of small planters who were not "the beneficiary" of the planting society as the rich were, but who had the distinction of being called planters, and who were "respectable citizens."

The *Pennsylvania Journal* wrote in 1756: "The people of this province are generally of the middling sort, and at present pretty much upon a level. They are chiefly industrious farmers, artificers or men in trade".... To call them "the people" was to omit black slaves, white servants, displaced Indians. And the term "middle class" concealed a fact long true about this country, that, as Richard Hofstadter said: "It was...a middle-class society governed for the most part by its upper classes."

Those upper classes, to rule, needed to make concessions to the middle class, without damage to their own wealth or power, at the expense of slaves, Indians, and poor whites. This bought loyalty. And to bind that loyalty with something more powerful even than material advantage, the ruling group found, in the 1760s and 1770s, a wonderfully useful device. That device was the language of liberty and equality, which could unite just enough whites to fight a revolution against England, without ending either slavery or inequality.

Exercises

1. What was the economic condition of Virginia in 1676?

2. What is the evidence that Bacon's Rebellion in 1676 "had the overwhelming support of the Virginia population"?

3. Why would a European man or woman sign an indenture? Was it a "choice" or were they compelled by "historical forces"?

4. Copy and fill in the chart below. Expand the chart by adding to the given criteria of comparison.

	AFRICAN SLAVE	INDENTURED SERVANT
I. PERIOD OF SERVITUDE		
II. CONDITIONS/RIGHTS DURING SERVITUDE		
III. CONDITIONS OF VOYAGE		
IV. REASONS FOR OR CAUSE OF SERVITUDE		
V. FORMS OF RESISTANCE		
VI. METHODS BY WHICH THEY WERE CONTROLLED		
VII.		
VIII.		

5. What happened when servants became free?

6. Which of the following is the most accurate characterization of the colonial economy, and WHY? Consider (without limiting yourself to) the following as criteria: closeness to actual event; how far removed from witnessing the event; degree of possibility of being an isolated event; degree of safety in generalizing from the specific; relevance of detail to question; how much the detail actually says about the entire colonial society.

   a. In Boston, by 1770, the top 1% of property owners owned 44% of the wealth.

   b. In New York [around 1750], the city almshouse, built for 100 poor, was housing over 400.

   c. In 1757, Boston officials spoke of "a great Number of Poor...who can scarcely procure from day to day daily Bread for themselves & Families."

   d. According to the present day historian Gary Nash, "Outbreaks of disorder punctuated the last quarter of the seventeenth century [1675–1700], toppling established governments in Massachusetts, New York, Maryland, Virginia, and North Carolina."

   e. In Boston in 1713, a town selectmen said that the "threatening scarcity of provisions" had led to such "extravagant prices that the necessities of the poor in the approaching winter must needs be very pressing."

   f. In New Jersey in 1745, Sam Baldwin was arrested for nonpayment of rent. "The People in general, supposing the Design of the Proprietors was to ruin them...went to the Prison, opened the Door, took out Baldwin."

7. What experiences besides economic deprivation or hardship might have caused colonists to resent their local or state governments?

8. What was the greatest threat to the elite's control over the colonists—a fear that was realized in Bacon's Rebellion? What tactics did the wealthy elite/rich rulers adopt to prevent another Bacon's Rebellion?

   Activity: Reenact a Virginia Company stockholders meeting, in London, England, circa 1678.

Chapter 4

Tyranny Is Tyranny

Around 1776, certain important people in the English colonies made a discovery that would prove enormously useful for the next two hundred years. They found that by creating a nation, a symbol, a legal unity called the United States, they could take over land, profits, and political power from favorites of the British Empire. In the process, they could hold back a number of potential rebellions and create a consensus of popular support for the rule of a new, privileged leadership.

When we look at the American Revolution this way, it was a work of genius, and the Founding Fathers deserve the awed tribute they have received over the centuries. They created the most effective system of national control devised in modern times and showed future generations of leaders the advantages of combining paternalism with command.

Starting with Bacon's Rebellion in Virginia, by 1760 there had been eighteen uprisings aimed at overthrowing colonial governments. There had also been six black rebellions, from South Carolina to New York, and forty riots of various origins.

By this time also, there emerged, according to Jack Greene, "stable, coherent, effective and acknowledged local political and social elites." And by the 1760s, this local leadership saw the possibility of directing much of the rebellious energy against England and her local officials. It was not a conscious conspiracy, but an accumulation of tactical responses.

After 1763, with England victorious in the Seven Years' War (known in America as the French and Indian War), expelling France from North

America, ambitious colonial leaders were no longer threatened by the French. They now had only two rivals left: the English and the Indians. The British, wooing the Indians, had declared Indian lands beyond the Appalachians out of bounds to whites (the Proclamation of 1763). Perhaps, once the British were out of the way, the Indians could be dealt with. Again, not a conscious, forethought strategy by the colonial elite, but a growing awareness as events developed.

With the French defeated, the British government could turn its attention to tightening control over the colonies. It needed revenues to pay for the war and looked to the colonies for that. Also, the colonial trade had become more and more important to the British economy, and more profitable: it had amounted to about 500,000 pounds in 1700 but by 1770 was worth 2,800,000 pounds.

So, the American leadership was less desirous of English rule, the English more in need of the colonists' wealth. The elements for conflict were there.

The war with France had brought glory to the generals, death to the privates, wealth for the merchants, unemployment for the poor. There were twenty-five thousand people living in New York (there had been seven thousand in 1720) when the war ended. A newspaper editor wrote about the growing "Number of Beggers and wandering Poor" in the streets of the city. Letters in the papers questioned the distribution of wealth: "How often have our Streets been covered with Thousands of Barrels of Flour for trade, while our near Neighbors can hardly procure enough to make a Dumplin to satisfy hunger?"

Gary Nash's study of city tax lists shows that by the early 1770s, the top 5 percent of Boston's taxpayers controlled 49 percent of the city's taxable assets. In Philadelphia and New York, too, wealth was more and more concentrated. Court-recorded wills show that by 1750 the wealthiest people in the cities were leaving twenty thousand pounds (equivalent to about $2.5 million today).

In Boston, the lower classes began to use the town meeting to vent their grievances. The governor of Massachusetts had written that in these town meetings "the meanest Inhabitants...by their constant Attendance there generally are the majority and outvote the Gentlemen, Merchants, Substantial Traders and all the better part of the Inhabitants."

What seems to have happened in Boston is that certain lawyers, editors, and merchants of the upper classes, but excluded from the ruling circles close to England—men like James Otis and Samuel Adams—

organized a "Boston Caucus" and through their oratory and their writing "molded laboring-class opinion, called the 'mob' into action, and shaped its behaviour." This is Gary Nash's description of Otis, who, he says, "keenly aware of the declining fortunes and the resentment of ordinary townspeople, was mirroring as well as molding popular opinion."

We have here a forecast of the long history of American politics, the mobilization of lower-class energy by upper-class politicians, for their own purposes. This was not purely deception; it involved, in part, a genuine recognition of lower-class grievances, which helps to account for its effectiveness as a tactic over the centuries.

In 1762, Otis, speaking against the conservative rulers of the Massachusetts colony represented by Thomas Hutchinson, gave an example of the kind of rhetoric that a lawyer could use in mobilizing city mechanics and artisans:

> I am forced to get my living by the labour of my hand; and the sweat of my brow, as most of you are and obliged to go thro' good report and evil report, for bitter bread, earned under the frowns of some who have no natural or divine right to be above me, and entirely owe their grandeur and honor to grinding the faces of the poor....

Boston seems to have been full of class anger in those days. In 1763, in the Boston *Gazette*, someone wrote that "a few persons in power" were promoting political projects "for keeping the people poor in order to make them humble."

This accumulated sense of grievance against the rich in Boston may account for the explosiveness of mob action after the Stamp Act of 1765. Through this act, the British were taxing the colonial population to pay for the French war, in which colonists had suffered to expand the British Empire. That summer, a shoemaker named Ebenezer MacIntosh led a mob in destroying the house of a rich Boston merchant named Andrew Oliver. Two weeks later, the crowd turned to the home of Thomas Hutchinson, symbol of the rich elite who ruled the colonies in the name of England. They smashed up his house with axes, drank the wine in his wine cellar, and looted the house of its furniture and other objects. A report by colony officials to England said that this was part of a larger scheme in which the houses of fifteen rich people were to be destroyed, as part of "a War of Plunder, of general levelling and taking away the Distinction of rich and poor."

It was one of those moments in which fury against the rich went further than leaders like Otis wanted. Could class hatred be focused against the pro-British elite, and deflected from the nationalist elite? In New York, that same year of the Boston house attacks, someone wrote to the New York *Gazette*, "Is it equitable that 99, rather 999, should suffer for the Extravagance or Grandeur of one, especially when it is considered that men frequently owe their Wealth to the impoverishment of their Neighbors?" The leaders of the Revolution would worry about keeping such sentiments within limits.

Mechanics were demanding political democracy in the colonial cities: open meetings of representative assemblies, public galleries in the legislative halls, and the publishing of roll-call votes, so that constituents could check on representatives. They wanted open-air meetings where the population could participate in making policy, more equitable taxes, price controls, and the election of mechanics and other ordinary people to government posts.

During elections for the 1776 convention to frame a constitution for Pennsylvania, a Privates Committee urged voters to oppose "great and overgrown rich men...they will be too apt to be framing distinctions in society." The Privates Committee drew up a bill of rights for the convention, including the statement that "an enormous proportion of property vested in a few individuals is dangerous to the rights, and destructive of the common happiness of mankind; and therefore every free state hath a right by its laws to discourage the possession of such property."

In the countryside, where most people lived, there was a similar conflict of poor against rich—which political leaders would use to mobilize the population against England, granting some benefits for the rebellious poor, and many more for themselves in the process. The tenant riots in New Jersey in the 1740s, the New York tenant uprisings of the 1750s and 1760s in the Hudson Valley, and the rebellion in northeastern New York that led to the carving of Vermont out of New York State were all more than sporadic rioting. They were long-lasting social movements, highly organized, involving the creation of countergovernments.

In North Carolina, a "Regulator Movement" of white farmers was organized against wealthy and corrupt officials in the period from 1766 to 1771, exactly those years when, in the cities of the Northeast, agitation was growing against the British, crowding out class issues. The Regulators referred to themselves as "poor Industrious peasants," as "labourers," "the wretched poor," "oppressed" by "rich and powerful...designing Monsters." They resented the tax system, which was especially burdensome on the poor, and the combination of merchants and lawyers who worked in the courts to collect debts from the harassed farmers. The Regulators did not represent servants or slaves, but they did speak for small owners, squatters, and tenants.

In Orange County, North Carolina, in the 1760s, the Regulators organized to prevent the collection of taxes and the confiscation of the property of tax delinquents. Officials said "an absolute Insurrection of a dangerous tendency has broke out in Orange County," and made military plans to suppress it. At one point seven hundred armed farmers forced the release of two arrested Regulator leaders. In another county, Anson, a local militia colonel complained of "the unparalleled tumults, Insurrections, and Commotions which at present distract this County." At one point a hundred men broke up the proceedings at a county court.

The result of all this was that the assembly passed some mild reform legislation, but also an act "to prevent riots and tumults," and the governor prepared to crush them militarily. In May of 1771 there was a decisive battle in which several thousand Regulators were defeated by a disciplined army using cannon. Six Regulators were hanged.

One consequence of this bitter conflict is that only a minority of the people in the Regulator counties seem to have participated as patriots in the Revolutionary War. Most of them probably remained neutral.

Fortunately for the Revolutionary movement, the key battles were being fought in the North, and here, in the cities, the colonial leaders had a divided white population; they could win over the mechanics, who were a kind of middle class, who had a stake in the fight against England, facing competition from English manufacturers. The biggest problem was to keep the propertyless people, who were unemployed and hungry in the crisis following the French war, under control.

In Boston, the economic grievances of the lowest classes mingled with anger against the British and exploded in mob violence. The leaders of the Independence movement wanted to use that mob energy against England, but also to contain it so that it would not demand too much from them.

A political group in Boston called the Loyal Nine—merchants, distillers, shipowners, and master craftsmen who opposed the Stamp Act—organized a procession in August 1765 to protest it. They put fifty master craftsmen at the head, but needed to mobilize shipworkers from the North End and mechanics and apprentices from the South End. Two or three thousand were in the procession (Negroes were excluded). They marched to the home of the stampmaster and burned his effigy. But after the "gentlemen" who organized the demonstration left, the crowd went further and destroyed some of the stampmaster's property.

Now a town meeting was called and the same leaders who had planned the demonstration denounced the violence and disavowed the actions of the crowd. And when the Stamp Act was repealed, due to overwhelming resistance, the conservative leaders severed their connections with the rioters. They held annual celebrations of the first anti–Stamp Act demonstration, to which they invited, according to Dirk Hoerder, not the rioters but "mainly upper and middle-class Bostonians, who traveled in coaches and carriages to Roxbury or Dorchester for opulent feasts."

When the British Parliament turned to its next attempt to tax the colonies, this time by a set of taxes which it hoped would not excite as much opposition, the colonial leaders organized boycotts. But, they stressed, "No Mobs or Tumults, let the Persons and Properties of your most inveterate Enemies be safe." Samuel Adams advised: "No Mobs— No Confusions—No Tumult." And James Otis said that "no possible circumstances, though ever so oppressive, could be supposed sufficient to justify private tumults and disorders...."

The quartering of troops by the British was directly hurtful to the sailors and other working people. After 1768, two thousand soldiers were quartered in Boston, and friction grew between the crowds and the soldiers. The soldiers began to take the jobs of working people when jobs were scarce, and on March 5, 1770, grievances of ropemakers against British soldiers taking their jobs led to a fight.

A crowd gathered in front of the customhouse and began provoking the soldiers, who fired and killed first Crispus Attucks, a mulatto worker, then others. This became known as the Boston Massacre. Feelings against the British mounted quickly at the acquittal of six of the British soldiers (two were punished by having their thumbs branded and were discharged from the army). The crowd at the massacre was described by John Adams, defense attorney for the British soldiers, as "a motley rabble of saucy boys, negroes, and molattoes, Irish teagues and outlandish jack tarrs." Perhaps ten thousand people marched in the funeral procession for the victims of the massacre, out of a total Boston population of sixteen thousand. This led England to remove the troops from Boston and try to quiet the situation.

Impressment—drafting colonists into military service—was the background of the massacre. There had been impressment riots through the 1760s in New York and in Newport, Rhode Island, where five hundred seamen, boys, and Negroes rioted. Six weeks before the Boston Massacre, there was a battle in New York of seamen against British soldiers taking their jobs, and one seaman was killed.

In the Boston Tea Party of December 1773 tea was seized from ships and dumped into Boston Harbor. The Boston Committee of Correspondence, formed a year before to organize anti-British actions, "controlled crowd action against the tea from the start," Dirk Hoerder says. The Tea Party led to the Coercive Acts by Parliament, virtually establishing martial law in Massachusetts, dissolving the colonial government, closing the port in Boston, and sending in troops. Mass meetings rose in opposition.

Pauline Maier, who studied the development of opposition to Britain in the decade before 1776 in her book *From Resistance to Revolution*, emphasizes the moderation of the leadership and, despite their desire for resistance, their "emphasis on order and restraint." She notes: "The officers and committee members of the Sons of Liberty were drawn almost entirely from the middle and upper classes of colonial society." Their aim, however, was to broaden their organization, to develop a mass base of wage earners.

In Virginia, it seemed clear to the educated gentry that something needed to be done to persuade the lower orders to join the revolutionary cause, to deflect their anger against England.

It was a problem for which the rhetorical talents of Patrick Henry were superbly fitted. He found language inspiring to all classes, specific enough in its listing of grievances to charge people with anger against the British, vague enough to avoid class conflict among the rebels, and stirring enough to build patriotic feeling for the resistance movement.

Tom Paine's *Common Sense*, which appeared in early 1776 and became the most popular pamphlet in the American colonies, did this. It made the first bold argument for independence, in words that any fairly literate person could understand: "Society in every state is a blessing, but Government even in its best state is but a necessary evil...."

Paine disposed of the idea of the divine right of kings by a pungent history of the British monarchy, going back to the Norman conquest of 1066, when William the Conqueror came over from France to set himself on the British throne: "A French bastard landing with an armed Banditti and establishing himself king of England against the consent of the natives, is in plain terms a very paltry rascally original. It certainly hath no divinity in it."

Paine dealt with the practical advantages of sticking to England or being separated:

I challenge the warmest advocate for reconciliation to show a single advantage that this continent can reap by being connected with Great Britain. I repeat the challenge; not a single advantage is derived. Our corn will fetch its price in any market in Europe, and our imported goods must be paid for by them where we will....

As for the bad effects of the connection with England, Paine appealed to the colonists' memory of all the wars in which England had involved them, wars costly in lives and money. He built slowly to an emotional pitch: "Everything that is right or reasonable pleads for separation. The blood of the slain, the weeping voice of nature cries, 'TIS TIME TO PART'."

Common Sense went through twenty-five editions in 1776 and sold hundreds of thousands of copies. It is probable that almost every literate colonist either read it or knew about its content. Pamphleteering had become by this time the chief theater of debate about relations with England. From 1750 to 1776 four hundred pamphlets had appeared arguing one or another side of the Stamp Act or the Boston Massacre or the Tea Party or the general questions of disobedience to law, loyalty to government, rights and obligations.

Paine's pamphlet appealed to a wide range of colonial opinion angered by England. But it caused some tremors in aristocrats like John Adams, who were with the patriot cause but wanted to make sure it didn't go too far in the direction of democracy. Popular assemblies needed to be checked, Adams thought, because they were "productive of hasty results and absurd judgements."

Paine himself came out of "the lower orders" of England—a staymaker, tax official, teacher, poor emigrant to America. But once the Revolution was under way, Paine more and more made it clear that he was not for the crowd action of lower-class people—like those militia who in 1779 attacked the house of James Wilson. Wilson was a Revolutionary leader who opposed price controls and wanted a more conservative government than was given by the Pennsylvania Constitution of 1776. Paine became an associate of one of the wealthiest men in Pennsylvania, Robert Morris, and a supporter of Morris's creation, the Bank of North America.

Later, during the controversy over adopting the Constitution, Paine would once again represent urban artisans, who favored a strong central government. He seemed to believe that such a government could represent some great common interest. In this sense, he lent himself perfectly to the myth of the Revolution—that it was on behalf of a united people.

The Declaration of Independence brought that myth to its peak of eloquence. Each harsher measure of British control—the Proclamation of 1763, which forbade colonists to settle beyond the Appalachians, the Stamp Tax, the Townshend taxes, including the one on tea, the stationing of troops and the Boston Massacre, the closing of the port of Boston and the dissolution of the Massachusetts legislature—escalated colonial rebellion to the point of revolution. The colonists had responded with the Stamp Act Congress, the Sons of Liberty, the Committees of Correspondence, the Boston Tea Party, and finally, in 1774, the setting up of a Continental Congress—an illegal body, forerunner of a future independent government.

It was after the military clash at Lexington and Concord in April 1775, between colonial minutemen and British troops, that the Continental Congress decided on separation. They organized a small committee to draw up the Declaration of Independence, which Thomas Jefferson wrote. It was adopted by the Congress on July 2, and officially proclaimed July 4, 1776.

By this time there was already a powerful sentiment for independence. Resolutions adopted in North Carolina in May of 1776, and sent to the Continental Congress, declared independence of England, asserted that all British law was null and void, and urged military preparations. About the same time, the town of Malden, Massachusetts, responding to a request from the Massachusetts House of Representatives that all towns in the state declare their views on independence, had met in town meeting and unanimously called for independence: "...we therefore renounce with disdain our connexion with a kingdom of slaves; we bid a final adieu to Britain."

"When in the Course of human events, it becomes necessary for one people to dissolve the political bands...they should declare the causes...." This was the opening of the Declaration of Independence. Then, in its second paragraph, came a powerful philosophical statement:

> We hold these truths to be self-evident, that all men are created equal, that they are endowed by their Creator with certain unalienable Rights, that among these are Life, Liberty and the pursuit of Happiness. That to secure these rights, Governments are instituted among Men, deriving their just powers from the consent of the governed, that whenever any Form of Government becomes destructive of these ends, it is the Right of the People to alter or to abolish it, and to institute new Government....

It then went on to list grievances against the king, "a history of repeated injuries and usurpations, all having in direct object the establishment of an absolute Tyranny over these States." The list accused the king of dissolving colonial governments, controlling judges, sending "swarms of Officers to harass our people," sending in armies of occupation, cutting off colonial trade with other parts of the world, taxing the colonists without their consent, and waging war against them, "transporting large Armies of foreign Mercenaries to compleat the works of death, desolation and tyranny."

All this, the language of popular control over governments, the right of rebellion and revolution, indignation at political tyranny, economic burdens, and military attacks, was language well suited to unite large numbers of colonists and persuade even those who had grievances against one another to turn against England.

Some Americans were clearly omitted from this circle of united interest drawn by the Declaration of Independence: Indians, black slaves, women. Indeed, one paragraph of the Declaration charged the king with inciting slave rebellions and Indian attacks:

> He has excited domestic insurrections amongst us, and has endeavoured to bring on the inhabitants of our frontiers, the merciless Indian Savages, whose known rule of warfare is an undistinguished destruction of all ages, sexes and conditions.

Twenty years before the Declaration, a proclamation of the legislature of Massachusetts of November 3, 1755, declared the Penobscot Indians "rebels, enemies and traitors" and provided a bounty: "For every scalp of a male Indian brought in...forty pounds. For every scalp of such female Indian or male Indian under the age of twelve years that shall be killed...twenty pounds...."

Thomas Jefferson had written a paragraph of the Declaration accusing the king of transporting slaves from Africa to the colonies and "suppressing every legislative attempt to prohibit or to restrain this execrable commerce." This seemed to express moral indignation against slavery and the slave trade (Jefferson's personal distaste for slavery must be put alongside the fact that he owned hundreds of slaves to the day he died). Behind it was the growing fear among Virginians and some other southerners about the growing number of black slaves in the colonies (20 percent of the total population) and the threat of slave revolts as the number of slaves increased.

Jefferson's paragraph was removed by the Continental Congress because slaveholders themselves disagreed about the desirability of ending the slave trade. So even that gesture toward the black slave was omitted from the American Revolution's great manifesto of freedom.

The use of the phrase "all men are created equal" was probably not a deliberate attempt to make a statement about women. It was just that women were beyond consideration as worthy of inclusion. They were politically invisible. Though practical needs gave women a certain authority in the home, on the farm, or in occupations such as midwifery, they were simply overlooked in any consideration of political rights, any notions of civic equality.

To say that the Declaration of Independence, even by its own language, was limited to life, liberty, and happiness for white males is not to denounce the makers and signers of the Declaration for holding the ideas expected of privileged males of the eighteenth century. Reformers and radicals, looking discontentedly at history, are often accused of expecting too much from a past political epoch—and sometimes they do. But the point of noting those outside the arc of human rights in the Declaration is not, centuries late and pointlessly, to denounce the moral failures of that time. It is to try to understand the way in which the Declaration functioned to mobilize certain groups of Americans, ignoring others. Surely, inspirational language to create a secure consensus is still used, in our time, to cover up serious conflicts of interest in that consensus, and to cover up, also, the omission of large parts of the human race.

The reality behind the words of the Declaration of Independence was that a rising class of important people needed to enlist on their side enough Americans to defeat England, without disturbing too much the relations of wealth and power that had developed over 150 years of colonial history. Indeed, 69 percent of the signers of the Declaration of Independence had held colonial office under England.

When the Declaration of Independence was read, with all its flaming radical language, from the town hall balcony in Boston, it was read by Thomas Crafts, a member of the Loyal Nine group, conservatives who had opposed militant action against the British. Four days after the reading, the Boston Committee of Correspondence ordered the townsmen to show up on the common for a military draft. The rich, it turned out, could avoid the draft by paying for substitutes; the poor had to serve. This led to rioting and shouting: "Tyranny is Tyranny let it come from whom it may."

Exercises

1. Before reading the chapter, make a time line which includes the following: the founding of Jamestown, Virginia; the passage of the first Navigation Act; Bacon's Rebellion; the French and Indian War; the Stamp Act; the Coercive Acts; the battles of Lexington and Concord; and the battle of Yorktown.

2. On page 47: What does Zinn mean by "… the advantages of combining paternalism with command"?

3. Zinn argues that "It was not a conscious conspiracy, but an accumulation of tactical responses."(p. 47) What is the difference between a "conscious conspiracy" and "tactical responses"?

4. Below are a series of arguments (a-k). For each argument, identify an example (detail/data) from the chapter that supports the argument (note: one example might be used to illustrate more than one of the arguments below, but try to find a different example for each argument):

    a. "…they [took] over land, profits, and political power from favorites of the British Empire."

    b. "…create a consensus of popular support for the rule of a new, privileged leadership."

    c. "…mirroring as well as molding popular opinion"

    d. "…mobilization of lower-class energy by upper-class politicians…"

    e. "…class hatred be focused against the pro-British elite…"

    f. "…class hatred be…deflected from the nationalist elite."

    g. "…they [won] over the mechanics…"

    h. "…[the local elites kept] the propertyless people…under control…[by using the] mob energy against England, but also [contained] it so that it would not demand too much from them."

    i. "…language…specific enough in its listing of grievances to charge people with anger against the British, vague enough to avoid class conflict among the rebels…"

j. "…language [to] persuade even those who had grievances against one another to turn against England."

k. "…without disturbing too much the relations of wealth and power that had developed over 150 years of colonial history."

5. *Research:* What role did each of the events listed below play in causing conflict between the colonial elites and England (or their representatives in America); the colonial people (lower orders) and colonial elites; OR the colonial people (lower orders) and England (or their representatives in America)?

[NOTE: You will have to go to texts other than Zinn for some of the answers.]

a. French and Indian War

b. growth of trade between England and its American colonies

c. Proclamation Line of 1763

d. "…six black rebellions…and forty riots" all occurring between 1676 and 1760

e. Stamp Act of 1765

f. mechanics' demand for political democracy in the cities

g. Privates Committee's bill of rights

h. tenant riots from the 1740s through the 1760s

i. Regulator Movement

j. Townshend Acts of 1767

k. quartering of British troops in 1768

l. impressment of sailors

m. impounding of ships in admiralty courts under the specifications of the Sugar Act

n. Tea Act of 1773

o. Boston Port Act of 1773

p. Massachusetts Government Act of 1774

6. Define the "lower orders" in terms of their:
   ★ percentage of community wealth controlled
   ★ occupations

       ★ political and economic interests
       ★ social labels/epithets

7. Define the "local political and social elite" in terms of their:
       ★ percentage of community wealth controlled
       ★ occupations
       ★ political and economic interests
       ★ social labels/epithets

8. *Debate Resolution:* The American Revolution was a war not for independence but consolidation.

Chapter 5

A Kind of Revolution

The American victory over the British army was made possible by the existence of an already-armed people. Just about every white male had a gun and could shoot. The Revolutionary leadership distrusted the mobs of poor. But they knew the Revolution had no appeal to slaves and Indians. They would have to woo the armed white population.

This was not easy. Yes, mechanics and sailors and some others were incensed against the British. But general enthusiasm for the war was not strong. John Shy, in his study of the Revolutionary army (*A People Numerous and Armed*), estimates that perhaps a fifth of the population was actively treasonous. John Adams had estimated a third opposed, a third in support, a third neutral.

The men who first joined the colonial militia were generally "hallmarks of respectability or at least of full citizenship" in their communities, Shy says. Excluded from the militia were friendly Indians, free Negroes, white servants, and free white men who had no stable home. But desperation led to the recruiting of the less respectable whites. Massachusetts and Virginia provided for drafting "strollers" (vagrants) into the militia. In fact, the military became a place of promise for the poor, who might rise in rank, acquire some money, and change their social status.

Here was the traditional device by which those in charge of any social order mobilize and discipline a recalcitrant population—offering the adventure and rewards of military service to get poor people to fight for a cause they may not see clearly as their own. A wounded American lieutenant at Bunker Hill, John Scott, told how he had joined the rebel forces:

I was a Shoemaker, & got my living by my Labor. When this Rebellion came on, I saw some of my Neighbors got into Commission, who were no better than myself. I was very ambitious, & did not like to see those Men above me. I was asked to enlist, as a private Soldier...I offered to enlist upon having a Lieutenants Commission; which was granted. I imagined myself now in a way of Promotion.

Scott was one of many Revolutionary fighters, usually of lower military ranks, from poor and obscure backgrounds. Shy's study of the Peterborough contingent shows that the prominent and substantial citizens of the town had served only briefly in the war. Other American towns show the same pattern. As Shy puts it: "Revolutionary America may have been a middle-class society, happier and more prosperous than any other in its time, but it contained a large and growing number of fairly poor people, and many of them did much of the actual fighting and suffering between 1775 and 1783: A very old story."

The military conflict itself, by dominating everything in its time, diminished other issues, made people choose sides in the one contest that was publicly important, forced people onto the side of the Revolution whose interest in independence was not at all obvious. War was making the ruling elite more secure against internal trouble.

Here, in the war for liberty, was conscription, as usual, cognizant of wealth. With the impressment riots against the British still remembered, impressment of seamen by the American navy was taking place by 1779. A Pennsylvania official said: "We cannot help observing how similar this Conduct is to that of the British Officers during our Subjection to Great Britain and are persuaded it will have the same unhappy effects viz. an estrangement of the Affections of the People from...Authority...which by an easy Progression will proceed to open Opposition...and bloodshed."

The Americans lost the first battles of the war: Bunker Hill, Brooklyn Heights, Harlem Heights, the Deep South; they won small battles at Trenton and Princeton, and then, in a turning point, a big battle at Saratoga, New York, in 1777. Washington's frozen army hung on at Valley Forge, Pennsylvania, while Benjamin Franklin negotiated an alliance with the French monarchy, which was anxious for revenge on England. The war turned to the South, where the British won victory after victory, until the Americans, aided by a large French army, with the French navy blocking off the British from supplies and reinforcements, won the final victory of the war at Yorktown, Virginia, in 1781.

Through all this, the suppressed conflicts between rich and poor among the Americans kept reappearing. The war, Eric Foner says, was "a time of immense profits for some colonists and terrible hardships for others."

In May 1779, the First Company of Philadelphia Artillery petitioned the Assembly about the troubles of "the midling and poor" and threatened violence against "those who are avariciously intent upon amassing wealth by the destruction of the more virtuous part of the community." In October came the "Fort Wilson riot," in which a militia group marched into the city and to the house of James Wilson, a wealthy lawyer and Revolutionary official who had opposed price controls and the democratic constitution adopted in Pennsylvania in 1776. The militia were driven away by a "silk stocking brigade" of well-off Philadelphia citizens.

The Continental Congress, which governed the colonies through the war, was dominated by rich men, linked together in factions and compacts by business and family connections. For instance, Richard Henry Lee of Virginia was connected with the Adamses of Massachusetts and the Shippens of Pennsylvania.

The Congress voted half-pay for life for those officers who stuck to the end. This ignored the common soldier, who was not getting paid, who was suffering in the cold, dying of sickness, watching the civilian profiteers get rich. On New Year's Day, 1781, the Pennsylvania troops near Morristown, New Jersey, perhaps emboldened by rum, dispersed their officers, killed one captain, wounded others, and were marching, fully armed, with cannon, toward the Continental Congress at Philadelphia.

George Washington handled it cautiously. A peace was negotiated, in which half the men were discharged; the other half got furloughs.

Shortly after this, a smaller mutiny took place in the New Jersey Line, involving two hundred men who defied their officers and started out for the state capital at Trenton. Now Washington was ready. Six hundred men, who themselves had been well fed and clothed, marched on the mutineers and surrounded and disarmed them. Three ringleaders were put on trial immediately, in the field. One was pardoned, and two were shot by firing squads made up of their friends, who wept as they pulled the triggers. It was "an example," Washington said.

Two years later, there was another mutiny in the Pennsylvania Line. The war was over and the army had disbanded, but eighty soldiers, demanding their pay, invaded the Continental Congress headquarters in Philadelphia and forced the members to flee across the river to Princeton— "ignominiously turned out of doors," as one historian sorrowfully wrote (John Fiske, *The Critical Period*), "by a handful of drunken mutineers."

What soldiers in the Revolution could do only rarely, rebel against their authorities, civilians could do much more easily. Ronald Hoffman says: "The Revolution plunged the states of Delaware, Maryland, North Carolina, South Carolina, Georgia, and, to a much lesser degree, Virginia into divisive civil conflicts that persisted during the entire period of struggle." The southern lower classes resisted being mobilized for the revolution. They saw themselves under the rule of a political elite, win or lose against the British.

With black slaves 20 percent of the population (and in some counties 50 percent), fear of slave revolts grew. George Washington had turned down the requests of blacks, seeking freedom, to fight in the Revolutionary army. So when the British military commander in Virginia, Lord Dunmore, promised freedom to Virginia slaves who joined his forces, this created consternation.

Even more unsettling was white rioting in Maryland against leading families supporting the Revolution, who were suspected of hoarding needed commodities. Despite this, Maryland authorities retained control. They made concessions, taxing land and slaves more heavily, letting debtors pay in paper money. It was a sacrifice by the upper class to maintain power, and it worked.

In the lower South, however, the general mood was to take no part in a war that seemed to have nothing for them. Washington's military commander there, Nathanael Greene, dealt with disloyalty by a policy of concessions to some, brutality to others. In a letter to Thomas Jefferson he described a raid by his troops on Loyalists. "They made a dreadful carnage of them, upwards of one hundred were killed and most of the rest cut to pieces. It has had a very happy effect on those disaffected persons of which there were too many in this country." In general, throughout the states, concessions were kept to a minimum. The new constitutions that were drawn up in all states from 1776 to 1780 were not much different from the old ones. Only Pennsylvania abolished property qualifications for voting and holding office.

One would look, in examining the Revolution's effect on class relations, at what happened to land confiscated from fleeing Loyalists. It was distributed in such a way as to give a double opportunity to the Revolutionary leaders: to enrich themselves and their friends, and to parcel out some land to small farmers to create a broad base of support for the new government. Indeed, this became characteristic of the new nation: finding itself possessed of enormous wealth, it could create the richest ruling class in history and still have enough for the middle classes to act as a buffer between the rich and the dispossessed.

Edmund Morgan sums up the class nature of the Revolution this way: "The fact that the lower ranks were involved in the contest should not obscure the fact that the contest itself was generally a struggle for office and power between members of an upper class: the new against the established."

Carl Degler says (*Out of Our Past*): "No new social class came to power through the door of the American revolution. The men who engineered the revolt were largely members of the colonial ruling class." George Washington was the richest man in America. John Hancock was a prosperous Boston merchant. Benjamin Franklin was a wealthy printer. And so on.

On the other hand, town mechanics, laborers, and seamen, as well as small farmers, were swept into "the people" by the rhetoric of the Revolution, by the camaraderie of military service, by the distribution of some land. Thus was created a substantial body of support, a national consensus, something that, even with the exclusion of ignored and oppressed people, could be called "America."

Staughton Lynd's close study of Dutchess County, New York, in the Revolutionary period corroborates this. There were tenant risings in 1766 against the huge feudal estates in New York. The Rensselaerwyck holding was a million acres. Tenants, claiming some of this land for themselves, unable to get satisfaction in the courts, turned to violence. In Poughkeepsie, seventeen hundred armed tenants closed the courts and broke open the jails. But the uprising was crushed.

Tenants became a threatening force in the midst of the war. Many stopped paying rent. The legislature, worried, passed a bill to confiscate Loyalist land and add four hundred new freeholders to the eighteen hundred already in the county. The new freeholders found that they had stopped being tenants, but were now mortgagees, paying back loans from banks instead of rent to landlords.

It seems that the rebellion against British rule allowed a certain group of the colonial elite to replace those loyal to England, give some benefits to small landholders, and leave poor white working people and tenant farmers in very much their old situation.

What did the Revolution mean to the native Americans, the Indians? They had been ignored by the fine words of the Declaration, had not been considered equal, certainly not in choosing those who would govern the

American territories in which they lived, nor in being able to pursue happiness as they had pursued it for centuries before the white Europeans arrived. Now, with the British out of the way, the Americans could begin the inexorable process of pushing the Indians off their lands, killing them if they resisted. In short, as Francis Jennings puts it, the white Americans were fighting against British imperial control in the East, and for their own imperialism in the West.

In New York, through intricate swindling, eight hundred thousand acres of Mohawk land were taken, ending the period of friendship between the Mohawks and the state. Chief Hendrick of the Mohawks is recorded speaking his bitterness to Gov. George Clinton and the provincial council of New York in 1753:

> Brother when we came here to relate our Grievances about our Lands, we expected to have something done for us, and we have told you that the Covenant Chain of our Forefathers was like to be broken, and brother you tell us that we shall be redressed at Albany, but we know them so well, we will not trust to them, for they [the Albany merchants] are no people but Devils so...as soon as we come home we will send up a Belt of Wampum to our Brothers the other 5 Nations to acquaint them the Covenant Chain is broken between you and us. So brother you are not to expect to hear of me any more, and Brother we desire to hear no more of you.

When the British fought the French for North America in the Seven Years' War, the Indians fought on the side of the French. The French were traders but not occupiers of Indian lands, while the British clearly coveted their hunting grounds and living space.

When that war ended in 1763, the French, ignoring their old allies, ceded to the British lands west of the Appalachians. The Indians therefore united to make war on the British western forts; this is called "Pontiac's Conspiracy" by the British, but "a liberation war for independence" in the words used by Francis Jennings. Under orders from the British general Jeffrey Amherst, the commander of Fort Pitts gave the attacking Indian chiefs, with whom he was negotiating, blankets from the smallpox hospital. It was a pioneering effort at what is now called biological warfare. An epidemic soon spread among the Indians.

Despite the burning of villages, the British could not destroy the will of the Indians, who continued guerrilla war. A peace was made, with the British agreeing to establish a line at the Appalachians, beyond which settlements would not encroach on Indian territory. This was the Royal

Proclamation of 1763, and it angered Americans (the original Virginia charter said its land went westward to the ocean). It helps to explain why most of the Indians fought for England during the Revolution. With their French allies, then their English allies, gone, the Indians faced a new land-coveting nation—alone.

With the eastern elite controlling the lands on the seaboard, the poor, seeking land, were forced to go West. They became a useful bulwark for the rich, because it was the frontiers people who were the first targets of the Indians.

The situation of black slaves as a result of the American Revolution was more complex. Thousands of blacks fought with the British. Five thousand were with the Revolutionaries.

In the northern states, the combination of blacks in the military, the lack of powerful economic need for slaves, and the rhetoric of Revolution led to the end of slavery—but very slowly. As late as 1810, thirty thousand blacks, one-fourth of the black population of the North, remained slaves. In 1840 there were still a thousand slaves in the North. In the upper South, there were more free Negroes than before, leading to more control legislation. In the lower South, slavery expanded with the growth of rice and cotton plantations.

What the Revolution did was to create space and opportunity for blacks to begin making demands of white society. Sometimes these demands came from the new, small black elites in Baltimore, Philadelphia, Richmond, and Savannah, sometimes from articulate and bold slaves. Pointing to the Declaration of Independence, blacks petitioned Congress and the state legislatures to abolish slavery, to give blacks equal rights. In 1780, seven blacks in Dartmouth, Massachusetts, petitioned the legislature for the right to vote, linking taxation to representation:

> ...we apprehend ourselves to be Aggreeved, in that while we are not allowed the Privilage of freemen of the State having no vote or Influence in the Election of those that Tax us yet many of our Colour (as is well known) have cheerfully Entered the field of Battle in the defense of the Common Cause and that (as we conceive) against a similar Exertion of Power (in Regard to taxation) too well known to need a recital in this place....

A black man, Benjamin Banneker, who taught himself mathematics and astronomy, accurately predicted a solar eclipse, and was appointed to plan the new city of Washington, wrote to Thomas Jefferson:

I suppose it is a truth too well attested to you, to need a proof here, that we are a race of beings, who have long labored under the abuse and censure of the world; that we have long been looked upon with an eye of contempt; and that we have long been considered rather as brutish than human, and scarcely capable of mental endowments.... I apprehend you will embrace every opportunity to eradicate that train of absurd and false ideas and opinions, which so generally prevails with respect to us; and that your sentiments are concurrent with mine, which are, that one universal Father hath given being to us all; and that he hath not only made us all of one flesh, but that he hath also, without partiality, afforded us all the same sensations and endowed us all with the same facilities....

Banneker asked Jefferson "to wean yourselves from those narrow prejudices which you have imbibed."

Jefferson tried his best, as an enlightened, thoughtful individual might. But the structure of American society, the power of the cotton plantation, the slave trade, the politics of unity between northern and southern elites, and the established culture of race prejudice in the colonies, as well as his own weaknesses—that combination of practical need and ideological fixation—kept Jefferson a slaveowner throughout his life.

The inferior position of blacks, the exclusion of Indians from the new society, the establishment of supremacy for the rich and powerful in the new nation—all this was already settled in the colonies by the time of the Revolution. With the English out of the way, it could now be put on paper, solidified, regularized, made legitimate, by the Constitution of the United States, drafted at a convention of Revolutionary leaders in Philadelphia.

To many Americans over the years, the Constitution drawn up in 1787 has seemed a work of genius put together by wise, humane men who created a legal framework for democracy and equality.

Another view of the Constitution was put forward early in the twentieth century by the historian Charles Beard (arousing anger and indignation, including a denunciatory editorial in the *New York Times*). In his book *An Economic Interpretation of the Constitution*, Beard studied the economic backgrounds and political ideas of the fifty-five men who gathered in Philadelphia in 1787 to draw up the Constitution. He found that a majority of them were lawyers by profession, that most of them were men of wealth, in land, slaves, manufacturing, or shipping, that half of them had money loaned out at interest, and that forty of the fifty-five held government bonds, according to the records of the Treasury Department.

Thus, Beard found that most of the makers of the Constitution had some direct economic interest in establishing a strong federal government: the manufacturers needed protective tariffs; the moneylenders wanted to stop the use of paper money to pay off debts; the land speculators wanted protection as they invaded Indian lands; slaveowners needed federal security against slave revolts and runaways; bondholders wanted a government able to raise money by nationwide taxation, to pay off those bonds.

Four groups, Beard noted, were not represented in the Constitutional Convention: slaves, indentured servants, women, and men without property. And so the Constitution did not reflect the interests of those groups.

He wanted to make it clear that he did not think the Constitution was written merely to benefit the Founding Fathers personally. Rather, it was to benefit the groups the founders represented, the "economic interests they understood and felt in concrete, definite form through their own personal experience."

By 1787 there was not only a positive need for strong central government to protect the large economic interests, but also immediate fear of rebellion by discontented farmers. The chief event causing this fear was an uprising in the summer of 1786 in western Massachusetts, known as Shays' Rebellion.

In the western towns of Massachusetts there was resentment against the legislature in Boston. The new constitution of 1780 had raised the property qualifications for voting. No one could hold state office without being quite wealthy. Furthermore, the legislature was refusing to issue paper money, as had been done in some other states, such as Rhode Island, to make it easier for debt-ridden farmers to pay off their creditors.

Illegal conventions began to assemble in some of the western counties to organize opposition to the legislature. At one of these, a man named Plough Jogger spoke his mind:

> I have been greatly abused, have been obliged to do more than my part in the war; been loaded with class rates, town rates, province rates, Continental rates and all rates ...been pulled and hauled by sheriffs, constables and collectors, and had my cattle sold for less than they were worth....
>
> ...The great men are going to get all we have and I think it is time for us to rise and put a stop to it, and have no more courts, nor sheriffs, nor collectors nor lawyers....

There were going to be court proceedings in Hampshire County, in the towns of Northampton and Springfield, to seize the cattle of farmers who hadn't paid their debts, to take away their land, now full of grain and ready for harvest. And so, veterans of the Continental army, also aggrieved because they had been treated poorly on discharge—given certificates for future redemption instead of immediate cash—began to organize the farmers into squads and companies. One of these veterans was Luke Day, who arrived the morning of court with a fife-and-drum corps, still angry with the memory of being locked up in debtors' prison in the heat of the previous summer.

The sheriff looked to the local militia to defend the court against these armed farmers. But most of the militia was with Luke Day. The sheriff did manage to gather five hundred men, and the judges put on their black silk robes, waiting for the sheriff to protect their trip to the courthouse. But there at the courthouse steps, Luke Day stood with a petition, asserting the people's constitutional right to protest the unconstitutional acts of the General Court, asking the judges to adjourn until the General Court could act on behalf of the farmers. Standing with Luke Day were fifteen hundred armed farmers. The judges adjourned.

Shortly after, at courthouses in Worcester and Athol, farmers with guns prevented the courts from meeting to take away their property, and the militia were too sympathetic to the farmers, or too outnumbered, to act. In Concord, a fifty-year-old veteran of two wars, Job Shattuck, led a caravan of carts, wagons, horses, and oxen onto the town green, while a message was sent to the judges: "The voice of the People of this county is such that the court shall not enter this courthouse until such time as the People shall have redress of the grievances they labor under at the present." A county convention then suggested the judges adjourn, which they did.

At Great Barrington, a militia of a thousand faced a square crowded with armed men and boys. But the militia was split in its opinion, most favoring the crowd, which, after obtaining the chief justice's promise to adjourn his court until the General Court met, went back to the square, broke open the county jail, and set the debtors free. The chief justice, a country doctor, said: "I have never heard anybody point out a better way to have their grievances redressed than the people have taken."

The governor and the political leaders of Massachusetts became alarmed. Samuel Adams, once looked on as a radical leader in Boston, now insisted people act within the law. He said "British emissaries" were stirring up the farmers. People in the town of Greenwich responded: You in Boston have the money, and we don't. And didn't you act illegally yourselves in the Revolution? The insurgents were now being called Regulators. Their emblem was a sprig of hemlock.

The problem went beyond Massachusetts. In Rhode Island, the debtors had taken over the legislature and were issuing paper money. In New Hampshire, several hundred men, in September of 1786, surrounded the legislature in Exeter, asking that taxes be returned and paper money issued; they dispersed only when military action was threatened.

Daniel Shays entered the scene in western Massachusetts. A poor farm hand when the Revolution broke out, he joined the Continental army, fought at Lexington, Bunker Hill, and Saratoga, and was wounded in action. In 1780, not being paid, he resigned from the army, went home, and soon found himself in court for nonpayment of debts. He also saw what was happening to others: a sick woman, unable to pay, had her bed taken from under her.

What brought Shays fully into the situation was that on September 19, the Supreme Judicial Court of Massachusetts indicted eleven leaders of the rebellion, including three of his friends, as "disorderly, riotous and seditious persons." Shays organized seven hundred armed farmers, most of them veterans of the war, and led them to Springfield. As they marched, their ranks grew. Some of the militia joined, and reinforcements began coming in from the countryside. The judges postponed hearings for a day, then adjourned the court.

Now the General Court, meeting in Boston, was told by Governor James Bowdoin to "vindicate the insulted dignity of government." The recent rebels against England, secure in office, were calling for law and order. Sam Adams helped draw up a riot act and a resolution suspending habeas corpus, to allow the authorities to keep people in jail without trial. At the same time, the legislature moved to make some concessions to the angry farmers, saying certain old taxes could now be paid in goods instead of money.

This didn't help. Confrontations between farmers and militia now multiplied. But the winter snows began to interfere with the farmers' trips to the courthouses. When Shays began marching a thousand men into Boston, a blizzard forced them back, and one of his men froze to death.

An army came into the field, led by Gen. Benjamin Lincoln, on money raised by Boston merchants. The rebels were outnumbered and on the run. Shays took refuge in Vermont, and his followers began to surrender. There were a few more deaths in battle, and then sporadic, disorganized, desperate acts of violence against authority: the burning of barns, the slaughter of a general's horses. One government soldier was killed in an eerie nighttime collision of two sleighs.

Captured rebels were put on trial in Northampton and six were sentenced to death. A note was left at the door of the high sheriff of Pittsfield: "I understand that there is a number of my countrymen condemned to die because they fought for justice.... Prepare for death with speed, for your life or mine is short."

Thirty-three more rebels were put on trial and six more condemned to death. General Lincoln urged mercy and a Commission of Clemency, but Samuel Adams said: "In monarchy the crime of treason may admit of being pardoned or lightly punished, but the man who dares rebel against the laws of a republic ought to suffer death." Several hangings followed; some of the condemned were pardoned. Shays, in Vermont, was pardoned in 1788 and returned to Massachusetts, where he died, poor and obscure, in 1825.

It was Thomas Jefferson, in France as ambassador at the time of Shays' Rebellion, who spoke of such uprisings as healthy for society. In a letter to a friend he wrote: "I hold it that a little rebellion now and then is a good thing.... It is a medicine necessary for the sound health of government.... God forbid that we should ever be twenty years without such a rebellion.... The tree of liberty must be refreshed from time to time with the blood of patriots and tyrants. It is its natural manure."

But Jefferson was far from the scene. The political and economic elite of the country were not so tolerant. They worried that the example might spread. A veteran of Washington's army, Gen. Henry Knox, founded an organization of army veterans, "The Order of the Cincinnati." Knox wrote to Washington in late 1786 about Shays' Rebellion, and in doing so expressed the thoughts of many of the wealthy and powerful leaders of the country: "The people who are the insurgents feel at once their own poverty, compared with the opulent.... Their creed is 'That the property of the United States has been protected from the confiscations of Britain by the joint exertions of all, and therefore ought to be the common property of all.'"

Alexander Hamilton, an aide to Washington during the war, was one of the most forceful and astute leaders of the new aristocracy. He voiced his political philosophy:

> All communities divide themselves into the few and the many. The first are the rich and well-born, the other the mass of the people.... The people are turbulent and changing; they seldom judge or determine right. Give therefore to the first class a distinct permanent share in the government.... Nothing but a permanent body can check the imprudence of democracy....

At the Constitutional Convention, Hamilton suggested a president and Senate chosen for life. The Convention did not take his suggestion. But neither did it provide for popular elections, except in the case of the House of Representatives, where the qualifications were set by the state legislatures (which required property holding for voting in almost every state), and excluded women, Indians, and slaves. The Constitution provided for senators to be elected by the state legislators, for the president to be elected by electors chosen by the state legislators, and for the Supreme Court to be appointed by the president.

The problem of democracy in the post-Revolutionary society was not, however, the Constitutional limitations on voting. It lay deeper, beyond the Constitution, in the division of society into rich and poor. For if some people had great wealth and great influence; if they had the land, the money, the newspapers, the church, the educational system—how could voting, however broad, cut into such power? There was still another problem: wasn't it the nature of representative government, even when most broadly based, to be conservative, to prevent tumultuous change?

It came time to ratify the Constitution, to submit to a vote in state conventions, with approval of nine of the thirteen required to ratify it. In New York, where debate over ratification was intense, a series of newspaper articles appeared, anonymously, and they tell us much about the nature of the Constitution. These articles, favoring adoption of the Constitution, were written by James Madison, Alexander Hamilton, and John Jay, and came to be known as the *Federalist Papers* (opponents of the Constitution became known as anti-Federalists).

In *Federalist Paper #10*, James Madison argued that representative government was needed to maintain peace in a society ridden by factional disputes. These disputes came from "the various and unequal distribution of property. Those who hold and those who are without property have ever formed distinct interests in society." The problem, he said, was how to control the factional struggles that came from inequalities in wealth. Minority factions could be controlled, he said, by the principle that decisions would be by vote of the majority.

So the real problem, according to Madison, was a majority faction, and here the solution was offered by the Constitution, to have "an extensive republic," that is, a large nation ranging over thirteen states, for then "it will be more difficult for all who feel it to discover their own strength, and to act in unison with each other...."

As part of his argument for a large republic to keep the peace, James Madison tells quite clearly, in *Federalist #10*, whose peace he wants to keep: "A rage for paper money, for an abolition of debts, for an equal division of property, or for any other improper or wicked project, will be less apt to pervade the whole body of the Union than a particular member of it."

When economic interest is seen behind the political clauses of the Constitution, then the document becomes not simply the work of wise men trying to establish a decent and orderly society, but the work of certain groups trying to maintain their privileges, while giving just enough rights and liberties to enough of the people to ensure popular support.

In the new government, Madison would belong to one party (the Democrat-Republicans) along with Jefferson and Monroe. Hamilton would belong to the rival party (the Federalists) along with Washington and Adams. But both agreed—one a slaveholder from Virginia, the other a merchant from New York—on the aims of this new government they were establishing. In this they anticipated the tradition of fundamental agreement between the two "opposing" political parties in the American system. Hamilton wrote elsewhere in the *Federalist Papers* that the new Union would be able "to repress domestic faction and insurrection." He referred directly to Shays' Rebellion: "The tempestuous situation from which Massachusetts has scarcely emerged evinces that dangers of this kind are not merely speculative."

It was either Madison or Hamilton (the authorship of the individual papers is not always known) who in *Federalist Paper # 63* argued the necessity of a "well-constructed Senate" as "sometimes necessary as a defence to the people against their own temporary errors and delusions." And: "In these critical moments, how salutary will be the interference of some temperate and respectable body of citizens in order to check the misguided career, and to suspend the blow meditated by the people against themselves, until reason, justice, and truth can regain their authority over the public mind?"

The Constitution was a compromise between slaveholding interests of the South and moneyed interests of the North. For the purpose of uniting the thirteen states into one great market for commerce, the northern delegates wanted laws regulating interstate commerce and urged that such laws require only a majority of Congress to pass. The South agreed to this, in return for allowing the trade in slaves to continue for twenty years before being outlawed.

Charles Beard warned us that governments—including the government of the United States—are not neutral, that they represent the dominant economic interests, and that their constitutions are intended to serve these interests.

True, there were many property owners. But some people had much more than others. A few people had great amounts of property; many people (roughly, one-third) had small amounts; others had none.

Still, one-third was a considerable number of people who felt they had something at stake in the stability of a new government. This was a larger base of support for government than anywhere in the world at the end of the eighteenth century. In addition, the city mechanics had an important interest in a government that would protect their work from foreign competition.

This was especially true in New York. When the ninth and tenth states had ratified the Constitution, four thousand New York City mechanics marched with floats and banners to celebrate. Bakers, blacksmiths, brewers, ship joiners and shipwrights, coopers, cartmen, and tailors all marched. They required a government that would protect them against the British hats and shoes and other goods that were pouring into the colonies after the Revolution. As a result, the mechanics often supported wealthy conservatives at the ballot box.

The Constitution, then, illustrates the complexity of the American system: that it serves the interests of a wealthy elite, but also does enough for small property owners, for middle-income workers and farmers, to build a broad base of support. The slightly prosperous people who make up this base of support are buffers against the blacks, the Indians, and the very poor whites. They enable the elite to keep control with a minimum of coercion, a maximum of law—all made palatable by the fanfare of patriotism and unity.

The Constitution became even more acceptable to the public at large after the first Congress, responding to criticism, passed a series of amendments known as the Bill of Rights. These amendments seemed to make the new government a guardian of people's liberties: to speak, to publish, to worship, to petition, to assemble, to be tried fairly, to be secure at home against official intrusion. It was, therefore, perfectly designed to build popular backing for the new government. What was not made clear—it was a time when the language of freedom was new and its reality untested—was the shakiness of anyone's liberty when entrusted to a government of the rich and powerful.

Indeed, the same problem existed for the other provisions of the Constitution, such as the clause forbidding states to "impair the obligation of contract," or that giving Congress the power to tax the people and to appropriate money. They all sound benign and neutral until one asks: Tax whom, for what? Appropriate what, for whom?

To protect everyone's contracts seems like an act of fairness, of equal treatment, until one considers that contracts made between rich and poor, between employer and employee, landlord and tenant, creditor and debtor, generally favor the more powerful of the two parties. Thus, to protect these contracts is to put the great power of the government, its laws, courts, sheriffs, police, on the side of the privileged—and to do it not, as in premodern times, as an exercise of brute force against the weak but as a matter of law.

The First Amendment of the Bill of Rights shows that quality of interest hiding behind innocence. Passed in 1791 by Congress, it provided that "Congress shall make no law... abridging the freedom of speech, or of the press...." Yet, seven years after the First Amendment became part of the Constitution, Congress passed a law very clearly abridging the freedom of speech.

This was the Sedition Act of 1798, passed under John Adams's administration, at a time when Irishmen and Frenchmen in the United States were looked on as dangerous revolutionaries because of the recent French Revolution and the Irish rebellions. The Sedition Act made it a crime to say or write anything "false, scandalous and malicious" against the government, Congress, or the President, with intent to defame them, bring them into disrepute, or excite popular hatreds against them.

This act seemed to violate the First Amendment directly. Yet, it was enforced. Ten Americans were put in prison for utterances against the government, and every member of the Supreme Court between 1798 and 1800, sitting as an appellate judge, held it constitutional.

Despite the First Amendment, the British common law of "seditious libel" still ruled in America. This meant that while the government could not exercise "prior restraint"—that is, prevent an utterance or publication in advance—it could legally punish the speaker or writer afterward. Thus, Congress has a convenient legal basis for the laws it has enacted since that time, making certain kinds of speech a crime. And, since punishment after the fact is a strong deterrent to the exercise of free expression, the claim of "no prior restraint" itself is destroyed. This leaves the First Amendment much less than the stone wall of protection it seems at first glance.

Are the economic provisions in the Constitution enforced just as weakly? We have an instructive example almost immediately in Washington's first administration, when Congress's power to tax and appropriate money was immediately put to use by the secretary of the treasury, Alexander Hamilton.

Hamilton, believing that government must ally itself with the richest elements of society to make itself strong, proposed to Congress a series of laws, which it enacted, expressing this philosophy. The Bank of the United States was set up as a partnership between the government and certain banking interests. A tariff was passed to help the manufacturers. It was agreed to pay bondholders—most of the war bonds were now concentrated among a small group of wealthy people—the full value of their bonds. Tax laws were passed to raise money for this bond redemption.

One of these tax laws was the Whiskey Tax, which especially hurt small farmers who raised grain that they converted into whiskey and then sold. In 1794 the farmers of western Pennsylvania took up arms and rebelled against the collection of this tax. Secretary of the Treasury Hamilton led the troops to put them down. We see then, in the first years of the Constitution, that some of its provisions—even those paraded most flamboyantly (like the First Amendment)—might be treated lightly. Others (like the power to tax) would be powerfully enforced.

Still, the mythology around the Founding Fathers persists. Were they wise and just men trying to achieve a balance of power? In fact, they did not want a balance, except one which kept things as they were, a balance among the dominant forces at that time. They certainly did not want an equal balance between slaves and masters, propertyless and property holders, Indians and white.

As many as half the people were not even considered by the Founding Fathers. They were not mentioned in the Declaration of Independence, they were absent in the Constitution, they were invisible in the new political democracy. They were the women of early America.

Exercises

1. How much colonial opposition was there to British rule in 1776?

2. What motivated the colonial poor to fight the British?

3. Zinn argues that the American Revolutionary "War was making the ruling elite more secure against internal trouble" (p. 62). What evidence does Zinn provide to support this assertion?

4. The Battle of Saratoga (1777) brought the French into the war on the side of the Americans. Why was this result significant enough to make the Battle of Saratoga the "turning point" of the war?

5. Which of the following is the most appropriate thesis for this chapter:

    a. The Americans won the war only with help from the French.

    b. The war was a struggle for power between members of an upper class.

    c. Rich men ran the war.

    d. General enthusiasm for the war was not strong.

Defend your choice and give your reasons for having eliminated the rest.

6. What were the grievances of the American troops who mutinied or rebelled during the American Revolution?

7. What were the methods of control used by the Revolutionary elite to control disobedient and rebellious colonists?

8. How did farmers resist impoverishment?

9. Why did the Indians fight with the British against the colonial rebels?

10. How did blacks respond to the opportunities presented by the Revolutionary War? How effective were their responses?

11. Why did the author of "All men are created equal," Thomas Jefferson, remain a slaveholder all his life?

12. The U.S. Constitution was: (Defend your choice with detail.)

a. "a work of genius put together by wise, humane men who created a legal framework for democracy and equality"

b. a work of genius put together by rich men to benefit their economic interests

c. a work of genius which balances the interests of slaves, indentured servants, women, men without property, and men with property

d. a compromise between slaveholding interests of the South and monied interests of the North

e. all of the above

13. Who benefits most from a strong central government? How?

14. In the months preceding Shays' Rebellion, what were the grievances of western Massachusetts farmers? What were the state government's responses (both judicial and legislative) to the grievances of these farmers? What were the Boston merchants' responses to Shays' resistance?

15. Did Shays' Rebellion have the salutary effect of "refreshing the tree of liberty"? Explain your response.

16. Explain the difference between Jefferson's and Hamilton's attitudes toward popular participation in the decision-making process. If one were to look only at *Federalist Paper #10*, does Madison agree with Hamilton or Jefferson on this issue?

17. Did the U.S. Constitution define a democratic government? Is a democratic government possible in an economically polarized society?

18. Why did city mechanics in New York support wealthy conservatives in promoting the ratification of the U.S. Constitution? Is it surprising that they did?

19. Many historians argue that the U.S. Constitution creates a neutral, level playing field on which contestants prove their worth (that any inequality in wealth is not due to unfair rules but to unequal abilities). For what reasons does Zinn disagree with this interpretation?

20. Why did Congress pass the Whiskey Tax? How did small farmers who manufactured whiskey respond? What is the difference between the means by which Shays' Rebellion was defeated and the Whiskey Rebellion was defeated? What is the significance of the answer to the previous question?

21. *Draw a map* that includes the following: Boston; Springfield; Massachusetts; New York City; New York; Washington, D.C.; Pennsylvania; Saratoga; Yorktown; Philadelphia; Hudson River; Proclamation Line of 1763.

Chapter 6

The Intimately Oppressed

It is possible, reading standard histories, to forget half the population of the country. The explorers were men, the landholders and merchants men, the political leaders men, the military figures men. The very invisibility of women, the overlooking of women, is a sign of their submerged status.

In this invisibility they were something like black slaves (and thus slave women faced a double oppression). The biological uniqueness of women, like skin color and facial characteristics for Negroes, became a basis for treating them as inferiors. It seems that their physical characteristics became a convenience for men, who could use, exploit, and cherish someone who was at the same time servant, sex mate, companion, and bearer-teacher-warden of his children.

Because of that intimacy and long-term connection with children, there was a special patronization, which on occasion, especially in the face of a show of strength, could slip over into treatment as an equal. An oppression so private would turn out hard to uproot.

Earlier societies—in America and elsewhere—in which property was held in common and families were extensive and complicated, with aunts and uncles and grandmothers and grandfathers all living together, seemed to treat women more as equals than did the white societies that later overran them, bringing "civilization" and private property.

In the Zuñi tribes of the Southwest, for instance, extended families—large clans—were based on the woman, whose husband came to live with her family. It was assumed that women owned the houses, and the fields belonged to the clans, and the women had equal rights to what was produced. A woman was more secure because she was with her own family, and she could divorce the man when she wanted to, keeping their property.

It would be an exaggeration to say that women were treated equally with men; but they were treated with respect, and the communal nature of the society gave them a more important place. The puberty ceremony of the Sioux was such as to give pride to a young Sioux maiden:

> Walk the good road, my daughter, and the buffalo herds wide and dark as cloud shadows moving over the prairie will follow you.... Be dutiful, respectful, gentle and modest, my daughter. And proud walking. If the pride and the virtue of the women are lost, the spring will come but the buffalo trails will turn to grass. Be strong, with the warm, strong heart of the earth. No people goes down until their women are weak and dishonored....

The conditions under which white settlers came to America created various situations for women. Where the first settlements consisted almost entirely of men, women were imported as sex slaves, childbearers, companions. In 1619, the year that the first black slaves came to Virginia, ninety women arrived at Jamestown on one ship: "Agreeable persons, young and incorrupt...sold with their own consent to settlers as wives, the price to be the cost of their own transportation."

Many women came in those early years as indentured servants—often teenaged girls—and lived lives not much different from slaves, except that the term of service had an end. They were to be obedient to masters and mistresses. Sexual abuse by their masters was common. According to the authors of *America's Working Women* (Baxandall, Gordon, and Reverby): "They were poorly paid and often treated rudely and harshly, deprived of good food and privacy."

In 1756, Elizabeth Sprigs wrote to her father about her servitude: "What we unfortunate English People suffer here is beyond the probibility of you in England to Conceive, let it suffice that I one of the unhappy Number, am toiling almost Day and Night...with only this comfort that you Bitch you do not halfe enough...."

Of course these terrible conditions provoked resistance. For instance, the General Court of Connecticut in 1645 ordered that a certain "Susan C., for her rebellious carriage toward her mistress, to be sent to the house of correction and be kept to hard labor and coarse diet...."

Whatever horrors can be imagined in the transport of black slaves to America must be multiplied for black women, who were often one-third of the cargo. Slave traders reported:

I saw pregnant women give birth to babies while chained to corpses which our drunken overseers had not removed.... [p]acked spoon-fashion they often gave birth to children in the scalding perspiration from the human cargo.... On board the ship was a young negro woman chained to the deck, who had lost her senses soon after she was purchased and taken on board.

A woman named Linda Brent who escaped from slavery told of another burden:

But I now entered on my fifteenth year—a sad epoch in the life of a slave girl. My master began to whisper foul words in my ear. Young as I was, I could not remain ignorant of their import.... My master met me at every turn, reminding me that I belonged to him, and swearing by heaven and earth that he would compel me to submit to him. If I went out for a breath of fresh air, after a day of unwearied toil, his footsteps dogged me. If I knelt by my mother's grave, his dark shadow fell on me even there. The light heart which nature had given me became heavy with sad forebodings....

Even free white women, not brought as servants or slaves but as wives of the early settlers, faced special hardships. Eighteen married women came over on the Mayflower. Three were pregnant, and one of them gave birth to a dead child before they landed. Childbirth and sickness plagued the women; by the spring, only four of those eighteen women were still alive.

All women were burdened with ideas carried over from England. English law was summarized in a document of 1632 entitled "The Lawes Resolutions of Womens Rights": "In this consolidation which we call wedlock is a locking together. It is true, that man and wife are one person, but understand in what manner.... Her new self is her superior; her companion, her master...."

Julia Spruill describes the woman's legal situation in the colonial period: "The husband's control over the wife's person extended to the right of giving her chastisement.... But he was not entitled to inflict permanent injury or death on his wife...."

As for property: "Besides absolute possession of his wife's personal property and a life estate in her lands, the husband took any other income that might be hers. He collected wages earned by her labor.... Naturally it followed that the proceeds of the joint labor of husband and wife belonged to the husband."

For a woman to have a child out of wedlock was a crime, and colonial

court records are full of cases of women being arraigned for "bastardy"—
the father of the child untouched by the law and on the loose. A colonial
periodical of 1747 reproduced a speech "of Miss Polly Baker before a
Court of Judicature, at Connecticut near Boston in New England; where
she was prosecuted the fifth time for having a Bastard Child."

> ...I take the liberty to say, that I think this law, by which I am punished,
> both unreasonable in itself, and particularly severe with regard to
> me.... Abstracted from the law, I cannot conceive...what the nature of
> my offense is. I have brought five fine children into the world, at the
> risque of my life; I have maintained them well by my own industry,
> without burthening the township, and would have done it better, if it
> had not been for the heavy charges and fines I have paid.... [n]or has
> anyone the least cause of complaint against me, unless, perhaps, the
> ministers of justice, because I have had children without being married,
> by which they missed a wedding fee. But can this be a fault of mine?

The father's position in the family was expressed in *The Spectator*, an
influential periodical in America and England: "Nothing is more gratify-
ing to the mind of man than power or dominion.... I look upon my family
as a patriarchal sovereignty in which I am myself both king and priest."

A best-selling "pocket book," published in London, was widely read
in the American colonies in the 1700s. It was called *Advice to a Daughter*:
"You must first lay it down for a Foundation in general, That there is
Inequality in Sexes, and that for the better Oeconomy of the World; the
Men, who were to be the Law-givers, had the larger share of Reason
bestow'd upon them...."

Against this powerful education, it is remarkable that women nevertheless rebelled. Women rebels have always faced special disabilities: they
live under the daily eye of their master; and they are isolated one from the
other in households, thus missing the daily camaraderie that has given
heart to rebels of other oppressed groups.

Anne Hutchinson was a religious woman, mother of thirteen children,
and knowledgeable about healing with herbs. She defied the church fathers
in the early years of the Massachusetts Bay Colony by insisting that she,
and other ordinary people, could interpret the Bible for themselves.

She was put on trial twice: by the church for heresy, and by the government for challenging their authority. At her civil trial she was pregnant and
ill, but they did not allow her to sit down until she was close to collapse. At
her religious trial she was interrogated for weeks, and again she was sick,
but challenged her questioners with expert knowledge of the Bible and

remarkable eloquence. When finally she repented in writing, they were not satisfied. They said: "Her repentance is not in her countenance."

She was banished from the colony, and when she left for Rhode Island in 1638, thirty-five families followed her. Then she went to the shores of Long Island, where Indians who had been defrauded of their land thought she was one of their enemies; they killed her and her family. Twenty years later, the one person back in Massachusetts Bay who had spoken up for her during her trial, Mary Dyer, was hanged by the government of the colony, along with two other Quakers, for "rebellion, sedition, and presumptuous obtruding themselves."

It remained rare for women to participate openly in public affairs, although on the southern and western frontiers conditions made this occasionally possible.

During the Revolution, the necessities of war brought women out into public affairs. Women formed patriotic groups, carried out anti-British actions, wrote articles for independence. In 1777 there was a women's counterpart to the Boston Tea Party—a "coffee party," described by Abigail Adams in a letter to her husband John:

> One eminent, wealthy, stingy merchant (who is a bachelor) had a hogshead of coffee in his store, which he refused to sell the committee under six shillings per pound. A number of females, some say a hundred, some say more, assembled with a cart and trunks, marched down to the warehouse, and demanded the keys, which he refused to deliver. Upon which one of them seized him by his neck and tossed him into the cart. Upon his finding no quarter, he delivered the keys when they tipped up the cart and discharged him; then opened the warehouse, hoisted out the coffee themselves, put it into the trunks and drove off.... A large concourse of men stood amazed, silent spectators of the whole transaction.

It has been pointed out by women historians recently that the contributions of working-class women in the American Revolution have been mostly ignored, unlike the genteel wives of the leaders (Dolley Madison, Martha Washington, and Abigail Adams, for example). Margaret Corbin, called "Dirty Kate," Deborah Sampson Garnet, and "Molly Pitcher" were rough, lower-class women, prettified into ladies by historians. While poor women, in the last years of the fighting, went to army encampments, helped, and fought, they were represented later as prostitutes, whereas Martha Washington was given a special place in history books for visiting her husband at Valley Forge.

When feminist impulses are recorded, they are, almost always, the writings of privileged women who had some status from which to speak freely, more opportunity to write and have their writings recorded. Abigail Adams, even before the Declaration of Independence, in March of 1776, wrote to her husband:

> ...in the new code of laws which I suppose it will be necessary for you to make... [d]o not put such unlimited power in the hands of husbands. Remember, all men would be tyrants if they could. If particular care and attention are not paid to the ladies, we are determined to foment a rebellion, and will not hold ourselves bound to obey the laws in which we have no voice of representation.

Nevertheless, Jefferson underscored his phrase "all men are created equal" by his statement that American women would be "too wise to wrinkle their foreheads with politics." And after the Revolution, none of the new state constitutions granted women the right to vote, except for New Jersey, and that state rescinded the right in 1807. New York's constitution specifically disfranchised women by using the word "male."

Working-class women had no means of recording whatever sentiments of rebelliousness they may have felt at their subordination. Not only were they bearing children in great numbers, under great hardships, but they were working in the home. Around the time of the Declaration of Independence, four thousand women and children in Philadelphia were spinning at home for local plants under the "putting out" system. Women also were shopkeepers and innkeepers and engaged in many trades.

Ideas of female equality were in the air during and after the Revolution. Tom Paine spoke out for the equal rights of women. And the pioneering book of Mary Wollstonecraft in England, *A Vindication of the Rights of Women*, was reprinted in the United States shortly after the Revolutionary War. She wrote: "I wish to persuade women to endeavor to acquire strength, both of mind and body...."

Between the American Revolution and the Civil War, so many elements of American society were being transformed that changes were bound to take place in the situation of women. In preindustrial America, the practical need for women in a frontier society had produced some measure of equality; women worked at important jobs—publishing newspapers, managing tanneries, keeping taverns, engaging in skilled work. A grandmother, Martha Moore Ballard, on a farm in Maine in 1795, in twenty-five years as a midwife delivered more than a thousand babies.

Now, women were being pulled out of the house and into industrial life, while at the same time there was pressure for women to stay home where they were more easily controlled. The idea of "the woman's place," promulgated by men, was accepted by many women. It became important to develop a set of ideas, taught in church, in school, and in the family, to keep women in their place even as that place became more and more unsettled. The woman was expected to be pious. One female writer said: "Religion is just what woman needs. Without it she is ever restless or unhappy."

Sexual purity was to be the special virtue of a woman. The role began early, with adolescence. Obedience prepared the girl for submission to the first proper mate. Barbara Welter describes this:

> The assumption is twofold: the American female was supposed to be so infinitely lovable and provocative that a healthy male could barely control himself when in the same room with her, and the same girl, as she "comes out" of the cocoon of her family's protectiveness, is so palpitating with undirected affection [that]...she is required to exert the inner control of obedience. The combination forms a kind of societal chastity belt which is not unlocked until the marriage partner has arrived, and adolescence is formally over.

When Amelia Bloomer in 1851 suggested in her feminist publication that women wear a kind of short skirt and pants, to free themselves from the encumbrances of traditional dress, this was attacked in the popular women's literature. One story has a girl admiring the "bloomer" costume, but her professor admonishes her that they are "only one of the many manifestations of that wild spirit of socialism and agrarian radicalism which is at present so rife in our land."

The woman's job was to keep the home cheerful, maintain religion, be nurse, cook, cleaner, seamstress, flower arranger. A woman shouldn't read too much, and certain books should be avoided.

A sermon preached in 1808 in New York: "How interesting and important are the duties devolved on females as wives...the counsellor and friend of the husband; who makes it her daily study to lighten his cares, to soothe his sorrows, and to augment his joys...."

Women were also urged, especially since they had the job of educating children, to be patriotic. One women's magazine offered a prize to the woman who wrote the best essay on "How May an American Woman Best Show Her Patriotism."

The cult of domesticity for the woman was a way of pacifying her with a doctrine of "separate but equal"—giving her work equally as important as the man's, but separate and different. Inside that "equality" there was the fact that the woman did not choose her mate, and once her marriage took place, her life was determined. Marriage enchained, and children doubled the chains.

The "cult of true womanhood" could not completely erase what was visible as evidence of woman's subordinate status: she could not vote, could not own property; when she did work, her wages were one-fourth to one-half what men earned in the same job. Women were excluded from the professions of law and medicine, from colleges, from the ministry.

Putting all women into the same category—giving them all the same domestic sphere to cultivate—created a classification (by sex) that blurred the lines of class. However, forces were at work to keep raising the issue of class. Samuel Slater had introduced industrial spinning machinery in New England in 1789, and now there was a demand for young girls literally, "spinsters"—to work the spinning machinery in factories. In 1814, the power loom was introduced in Waltham, Massachusetts, and now all the operations needed to turn cotton fiber into cloth were under one roof. The new textile factories swiftly multiplied, with women 80 to 90 percent of their operatives—most of these women between fifteen and thirty.

Some of the earliest industrial strikes took place in these textile mills in the 1830s. Women's daily average earnings in 1836 were less than thirty-seven cents, and thousands earned twenty-five cents a day, working twelve to sixteen hours a day. In Pawtucket, Rhode Island, in 1824, came the first known strike of women factory workers; 202 women joined men in protesting a wage cut and longer hours, but they met separately. Four years later, women in Dover, New Hampshire, struck alone.

In Lowell, Massachusetts, in 1834, when a young woman was fired from her job, other girls left their looms, one of them then climbing the town pump and making, according to a newspaper report, "a flaming Mary Wollstonecraft speech on the rights of women and the iniquities of the 'moneyed aristocracy' which produced a powerful effect on her auditors and they determined to have their own way, if they died for it."

Several times in those strikes, women armed with sticks and stones broke through the wooden gates of a textile mill and stopped the looms.

Catharine Beecher, a woman reformer of the time, wrote about the factory system:

> I was there in mid-winter, and every morning I was awakened at five, by the bells calling to labor.... Then half an hour only allowed for dinner, from which the time for going and returning was deducted. Then back to the mills, to work till seven o'clock.... [I]t must be remembered that

all the hours of labor are spent in rooms where oil lamps, together with from 40 to 80 persons, are exhausting the healthful principle of the air...and where the air is loaded with particles of cotton thrown from thousands of cards, spindles, and looms.

And the life of upper-class women? Frances Trollope, an English-woman, wrote in her book *Domestic Manners of the Americans*:

Let me be permitted to describe the day of a Philadelphian lady of the first class.... She rises, and her first hour is spent in the scrupulously nice arrangement of her dress; she descends to her parlor, neat, stiff, and silent; her breakfast is brought in by her free black footman.... Twenty minutes before her carriage should appear, she retires to her chamber, as she calls it; shakes and folds up her still snow-white apron, smooths her rich dress, and...sets on her elegant bonnet...then walks downstairs, just at the moment that her free black coachman announces to her free black footman that the carriage waits. She steps into it, and gives the word: "Drive to the Dorcas Society."

At Lowell, the Female Labor Reform Association put out a series of "Factory Tracts." The first was entitled "Factory Life as It Is By an Operative" and spoke of the textile mill women as "nothing more nor less than slaves in every sense of the word! Slaves, to a system of labor which requires them to toil from five until seven o'clock, with one hour only to attend to the wants of nature—slaves to the will and requirements of the 'powers that be.'"

Around that time, the *New York Herald* carried a story about "700 females, generally of the most interesting state and appearance," meeting "in their endeavor to remedy the wrongs and oppressions under which they labor." The *Herald* editorialized: "we very much doubt whether it will terminate in much good to female labor of any description.... All combinations end in nothing."

Middle-class women, barred from higher education, began to monopolize the profession of primary-school teaching. As teachers, they read more, communicated more, and education itself became subversive of old ways of thinking. They began to write for magazines and newspapers, and started some ladies' publications. Literacy among women doubled between 1780 and 1840. Women became health reformers. They formed movements against double standards in sexual behavior and the victimization of prostitutes. They joined in religious organizations. Some of the most powerful of them joined the antislavery movement. So, by the time a clear feminist movement emerged in the 1840s, women had become practiced organizers, agitators, and speakers.

When Emma Willard addressed the New York legislature in 1819, she told them that the education of women "has been too exclusively directed to fit them for displaying to advantage the charms of youth and beauty." The problem, she said, was that "the taste of men, whatever it might happen to be, has been made into a standard for the formation of the female character." Reason and religion teach us, she said, that "we too are primary existences...not the satellites of men."

In 1821, Willard founded the Troy Female Seminary, the first recognized institution for the education of girls. She wrote later of how she upset people by teaching her students about the human body: "Mothers visiting a class at the Seminary in the early thirties were so shocked.... To preserve the modesty of the girls, and spare them too frequent agitation, heavy paper was pasted over the pages in their textbooks which depicted the human body."

Women struggled to enter the all-male professional schools. Elizabeth Blackwell got her medical degree in 1849, having overcome many rebuffs before being admitted to Geneva College. She then set up the New York Dispensary for Poor Women and Children "to give to poor women an opportunity of consulting physicians of their own sex." In her first annual report, she wrote:

> My first medical consultation was a curious experience. In a severe case of pneumonia in an elderly lady I called in consultation a kind-hearted physician of high standing.... This gentleman, after seeing the patient, went with me into the parlour. There he began to walk about the room in some agitation, exclaiming, "A most extraordinary case! Such a one never happened to me before; I really do not know what to do!" I listened in surprise and much perplexity, as it was a clear case of pneumonia and of no unusual degree of danger, until at last I discovered that his perplexity related to me, not to the patient, and to the propriety of consulting with a lady physician!

Oberlin College pioneered in the admission of women. But the first girl admitted to the theology school there, Antoinette Brown, who graduated in 1850, found that her name was left off the class list. With Lucy Stone, Oberlin found a formidable resister. She was active in the peace society and in antislavery work, taught colored students, and organized a debating club for girls. She was chosen to write the commencement address, then was told it would have to be read by a man. She refused to write it.

Lucy Stone began lecturing on women's rights in 1847 in a church in Gardner, Massachusetts, where her brother was a minister. She was tiny, weighed about one hundred pounds, was a marvelous speaker. As lecturer for the American Anti-Slavery Society, she was, at various times, deluged with cold water, sent reeling by a thrown book, and attacked by mobs.

When she married Henry Blackwell, they joined hands at their wedding and read a statement:

> ...we deem it a duty to declare that this act on our part implies no sanction of, nor promise of voluntary obedience to such of the present laws of marriage as refuse to recognize the wife as an independent, rational being, while they confer upon the husband an injurious and unnatural superiority....

She was one of the first to refuse to give up her name after marriage. She was "Mrs. Stone." When she refused to pay taxes because she was not represented in the government, officials took all her household goods in payment, even her baby's cradle.

After Amelia Bloomer, a postmistress in a small town in New York, developed the bloomer, women activists adopted it in place of the old whale-boned bodice, the corsets and petticoats. The Reverend John Todd (one of his many best-selling books gave advice to young men on the results of masturbation: "the mind is greatly deteriorated") commented on the new feminist mode of dress:

> Some have tried to become semi-men by putting on the Bloomer dress. Let me tell you in a word why it can never be done. It is this: woman, robed and folded in her long dress, is beautiful. She walks gracefully.... If she attempts to run, the charm is gone.... Take off the robes, and put on pants, and show the limbs, and grace and mystery are all gone.

Women, after becoming involved in other movements of reform—antislavery, temperance, dress styles, prison conditions—turned, emboldened and experienced, to their own situation. Angelina Grimké, a southern white woman who became a fierce speaker and organizer against slavery, saw that movement leading further:

> Let us all first wake up the nation to lift millions of slaves of both sexes from the dust, and turn them into men and then...it will be an easy matter to take millions of females from their knees and set them on their feet, or in other words transform them from babies into women.

Sarah Grimké, Angelina's sister, wrote:

During the early part of my life, my lot was cast among the butterflies of the fashionable world; and of this class of women, I am constrained to say, both from experience and observation, that their education is miserably deficient; that they are taught to regard marriage as the one thing needful, the only avenue to distinction....

She said:

All I ask of our brethren is that they will take their feet from off our necks, and permit us to stand upright on the ground which God has designed us to occupy.... To me it is perfectly clear that whatsoever it is morally right for a man to do, it is morally right for a woman to do.

Sarah could write with power; Angelina was the firebrand speaker. Once she spoke six nights in a row at the Boston Opera House. She was the first woman (in 1838) to address a committee of the Massachusetts state legislature on antislavery petitions. Her talk attracted a huge crowd, and a representative from Salem proposed that "a Committee be appointed to examine the foundations of the State House of Massachusetts to see whether it will bear another lecture from Miss Grimké!"

Speaking out on other issues prepared the way for speaking on the situation of women: Dorothea Dix, in 1843, addressed the legislature of Massachusetts on what she saw in the prisons and almshouses in the Boston area:

I tell what I have seen, painful and shocking as the details often are.... I proceed, gentlemen, briefly to call your attention to the present state of insane persons confined within this Commonwealth in cages, closets, cellars, stalls, pens; chained, naked, beaten with rods, and lashed into obedience!

Frances Wright was a writer, founder of a utopian community, immigrant from Scotland in 1824, a fighter for the emancipation of slaves and for birth control and sexual freedom. She wanted free public education for all children over two years of age in state-supported boarding schools. She expressed in America what the utopian socialist Charles Fourier had said in France, that the progress of civilization depended on the progress of women.

I shall venture the assertion, that, until women assume the place in society which good sense and good feeling alike assign to them, human improvement must advance but feebly.... men will ever rise or fall to the level of the other sex.... Until power is annihilated on one side, fear and obedience on the other, and both restored to their birthright—equality.

Women put in enormous work in antislavery societies all over the country, gathering thousands of petitions to Congress. In the course of this work, events were set in motion that carried the movement of women for their own equality racing alongside the movement against slavery. In 1840, a World Anti-Slavery Society Convention met in London. After a fierce argument, it was voted to exclude women, but it was agreed they could attend meetings in a curtained enclosure. The women sat in silent protest in the gallery, and William Lloyd Garrison, one abolitionist who had fought for the rights of women, sat with them.

It was at that time that Elizabeth Cady Stanton met Lucretia Mott and others, and began to lay the plans that led to the first Women's Rights Convention in history. It was held at Seneca Falls, New York, where Elizabeth Cady Stanton lived as a mother, a housewife, full of resentment at her condition, declaring: "A woman is a nobody. A wife is everything." She wrote later:

> My experiences at the World Anti-Slavery Convention, all I had read of the legal status of women, and the oppression I saw everywhere, together swept across my soul.... I could not see what to do or where to begin— my only thought was a public meeting for protest and discussion.

An announcement was put in the Seneca County Courier calling for a meeting to discuss the "rights of woman" the 19th and 20th of July. Three hundred women and some men came. A Declaration of Principles was signed at the end of the meeting by sixty-eight women and thirty-two men. It made use of the language and rhythm of the Declaration of Independence:

> When in the course of human events, it becomes necessary for one portion of the family of man to assume among the people of the earth a position different from that they have hitherto occupied...
>
> We hold these truths to be self-evident: that all men and women are created equal; that they are endowed by their Creator with certain inalienable rights; that among these are life, liberty and the pursuit of happiness....
>
> The history of mankind is a history of repeated injuries and usurpations on the part of man toward woman, having in direct object the establishment of an absolute tyranny over her. To prove this, let facts be submitted to a candid world....

Then came the list of grievances. And then a series of resolutions. Women's conventions in various parts of the country followed the one at Seneca Falls. At one of these, in 1851, an aged black woman, who had been born a slave in New York, tall, thin, wearing a gray dress and white turban, listened to some male ministers who had been dominating the discussion. This was Sojourner Truth. She rose to her feet and joined the indignation of her race to the indignation of her sex:

> That man over there says that woman needs to be helped into carriages and lifted over ditches.... Nobody ever helps me into carriages, or over mud-puddles or gives me any best place. And a'nt I a woman?
>
> Look at my arm! I have ploughed, and planted, and gathered into barns, and no man could head me! And a'nt I a woman?
>
> I would work as much and eat as much as a man, when I could get it, and bear the lash as well. And a'nt I a woman?
>
> I have borne thirteen children and seen em most all sold off to slavery, and when I cried out with my mother's grief, none but Jesus heard me! And a'nt I a woman?

Thus were women beginning to resist, in the 1830s and 1840s and 1850s, the attempt to keep them in their "woman's sphere." They were taking part in all sorts of movements, for prisoners, for the insane, for black slaves, and also for all women.

In the midst of these movements, there exploded, with the force of government and the authority of money, a quest for more land, an urge for national expansion.

Exercises

1. What effect does private property seem to have on the position of women in society?

2. How did European women manage to pay for their voyage to the American colonies?

3. How did masters exercise their control over female servants and slaves? How did husbands exercise control over their wives?

4. Was it better for a woman to be married or single in colonial America?

5. What was a fundamental obstacle preventing women from rebelling against their subordinate status?

6. Why was Anne Hutchinson banished from the Massachusetts Bay Colony?

7. Why was Mary Dyer hanged?

8. What role did American women play during the American Revolution?

9. What was Abigail Adams's argument in favor of giving women the vote? To whom did she make this argument?

10. What might one of Thomas Jefferson's reasons have been for excluding women from politics?

11. In the periods before, during, and after the American Revolution, what factors caused some women to demand greater rights for themselves (or their sex)?

12. Why would women editors of a women's magazine write a story discrediting the wearing of bloomers?

13. How did the proponents of the Cult of Domesticity (or the Cult of Womanhood) argue that the women's sphere was separate but equal? One aspect of the "Cult" defined the role of women as being as responsible for the moral fabric of her family. How might a middle-class woman have used the ideology of being responsible for the moral fabric of her family to justify her involvement, outside the home, in the reform movements—abolition, peace, communitarianism, education, temperance?

14. What is the origin of the word "spinster"?

15. What evidence does Zinn provide to indicate that single women were perhaps lured to the factory by attractive wages and conditions only to see those wages and conditions deteriorate?

16. Did the emergence of an idle, educated, middle-class female population in the midst of politically charged reform movements lead to the first organized feminist movement? Explain your answer.

17. Why did middle-class women activists gravitate to the reform movements (antislavery, temperance, dress styles, prison conditions, peace, education, communitarianism)? How were the reform movements excellent training grounds from which to promote and pursue a women's rights movement?

18. Why was the World Anti-Slavery Society Convention of 1840 the birthplace of the women's rights movement?

19. Take a standard American history text and compare its treatment of the following points with Zinn's teatment of them in this chapter. (If the traditional text does not address one of the points below, speculate as to why the text excluded it.)

        a. means by which women came to colonial America

        b. the unique experiences of indentured women (as distinct from indentured men)

        c. the different legal status of single and married women in colonial America

        d. the significance of Anne Hutchinson's story

        e. the role of women in the American Revolution

        f. Abigail Adams

        g. women's magazines

        h. "cult of true womanhood" ("cult of domesticity")

        i. the reasons women became mill workers

        j. the experiences of women mill workers in the 1830s and 1840s

        k. Frances Wright

        l. Emma Willard

        m. Elizabeth Blackwell

        n. Lucy Stone, Lucretia Mott, Elizabeth Cady Stanton

        o. Sojourner Truth

        p. Sarah and Angelina Grimké

        q. Seneca Falls

What points does your chosen traditional text make about women (1619–1848) that Zinn leaves out?

Chapter 7

As Long as Grass Grows
or Water Runs

If women, of all the subordinate groups in a society dominated by rich white males, were closest to home (indeed, *in* the home), the most interior, then the Indians were the most foreign, the most exterior. Women, because they were so near and so needed, were dealt with more by patronization than by force. The Indian, not needed—indeed, an obstacle—could be dealt with by sheer force, except that sometimes the language of paternalism preceded the burning of villages.

And so, "Indian removal," as it has been politely called, cleared the land for white occupancy between the Appalachians and the Mississippi, cleared it for cotton in the South and grain in the North, for expansion, immigration, canals, railroads, new cities, and the building of a huge continental empire clear across to the Pacific Ocean. The cost in human life cannot be accurately measured, in suffering not even roughly measured. Most of the history books given to children pass quickly over it.

In the Revolutionary War, almost every important Indian nation fought on the side of the British. They knew that if the British, who had set a limit on the colonists' expansion westward, lost the war, there would be no holding back the Americans. Indeed, by the time Jefferson became president in 1800, there were 700,000 white settlers west of the mountains. Jefferson now committed the federal government to promote future removal of the Creek and the Cherokee from Georgia. Aggressive activity against the Indians mounted in the Indiana Territory under Gov. William Henry Harrison.

When Jefferson doubled the size of the nation by purchasing the Louisiana Territory from France in 1803—thus extending the western frontier from the Appalachians across the Mississippi to the Rocky Mountains—he proposed to Congress that Indians should be encouraged to settle down on smaller tracts and do farming. "Two measures are deemed expedient. First to encourage them to abandon hunting.... Secondly, to Multiply trading houses among them...leading them thus to agriculture, to manufactures, and civilization...."

Jefferson's talk of "agriculture... manufactures... civilization" is crucial. Indian removal was necessary for the opening of the vast American lands to agriculture, to commerce, to markets, to money, to the development of the modern capitalist economy. Land was indispensable for all this, and after the Revolution, huge tracts of land were bought up by rich speculators, including George Washington and Patrick Henry. John Donelson, a North Carolina surveyor, ended up with twenty thousand acres of land near what is now Chattanooga. His son-in-law made twenty-two trips out of Nashville in 1795 for land deals. This was Andrew Jackson.

Jackson was a land speculator, merchant, slave trader, and the most aggressive enemy of the Indians in early American history. He became a hero of the War of 1812, which was not (as often depicted in American textbooks) just a war against England for survival, but a war for the expansion of the new nation, into Florida, into Canada, into Indian territory.

Tecumseh, a Shawnee chief and noted orator, tried to unite the Indians against the white invasion. "The land," he said, "belongs to all, for the use of each...." Angered when fellow Indians were induced to cede a great tract of land to the United States government, in 1811 Tecumseh organized an Indian gathering of five thousand, on the bank of the Tallapoosa River in Alabama, and told them: "Let the white race perish. They seize your land; they corrupt your women, they trample on the ashes of your dead! Back whence they came, upon a trail of blood, they must be driven."

The Creek Indians occupied most of Georgia, Alabama, and Mississippi. In 1813 some of their warriors massacred 250 people at Fort Mims, whereupon Jackson's troops burned down a Creek village, killing men, women, children. Jackson established the tactic of promising rewards in land and plunder.

But among Jackson's men there were mutinies. They were tired of fighting and wanted to go home. Jackson wrote to his wife about "the once brave and patriotic volunteers...sunk...to mere whining, complaining, seditioners and mutineers...." When a seventeen-year-old soldier who had refused to clean up his food and threatened his officer with a gun was sentenced to death by a court-martial, Jackson turned down his plea and ordered the execution to proceed. He then walked out of earshot of the firing squad.

Jackson became a national hero when in 1814 he fought the Battle of Horseshoe Bend against a thousand Creeks and killed eight hundred of them, with few casualties on his side. His white troops had failed in a frontal attack on the Creeks, but the Cherokees with him, promised governmental friendship if they joined the war, swam the river, came up behind the Creeks, and won the battle for Jackson.

When the war ended, Jackson and friends of his began buying up the seized Creek lands. He got himself appointed treaty commissioner and dictated a treaty in 1814 which took away half the land of the Creek nation.

This treaty started something new and important. It granted Indians individual ownership of land, thus splitting Indian from Indian, breaking up communal landholding, bribing some with land, leaving others out—introducing the competition and conniving that marked the spirit of Western capitalism. It fitted well the old Jeffersonian idea of how to handle the Indians, by bringing them into "civilization."

From 1814 to 1824, in a series of treaties with the southern Indians, whites took over three-fourths of Alabama and Florida, one-third of Tennessee, one-fifth of Georgia and Mississippi, and parts of Kentucky and North Carolina. Jackson played a key role in those treaties, using bribery, deception, and force to get more and more land, and giving jobs to his friends and relatives.

These treaties, these land grabs, laid the basis for the cotton kingdom, the slave plantations. Jackson's work had brought the white settlements to the border of Florida, owned by Spain. Here were the villages of the Seminole Indians, where some escaped black slaves were taking refuge. Jackson began raids into Florida, arguing it was a sanctuary for escaped slaves and for marauding Indians. Florida, he said, was essential to the defense of the United States. It was that classic modern preface to a war of conquest.

Thus began the Seminole War of 1818, leading to the American acquisition of Florida. It appears on classroom maps politely as "Florida Purchase, 1819," but it came from Andrew Jackson's military campaign across the Florida border, burning Seminole villages, seizing Spanish forts, until Spain was "persuaded" to sell. He acted, he said, by the "immutable laws of self-defense."

Jackson then became governor of the Florida Territory. He was able now to give good business advice to friends and relatives. To a nephew, he suggested holding on to property in Pensacola. To a friend, a surgeon-general in the army, he suggested buying as many slaves as possible, because the price would soon rise.

Leaving his military post, he also gave advice to officers on how to deal with the high rate of desertion. (Poor whites—even if willing to give their lives at first—may have discovered the rewards of battle going to the rich.) Jackson suggested whipping for the first two attempts, and the third time, execution.

If you look through high school textbooks and elementary school textbooks in American history you will find Jackson the frontiersman, soldier, democrat, man of the people—not Jackson the slaveholder, land speculator, executioner of dissident soldiers, exterminator of Indians.

After Jackson was elected president in 1828 (following John Quincy Adams, who had followed Monroe, who had followed Madison, who had followed Jefferson), the two political parties were the Democrats and Whigs, who disagreed on banks and tariffs, but not on issues crucial for the white poor, the blacks, the Indians—although some white working people saw Jackson as their hero, because he opposed the rich man's bank.

Under Jackson, and the man he chose to succeed him, Martin Van Buren, seventy thousand Indians east of the Mississippi were forced westward. In New York, the Iroquois Confederation stayed. But the Sac and Fox Indians of Illinois were removed, after the Black Hawk War. When Chief Black Hawk was defeated and captured in 1832, he made a surrender speech:

> [Black Hawk] is now a prisoner to the white men.... He has done nothing for which an Indian ought to be ashamed. He has fought for his countrymen, the squaws and papooses, against white men, who came year after year, to cheat them and take away their lands.... The white men are bad schoolmasters; they carry false books, and deal in false actions; they smile in the face of the poor Indian to cheat him; they shake them by the hand to gain their confidence, to make them drunk, to deceive them, and ruin our wives....
>
> The white men do not scalp the head; but they do worse—they poison the heart.... Farewell, my nation!... Farewell to Black Hawk.

The removal of the Indians was explained by Lewis Cass, who served variously as secretary of war, governor of the Michigan Territory, minister to France, and a presidential candidate:

> A principle of progressive improvement seems almost inherent in human nature.... We are all striving in the career of life to acquire riches

of honor, or power, or some other object, whose possession is to realize the day dreams of our imaginations; and the aggregate of these efforts constitutes the advance of society. But there is little of this in the constitution of our savages.

Cass, pompous, pretentious, honored (Harvard gave him an honorary doctor of laws degree in 1836, at the height of Indian removal), took millions of acres from the Indians by treaty when he was governor of the Michigan Territory: "We must frequently promote their interest against their inclination.... A barbarous people, depending for subsistence upon the scanty and precarious supplies furnished by the chase, cannot live in contact with a civilized community."

If the Indians would only move to new lands across the Mississippi, Cass promised in 1825 at a treaty council with Shawnees and Cherokees, "The United States will never ask for your land there. This I promise you in the name of your great father, the President. That country he assigns to his red people, to be held by them and their children's children forever."

Everything in the Indian heritage spoke out against leaving their land. An old Choctaw chief said, responding, years before, to President Monroe's talk of removal: "I am sorry I cannot comply with the request of my father.... We wish to remain here, where we have grown up as the herbs of the woods; and do not wish to be transplanted into another soil." A Seminole chief had said to John Quincy Adams: "Here our navel strings were first cut and the blood from them sunk into the earth, and made the country dear to us."

Not all the Indians responded to the white officials' common designation of them as "children" and the president as "father." It was reported that when Tecumseh met with William Henry Harrison, Indian fighter and future president, the interpreter said: "Your father requests you to take a chair." Tecumseh replied: "My father! The sun is my father, and the earth is my mother; I will repose upon her bosom."

As soon as Jackson was elected president, Georgia, Alabama, and Mississippi began to pass laws to extend the states' rule over the Indians in their territory. Indian land was divided up, to be distributed by state lottery. Federal treaties and federal laws gave Congress, not the states, authority over the tribes. Jackson ignored this, and supported state action.

He had now found the right tactic. The Indians would not be "forced" to go west. But if they chose to stay they would have to abide by state laws, which destroyed their tribal and personal rights and made them subject to endless harassment and invasion by white settlers coveting their land. If they left, however, the federal government would give them financial support and promise them lands beyond the Mississippi. Jackson's instructions to an army major sent to talk to the Choctaws and Cherokees put it this way:

> Say to the chiefs and warriors that I am their friend...but they must, by removing from the limits of the States of Mississippi and Alabama and by being settled on the lands I offer them, put it in my power to be such—There, beyond the limits of any State, in possession of land of their own, which they shall possess as long as Grass grows or water runs. I am and will protect them and be their friend and father.

That phrase "as long as Grass grows or water runs" was to be recalled with bitterness by generations of Indians. (An Indian GI, veteran of Vietnam, testifying publicly in 1970 not only about the horror of the war but about his own maltreatment as an Indian, repeated that phrase and began to weep.)

As Jackson took office in 1829, gold was discovered in Cherokee territory in Georgia. Thousands of whites invaded, destroyed Indian property, staked out claims. Jackson ordered federal troops to remove them, but also ordered Indians as well as whites to stop mining. Then he removed the troops, the whites returned, and Jackson said he could not interfere with Georgia's authority. The white invaders seized land and stock, forced Indians to sign leases, beat up Indians who protested, sold alcohol to weaken resistance, and killed game that Indians needed for food.

Treaties made under pressure and by deception broke up Creek, Choctaw, and Chickasaw tribal lands into individual holdings, making each person a prey to contractors, speculators, and politicians. The Creeks and Choctaws remained on their individual plots, but great numbers of them were defrauded by land companies. According to one Georgia bank president, a stockholder in a land company, "Stealing is the order of the day."

The Creeks, defrauded of their land, short of money and food, refused to go west. Starving Creeks began raiding white farms, while Georgia militia and settlers attacked Indian settlements. Thus began the Second Creek War. One Alabama newspaper sympathetic to the Indians wrote: "The war with the Creeks is all humbug. It is a base and diabolical scheme, devised by interested men, to keep an ignorant race of people from maintaining their just rights, and to deprive them of the small remaining pittance placed under their control."

A Creek man more than a hundred years old, named Speckled Snake, reacted to Andrew Jackson's policy of removal:

Brothers! I have listened to many talks from our great white father. When he first came over the wide waters, he was but a little man...very little. His legs were cramped by sitting long in his big boat, and he begged for a little land to light his fire on.... But when the white man had warmed himself before the Indians' fire and filled himself with their hominy, he became very large. With a step he bestrode the mountains, and his feet covered the plains and the valleys. His hand grasped the eastern and the western sea, and his head rested on the moon. Then he became our Great Father. He loved his red children, and he said, "Get a little further, lest I tread on thee."

Dale Van Every, in his book *The Disinherited*, sums up what removal meant to the Indian:

The Indian was peculiarly susceptible to every sensory attribute of every natural feature of his surroundings. He lived in the open. He knew every marsh, glade, hill top, rock, spring, creek, as only the hunter can know them. He had never fully grasped the principle establishing private ownership of land as any more rational than private ownership of air but he loved the land with a deeper emotion than could any proprietor. He felt himself as much a part of it as the rocks and trees, the animals and birds. His homeland was holy ground, sanctified for him as the resting place of the bones of his ancestors and the natural shrine of his religion.

Just before Jackson became president, in the 1820s, after the tumult of the War of 1812 and the Creek War, the southern Indians and the whites had settled down, often very close to one another, and were living in peace in a natural environment that seemed to have enough for all of them. White men were allowed to visit the Indian communities and Indians often were guests in white homes. Frontier figures like Davy Crockett and Sam Houston came out of this setting, and both—unlike Jackson— became lifelong friends of the Indian.

The forces that led to removal did not come from the poor white frontiersmen who were neighbors of the Indians. They came from industrialization and commerce, the growth of populations, of railroads and cities, the rise in value of land, and the greed of businessmen. The Indians were to end up dead or exiled, the land speculators richer, the politicians more powerful. As for the poor white frontiersman, he played the part of a pawn, pushed into the first violent encounters, but soon dispensable.

With 17,000 Cherokees surrounded by 900,000 whites in Georgia, Alabama, and Tennessee, the Cherokees decided that survival required adaptation to the white man's world. They became farmers, blacksmiths, carpenters, masons, owners of property.

The Cherokees' language—heavily poetic, metaphorical, beautifully expressive, supplemented by dance, drama, and ritual—had always been a language of voice and gesture. Now their chief, Sequoyah, invented a written language, which thousands learned. The Cherokees' newly established Legislative Council voted money for a printing press, which on February 21, 1828, began publishing a newspaper, the *Cherokee Phoenix*, printed in both English and Sequoyah's Cherokee.

Before this, the Cherokees had, like Indian tribes in general, done without formal government. As Van Every puts it:

> The foundation principle of Indian government had always been the rejection of government. The freedom of the individual was regarded by practically all Indians north of Mexico as a canon infinitely more precious than the individual's duty to his community or nation. This anarchistic attitude ruled all behavior, beginning with the smallest social unit, the family. The Indian parent was constitutionally reluctant to discipline his children. Their every exhibition of self-will was accepted as a favorable indication of the development of maturing character....

There was an occasional assembling of a council, with a very loose and changing membership, whose decisions were not enforced except by the influence of public opinion. Now, surrounded by white society, all this began to change. The Cherokees even started to emulate the slave society around them: they owned more than a thousand slaves. They were beginning to resemble that "civilization" the white men spoke about. They even welcomed missionaries and Christianity. None of this made them more desirable than the land they lived on.

Jackson's 1829 message to Congress made his position clear: "I informed the Indians inhabiting parts of Georgia and Alabama that their attempt to establish an independent government would not be countenanced by the Executive of the United States, and advised them to emigrate beyond the Mississippi or submit to the laws of those States." Congress moved quickly to pass a removal bill. It did not mention force, but provided for helping the Indians to move. What it implied was that if they did not, they were without protection, without funds, and at the mercy of the states.

There were defenders of the Indians. Perhaps the most eloquent was Sen. Theodore Frelinghuysen of New Jersey, who told the Senate, debating removal: "We have crowded the tribes upon a few miserable acres on our southern frontier; it is all that is left to them of their once boundless forest: and still, like the horse-leech, our insatiated cupidity cries, give! give!... Sir...Do the obligations of justice change with the color of the skin?"

Now the pressures began on the tribes, one by one. The Choctaws did not want to leave, but fifty of their delegates were offered secret bribes of money and land, and the Treaty of Dancing Rabbit Creek was signed: Choctaw land east of the Mississippi was ceded to the United States in return for financial help in leaving. Whites, including liquor dealers and swindlers, came swarming onto their lands.

In late 1831, thirteen thousand Choctaws began the long journey west to a land and climate totally different from what they knew. They went on ox wagons, on horses, on foot, then to be ferried across the Mississippi River. The army was supposed to organize their trek but there was chaos. Food disappeared. Hunger came.

The first winter migration was one of the coldest on record, and people began to die of pneumonia. In the summer, a major cholera epidemic hit Mississippi, and Choctaws died by the hundreds. The seven thousand Choctaws left behind now refused to go, choosing subjugation over death. Many of their descendants still live in Mississippi.

As for the Cherokees, they faced a set of laws passed by Georgia: their lands were taken, their government abolished, all meetings prohibited. Cherokees advising others not to migrate were to be imprisoned. Cherokees could not testify in court against any white. Cherokees could not dig for the gold recently discovered on their land.

The Cherokee nation addressed a memorial to the nation, a public plea for justice:

> We are aware that some persons suppose it will be for our advantage to remove beyond the Mississippi. We think otherwise. Our people universally think otherwise.... We wish to remain on the land of our fathers.... The treaties with us, and laws of the United States made in pursuance of treaties, guarantee our residence and our privileges, and secure us against intruders. Our only request is, that these treaties may be fulfilled, and these laws executed....

Now they went beyond history, beyond law:

> We intreat those to whom the foregoing paragraphs are addressed, to remember the great law of love. "Do to others as ye would that others should do to you."...We pray them to remember that, for the sake of principle, their forefathers were compelled to leave, therefore driven from the old world, and that the winds of persecution wafted them over

the great waters and landed them on the shores of the new world, when the Indian was the sole lord and proprietor of these extensive domains— Let them remember in what way they were received by the savage of America, when power was in his hand.... Let them bring to remembrance all these facts, and they cannot, and we are sure, they will not fail to remember, and sympathize with us in these our trials and sufferings.

Jackson's response to this, in his second annual message to Congress in December 1830, was to point to the fact that the Choctaws and Chickasaws had already agreed to removal, and that "a speedy removal" of the rest would offer many advantages to everyone. He reiterated a familiar theme. "Toward the aborigines of the country no one can indulge a more friendly feeling than myself...." However: "The waves of population and civilization are rolling to the westward, and we now propose to acquire the countries occupied by the red men of the South and West by a fair exchange...."

Georgia passed a law making it a crime for a white person to stay in Indian territory without taking an oath to the state of Georgia. When the white missionaries in the Cherokee territory declared their sympathies openly for the Cherokees to stay, Georgia militia entered the territory in the spring of 1831 and arrested three of the missionaries, including Samuel Worcester. Refusing to swear allegiance to Georgia's laws, Worcester and Elizar Butler were sentenced to four years at hard labor. The Supreme Court ordered Worcester freed, but President Jackson refused to enforce the court order.

Jackson, reelected in 1832, now moved to speed up Indian removal. Most of the Choctaws and some of the Cherokees were gone, but there were still 22,000 Creeks in Alabama, 18,000 Cherokees in Georgia, and 5,000 Seminoles in Florida.

The Creeks had been fighting for their land ever since the years of Columbus, against Spaniards, English, French, and Americans. But by 1832 they had been reduced to a small area in Alabama, while the population of Alabama, growing fast, was now over 300,000. On the basis of extravagant promises from the federal government, Creek delegates in Washington signed the Treaty of Washington, agreeing to removal beyond the Mississippi. They gave up five million acres, with the provision that two million of these would go to individual Creeks, who could either sell or remain in Alabama with federal protection.

Almost immediately, the promises made in the treaty were broken. A white invasion of Creek lands began—looters, land seekers, defrauders, whiskey sellers, thugs—driving thousands of Creeks from their homes into the swamps and forests. The federal government did nothing. Instead it negotiated a new treaty providing for prompt emigration west, managed by the Creeks themselves, financed by the national government. An army colonel, dubious that this would work, wrote:

> They fear starvation on the route; and can it be otherwise, when many of them are nearly starving now.... You cannot have an idea of the deterioration which these Indians have undergone during the last two or three years, from a general state of comparative plenty to that of unqualified wretchedness and want.... They are brow beat, and cowed, and imposed upon, and depressed with the feeling that they have no adequate protection in the United States, and no capacity of self-protection in themselves.

Despite the hardships, the Creeks refused to budge, but by 1836, both state and federal officials decided they must go. Using as a pretext some attacks by desperate Creeks on white settlers, it was declared that the Creek nation, by making "war," had forfeited its treaty rights.

The army would now force it to migrate west. An army of eleven thousand was sent after them. The Creeks did not resist, no shots were fired, they surrendered. Those Creeks presumed by the army to be rebels or sympathizers were assembled, the men manacled and chained together to march westward under military guard, their women and children trailing after them. Creek communities were invaded by military detachments, the inhabitants driven to assembly points and marched westward in batches of two or three thousand. No talk of compensating them for land or property left behind.

Private contracts were made for the march, the same kind that had failed for the Choctaws. Again, delays and lack of food, shelter, clothing, blankets, medical attention. Again, old, rotting steamboats and ferries, crowded beyond capacity, taking them across the Mississippi. Starvation and sickness began to cause large numbers of deaths.

Eight hundred Creek men had volunteered to help the United States army fight the Seminoles in Florida in return for a promise that their families could remain in Alabama, protected by the federal government until the men returned. The promise was not kept. The Creek families were attacked by land-hungry white marauders—robbed, driven from their homes, women raped. Then the army, claiming it was for their safety, removed them from Creek country to a concentration camp on Mobile Bay. Hundreds died there from lack of food and from sickness.

When the warriors returned from the Seminole War, they and their families were hustled west. Moving through New Orleans, they encountered a yellow fever plague. They crossed the Mississippi—611 Indians crowded onto the aged steamer *Monmouth*. It went down in the Mississippi River and 311 people died, four of them the children of the Indian commander of the Creek volunteers in Florida.

The Choctaws and Chickasaws had quickly agreed to migrate. The Creeks were stubborn and had to be forced. The Cherokees were practicing a nonviolent resistance. One tribe—the Seminoles—decided to fight.

With Florida now belonging to the United States, Seminole territory was open to American land grabbers. In 1834 Seminole leaders were assembled and the U.S. Indian agent told them they must move west. The Seminoles replied:

> We were all made by the same Great Father, and are all alike His Children. We all came from the same Mother, and were suckled at the same breast. Therefore, we are brothers, and as brothers, should treat together in an amicable way.... If suddenly we tear our hearts from the homes around which they are twined, our heart-strings will snap.

When, in December 1835, the Seminoles were ordered to assemble for the journey, no one came. Instead, the Seminoles began a series of guerrilla attacks on white coastal settlements, all along the Florida perimeter, striking in surprise and in succession from the interior. They murdered white families, captured slaves, destroyed property.

One December day in 1835, a column of 110 soldiers was attacked by Seminoles, and all but three soldiers were killed. One of the survivors later told the story:

> It was 8 o'clock. Suddenly I heard a rifle shot...followed by a musket shot.... I had not time to think of the meaning of these shots, before a volley, as if from a thousand rifles, was poured in upon us from the front, and all along our left flank.... I could only see their heads and arms, peering out from the long grass, far and near, and from behind the pine trees....

It was the classic Indian tactic against a foe with superior firearms. Gen. George Washington had once given parting advice to one of his officers: "General St. Clair, in three words, beware of surprise.... [A]gain and again, General, beware of surprise."

Congress now appropriated money for a war against the Seminoles. Gen. Winfield Scott took charge, but his columns of troops, marching impressively into Seminole territory, found no one. They became tired of the mud, the swamps, the heat, the sickness, the hunger—the classic fatigue of a civilized army fighting people on their own land. In 1836, 103 commissioned officers resigned from the regular army, leaving only forty-six.

It was an eight-year war. It cost $20 million and 1,500 American lives. Finally, in the 1840s, the Seminoles began to get tired. They were a tiny group against a huge nation with great resources. They asked for truces. But when they went forward under truce flags, they were arrested, again and again. In 1837, their leader Osceola, under a flag of truce, had been seized and put in irons, then died of illness in prison. The war petered out.

Meanwhile the Cherokees had not fought back with arms, but had resisted in their own way. And so the government began to play Cherokee against Cherokee, the old game. The pressures built up on the Cherokee community—their newspaper suppressed, their government dissolved, the missionaries in jail, their land parceled among whites by the land lottery. In 1834, seven hundred Cherokees, weary of the struggle, agreed to go west; eighty-one died en route, including forty-five children—mostly from measles and cholera. Those who lived arrived at their destination across the Mississippi in the midst of a cholera epidemic and half of them died within a year. Now the Georgia whites stepped up their attacks to speed the removal.

In April 1838, Ralph Waldo Emerson addressed an open letter to President Van Buren, referring with indignation to the removal treaty with the Cherokees (signed behind the backs of an overwhelming majority of them) and asked what had happened to the sense of justice in America: "You, sir, will bring down that renowned chair in which you sit into infamy if your seal is set to this instrument of perfidy; and the name of this nation, hitherto the sweet omen of religion and liberty, will stink to the world."

Thirteen days before Emerson sent this letter, Martin Van Buren had ordered Maj. Gen. Winfield Scott into Cherokee territory to use whatever military force was required to move the Cherokees west. Five regiments of regulars and four thousand militia and volunteers began pouring into Cherokee country.

Some Cherokees had apparently given up on nonviolence: three chiefs who signed the Removal Treaty were found dead. But the seventeen thousand Cherokees were soon rounded up and crowded into stockades. On October 1, 1838, the first detachment set out in what was to be known as the Trail of Tears. As they moved westward, they began to die—of sickness, of drought, of the heat, of exposure. There were 645 wagons, and people marching alongside. Survivors, years later, told of halting at the edge of the Mississippi in the middle of winter, the river running full of ice, "hundreds of sick and dying penned up in wagons or stretched upon the ground." During confinement in the stockade or on the march westward four thousand Cherokees died.

In December 1838, President Van Buren spoke to Congress:

> It affords sincere pleasure to apprise the Congress of the entire removal of the Cherokee Nation of Indians to their new homes west of the Mississippi. The measures authorized by Congress at its last session have had the happiest effects.

Exercises

1. Why did almost every important Indian nation fight on the side of the British during the American Revolutionary War?

2. What was Jefferson's policy toward the Indians?

3. What prompted Tecumseh's rebellion?

4. How was the Battle of Horseshoe Bend won?

5. Why would demanding that Indians own private property make them more vulnerable to losing their land than if they continued to use the land in common?

6. What reasons did Jackson give to explain his invasion of Spanish-owned Florida? What resulted from the Seminole War of 1818?

7. How did President Jackson's Indian policy compare (in practice, rationale, and effect) to his predecessors'?

8. How did Jackson act unconstitutionally?

9. What caused the outbreak of the Second Creek War?

10. How did Speckled Snake describe the history of European-Indian relations? Do you agree with his synopsis? If not, how would you alter it?

11. If you went up to a Creek or Cherokee in the 1830s and asked if you could buy some of his or her land, what would he or she say to you?

12. Is there any parallel between Bacon's Rebellion and the Indian Wars preceeding the War of 1812 with respect to the dynamics among Indians, poor whites, and rich whites? If so, explain how the situations are parallel. If not, what factors are different enough so that there is no structural parallel?

13. What strategy(ies) did the Cherokees adopt to fight removal?

14. What position did Senator Frelinghuysen take regarding Indian removal? What action did Ralph Waldo Emerson take to oppose the removal of the Cherokees? Does Frelinghuysen remind you of Bartolomé de las Casas (chapter 1)? Why or why not? Does the existence of ineffective white opposition to Indian removal indicate that white Americans were swept away by historical forces? Why or why not?

15. What happened to the Choctaws after they signed their treaty of removal? Were the terms of the Treaty of Dancing Rabbit Creek observed by both sides?

16. Why did the Georgia militia arrest Sam Worcester and Elizar Butler? Were the actions of the militia consistent with the Supreme Court's interpretation of the U.S. Constitution? Why did it not matter whether the Supreme Court ruled in favor of or against the Cherokees?

17. By 1832, how long had the Creeks been defending their lands against the Europeans?

18. Place the following events in the order in which they usually happened:

  a. Indians appeal to federal government to enforce treaty that protected the integrity of Indian land.

  b. White settlers encroach on/invade Indian land.

  c. Federal government does nothing.

  d. On Indian land (by federal treaty) whites and Indians attack each other.

  e. Federal government orders Indians to move farther west.

  f. [Are any steps missing?]

  Why did this process repeat itself over and over again?

19. What were the conditions under which the Creeks moved west?

20. How did the Seminoles resist removal? How effective was the Seminole form of resistance?

21. If the Cherokee removal was so dreadful that it was to be known as the Trail of Tears, why did Van Buren feel that it had the "happiest effects?"

22. *Draw a map* that includes the following: Appalachians, Mississippi River, Rocky Mountains, Florida Territory, Tallapoosa River in Alabama, the state borders of Georgia, Mississippi, and Alabama, the location of the Battle of Horshoe Bend, the Trail of Tears.

23. *Debate Resolution:* Andrew Jackson's Indian policy represented a fundamental change from the Indian policies of previous U.S. presidents.

Chapter 8

We Take Nothing by Conquest, Thank God

Col. Ethan Allen Hitchcock, a professional soldier, graduate of the Military Academy, commander of the Third Infantry Regiment, a reader of Shakespeare, Chaucer, Hegel, Spinoza, wrote in his diary:

> Fort Jesup, La., June 30, 1845. Orders came last evening by express from Washington City directing General Taylor to move without any delay to...take up a position on the banks of or near the Rio Grande, and he is to expel any armed force of Mexicans who may cross that river. Bliss read the orders to me last evening hastily at tattoo. I have scarcely slept a wink, thinking of the needful preparations.... Violence leads to violence, and if this movement of ours does not lead to others and to bloodshed, I am much mistaken.

Hitchcock was not mistaken. Jefferson's Louisiana Purchase had doubled the territory of the United States, extending it to the Rocky Mountains. To the southwest was Mexico, which had won its independence in a revolutionary war against Spain in 1821. Mexico was then an even larger country than it is now, since it included what are now Texas, New Mexico, Utah, Nevada, Arizona, California, and part of Colorado. After agitation, and aid from the United States, Texas broke off from Mexico in 1836 and declared itself the "Lone Star Republic." In 1845, the U.S. Congress brought it into the Union as a state.

In the White House now was James Polk, a Democrat, an expansionist, who, on the night of his inauguration, confided to his secretary of the navy that one of his main objectives was the acquisition of California. His order to General Taylor to move troops to the Rio Grande was a challenge to the Mexicans. It was not at all clear that the Rio Grande was the southern boundary of Texas, although Texas had forced the defeated Mexican general Santa Anna to say so when he was a prisoner. The traditional border between Texas and Mexico had been the Nueces River, about 150 miles to the north, and both Mexico and the United States had recognized that as the border. However, Polk, encouraging the Texans to accept annexation, had assured them he would uphold their claims to the Rio Grande.

Ordering troops to the Rio Grande, into territory inhabited by Mexicans, was clearly a provocation. Taylor's army marched in parallel columns across the open prairie, scouts far ahead and on the flanks, a train of supplies following. Then, along a narrow road, through a belt of thick chaparral, they arrived, March 28, 1846, in cultivated fields and thatched-roof huts hurriedly abandoned by the Mexican occupants, who had fled across the river to the city of Matamoros. Taylor set up camp, began construction of a fort, and implanted his cannons facing the white houses of Matamoros, whose inhabitants stared curiously at the sight of an army on the banks of a quiet river.

The *Washington Union*, a newspaper expressing the position of President Polk and the Democratic party, had spoken early in 1845 on the meaning of Texas annexation: "Let the great measure of annexation be accomplished, and with it the questions of boundary and claims. For who can arrest the torrent that will pour onward to the West? The road to California will be open to us. Who will stay the march of our western people?"

It was shortly after that, in the summer of 1845, that John O'Sullivan, editor of the *Democratic Review*, used the phrase that became famous, saying it was "Our manifest destiny to overspread the continent allotted by Providence for the free development of our yearly multiplying millions." Yes, manifest destiny.

All that was needed in the spring of 1846 was a military incident to begin the war that Polk wanted. It came in April, when General Taylor's quartermaster, Colonel Cross, while riding up the Rio Grande, disappeared. His body was found eleven days later, his skull smashed by a heavy blow. It was assumed he had been killed by Mexican guerrillas crossing the river.

The next day (April 25), a patrol of Taylor's soldiers was surrounded and attacked by Mexicans, and wiped out: sixteen dead, others wounded, the rest captured. Taylor sent a dispatch to Polk: "Hostilities may now be considered as commenced."

The Mexicans had fired the first shot. But they had done what the American government wanted, according to Colonel Hitchcock, who wrote in his diary, even before those first incidents:

> I have said from the first that the United States are the aggressors.... We have not one particle of right to be here.... It looks as if the government sent a small force on purpose to bring on a war, so as to have a pretext for taking California and as much of this country as it chooses.... My heart is not in this business...but, as a military man, I am bound to execute orders.

On May 9, before news of any battles, Polk was suggesting to his cabinet a declaration of war. Polk recorded in his diary what he said to the cabinet meeting:

> I stated...that up to this time, as we knew, we had heard of no open act of aggression by the Mexican army, but that the danger was imminent that such acts would be committed. I said that in my opinion we had ample cause of war, and that it was impossible...that I could remain silent much longer...that the country was excited and impatient on the subject....

The country was not "excited and impatient." But the president was. When the dispatches arrived from General Taylor telling of casualties from the Mexican attack, Polk summoned the cabinet to hear the news, and they unanimously agreed he should ask for a declaration of war. Polk's message to Congress was indignant: "Mexico has passed the boundary of the United States, has invaded our territory and shed American blood upon the American soil...."

Congress then rushed to approve the war message. The bundles of official documents accompanying the war message, supposed to be evidence for Polk's statement, were not examined, but were tabled immediately by the House. Debate on the bill providing volunteers and money for the war was limited to two hours, and most of this was used up reading selected portions of the tabled documents, so that barely half an hour was left for discussion of the issues.

The Whig party also wanted California, but preferred to do it without war. Nevertheless, they would not deny men and money for the operation and so joined Democrats in voting overwhelmingly for the war resolution, 174 to 14. In the Senate there was debate, but it was limited to one day, and the war measure passed, 40 to 2, Whigs joining Democrats. John Quincy Adams of Massachusetts, who originally voted with "the stubborn 14," later voted for war appropriations.

Abraham Lincoln of Illinois was not yet in Congress when the war began, but after his election in 1846 he had occasion to vote and speak on the war. His "spot resolutions" became famous—he challenged Polk to specify the exact spot where American blood was shed "on the American soil." But he would not try to end the war by stopping funds for men and supplies. Speaking in the House on July 27, 1848, he said:

> If to say "the war was unnecessarily and unconstitutionally commenced by the President" be opposing the war, then the Whigs have very generally opposed it…. The marching an army into the midst of a peaceful Mexican settlement, frightening the inhabitants away, leaving their growing crops and other property to destruction, to you may appear a perfectly amiable, peaceful, unprovoking procedure; but it does not appear so to us…. But if, when the war had begun, and had become the cause of the country, the giving of our money and our blood, in common with yours, was support of the war, then it is not true that we have always opposed the war. With few individual exceptions, you have constantly had our votes here for all the necessary supplies….

A handful of antislavery Congressmen voted against all war measures, seeing the Mexican campaign as a means of extending the southern slave territory. One of these was Joshua Giddings of Ohio, a fiery speaker, physically powerful, who called it "an aggressive, unholy, and unjust war."

After Congress acted in May of 1846, there were rallies and demonstrations for the war in New York, Baltimore, Indianapolis, Philadelphia,and many other places. Thousands rushed to volunteer for the army. The poet Walt Whitman wrote in the *Brooklyn Eagle* in the early days of the war: "Yes: Mexico must be thoroughly chastised!…Let our arms now be carried with a spirit which shall teach the world that, while we are not forward for a quarrel, America knows how to crush, as well as how to expand!"

Accompanying all this aggressiveness was the idea that the United States would be giving the blessings of liberty and democracy to more people. This was intermingled with ideas of racial superiority, longings for the beautiful lands of New Mexico and California, and thoughts of commercial enterprise across the Pacific. The *New York Herald* said, in 1847: "The universal Yankee nation can regenerate and disenthrall the people of Mexico in a few years; and we believe it is a part of our destiny to civilize that beautiful country."

The *Congressional Globe* of February 11, 1847, reported:

> Mr. Giles, of Maryland—I take it for granted, that we shall gain territory, and must gain territory, before we shut the gates of the temple of

Janus.... We must march from ocean to ocean.... We must march from Texas straight to the Pacific ocean, and be bounded only by its roaring wave.... It is the destiny of the white race, it is the destiny of the Anglo-Saxon race....

The American Anti-Slavery Society, on the other hand, said the war was "waged solely for the detestable and horrible purpose of extending and perpetuating American slavery throughout the vast territory of Mexico." A twenty-seven-year-old Boston poet and abolitionist, James Russell Lowell, began writing satirical poems in the *Boston Courier* (they were later collected as the *Biglow Papers*). In them, a New England farmer, Hosea Biglow, spoke, in his own dialect, on the war:

> Ez fer war, I call it murder,—
> —There you hev it plain an' flat;
> I don't want to go no furder
> —Than my Testyment fer that....
>
> They jest want this Californy
> —So's to lug new slave-states in
> To abuse ye, an' to scorn ye,
> —An' to plunder ye like sin.

The war had barely begun, the summer of 1846, when a writer, Henry David Thoreau, who lived in Concord, Massachusetts, refused to pay his Massachusetts poll tax, denouncing the Mexican war. He was put in jail and spent one night there. His friends, without his consent, paid his tax, and he was released. Two years later, he gave a lecture, "Resistance to Civil Government," which was then printed as an essay, "Civil Disobedience":

> It is not desirable to cultivate a respect for the law, so much as for the right.... Law never made men a whit more just; and, by means of their respect for it, even the well-disposed are daily made the agents of injustice. A common and natural result of an undue respect for law is, that you may see a file of soldiers...marching in admirable order over hill and dale to the wars, against their wills, ay, against their common sense and consciences, which makes it very steep marching indeed, and produces a palpitation of the heart.

His friend and fellow writer Ralph Waldo Emerson agreed, but thought it futile to protest. When Emerson visited Thoreau in jail and asked, "What are you doing in there?" it was reported that Thoreau replied, "What are you doing out there?"

The churches, for the most part, were either outspokenly for the war or timidly silent. The Reverend Theodore Parker, a Unitarian minister in Boston, combined eloquent criticism of the war with contempt for the Mexican people, whom he called "a wretched people; wretched in their origin, history, and character," who must eventually give way as the Indians did. Yes, the United States should expand, he said, but not by war, rather by the power of her ideas, the pressure of her commerce, by "the steady advance of a superior race, with superior ideas and a better civilization...."

The racism of Parker was widespread. Congressman Delano of Ohio, an antislavery Whig, opposed the war because he was afraid of Americans mingling with an inferior people who "embrace all shades of color.... a sad compound of Spanish, English, Indian, and negro bloods...and resulting, it is said, in the production of a slothful, ignorant race of beings."

As the war went on, opposition grew. The American Peace Society printed a newspaper, the *Advocate of Peace*, which published poems, speeches, petitions, sermons against the war, and eyewitness accounts of the degradation of army life and the horrors of battle. Considering the strenuous efforts of the nation's leaders to build patriotic support, the amount of open dissent and criticism was remarkable. Antiwar meetings took place in spite of attacks by patriotic mobs.

As the army moved closer to Mexico City, the antislavery newspaper *The Liberator* daringly declared its wishes for the defeat of the American forces: "Every lover of Freedom and humanity, throughout the world, must wish them [the Mexicans] the most triumphant success...."

Frederick Douglass, a former slave and an extraordinary speaker and writer, wrote in his Rochester newspaper the *North Star*, January 21, 1848, of "the present disgraceful, cruel, and iniquitous war with our sister republic. Mexico seems a doomed victim to Anglo Saxon cupidity and love of dominion." Douglass was scornful of the unwillingness of opponents of the war to take real action (even the abolitionists kept paying their taxes):

> No politician of any considerable distinction or eminence seems willing to hazard his popularity with his party...by an open and unqualified disapprobation of the war. None seem willing to take their stand for peace at all risks; and all seem willing that the war should be carried on, in some form or other.

Where was popular opinion? It is hard to say. After the first rush, enlistments began to dwindle. Historians of the Mexican war have talked easily about "the people" and "public opinion." Their evidence, however, is not from "the people" but from the newspapers, claiming to be the voice of the people. The *New York Herald* wrote in August 1845: "The multitude cry aloud for war." The *New York Morning News* said "young and ardent spirits that throng the cities...want but a direction to their restless energies, and their attention is already fixed on Mexico."

It is impossible to know the extent of popular support of the war. But there is evidence that many organized workingmen opposed the war. There were demonstrations of Irish workers in New York, Boston, and Lowell against the annexation of Texas. In May, when the war against Mexico began, New York workingmen called a meeting to oppose the war, and many Irish workers came. The meeting called the war a plot by slave owners and asked for the withdrawal of American troops from disputed territory. That year, a convention of the New England Workingmen's Association condemned the war and announced they would "not take up arms to sustain the Southern slaveholder in robbing one-fifth of our countrymen of their labor."

Some newspapers, at the very start of the war, protested. Horace Greeley wrote in the *New York Tribune*, May 12, 1846:

> We can easily defeat the armies of Mexico, slaughter them by thousands.... Who believes that a score of victories over Mexico, the "annexation" of half her provinces, will give us more Liberty, a purer Morality, a more prosperous Industry, than we now have?...Is not Life miserable enough, comes not Death soon enough, without resort to the hideous enginery of War?

What of those who fought the war—the soldiers who marched, sweated, got sick, died? The Mexican soldiers. The American soldiers. We know little of the reactions of Mexican soldiers. We know much more about the American army—volunteers, not conscripts, lured by money and opportunity for social advancement via promotion in the armed forces. Half of General Taylor's army were recent immigrants—Irish and German mostly. Their patriotism was not very strong. Indeed, many of them deserted to the Mexican side, enticed by money. Some enlisted in the Mexican army and formed their own battalion, the San Patricio (St. Patrick's) Battalion.

At first there seemed to be enthusiasm in the army, fired by pay and patriotism. Martial spirit was high in New York, where the legislature authorized the governor to call fifty thousand volunteers. Placards read "Mexico or Death." There was a mass meeting of twenty thousand people in Philadelphia. Three thousand volunteered in Ohio.

This initial spirit soon wore off. One young man wrote anonymously to the *Cambridge Chronicle*:

> Neither have I the least idea of "joining" you, or in any way assisting the unjust war waging against Mexico. I have no wish to participate in such "glorious" butcheries of women and children as were displayed in the capture of Monterey, etc. Neither have I any desire to place myself under the dictation of a petty military tyrant, to every caprice of whose will I must yield implicit obedience. No sir-ee!...Human butchery has had its day.... And the time is rapidly approaching when the professional soldier will be placed on the same level as a bandit, the Bedouin, and the Thug.

There were extravagant promises and outright lies to build up the volunteer units. A man who wrote a history of the New York Volunteers declared: "Many enlisted for the sake of their families, having no employment, and having been offered 'three months' advance,' and were promised that they could leave part of their pay for their families to draw in their absence.... I boldly pronounce, that the whole Regiment was got up by fraud."

By late 1846, recruitment was falling off, so physical requirements were lowered, and anyone bringing in acceptable recruits would get two dollars a head. Even this didn't work. Congress in early 1847 authorized ten new regiments of regulars, to serve for the duration of the war, promising them one hundred acres of public land upon honorable discharge. But dissatisfaction continued.

And soon, the reality of battle came in upon the glory and the promises. On the Rio Grande before Matamoros, as a Mexican army of five thousand under General Arista faced Taylor's army of three thousand, the shells began to fly, and artilleryman Samuel French saw his first death in battle. John Weems describes it: "He happened to be staring at a man on horseback nearby when he saw a shot rip off the pommel of the saddle, tear through the man's body, and burst out with a crimson gush on the other side."

When the battle was over, five hundred Mexicans were dead or wounded. There were perhaps fifty American casualties. Weems describes the aftermath: "Night blanketed weary men who fell asleep where they dropped on the trampled prairie grass, while around them other prostrate men from both armies screamed and groaned in agony from wounds. By the eerie light of torches the surgeon's saw was going the livelong night."

Away from the battlefield, in the army camps, the romance of the recruiting posters was quickly forgotten. The Second Regiment of Mississippi Rifles, moving into New Orleans, was stricken by cold and sickness. The regimental surgeon reported: "Six months after our regiment had entered the service we had sustained a loss of 167 by death, and 134 by discharges." The regiment was packed into the holds of transports, eight hundred men into three ships. The surgeon continued:

> The dark cloud of disease still hovered over us. The holds of the ships...were soon crowded with the sick. The effluvia was intolerable.... The sea became rough.... Through the long dark night the rolling ship would dash the sick man from side to side bruising his flesh upon the rough corners of his berth. The wild screams of the delirious, the lamentations of the sick, and the melancholy groans of the dying, kept up one continual scene of confusion.... Four weeks we were confined to the loathsome ships and before we had landed at the Brasos, we consigned twenty-eight of our men to the dark waves.

Meanwhile, by land and by sea, Anglo-American forces were moving into California. A young naval officer, after the long voyage around the southern cape of South America, and up the coast to Monterey in California, wrote in his diary:

> Asia...will be brought to our very doors. Population will flow into the fertile regions of California. The resources of the entire country...will be developed.... The public lands lying along the route [of railroads] will be changed from deserts into gardens, and a large population will be settled....

It was a separate war that went on in California, where Anglo-Americans raided Spanish settlements, stole horses, and declared California separated from Mexico—the "Bear Flag Republic." Indians lived there, and naval officer Revere gathered the Indian chiefs and spoke to them (as he later recalled):

> I have called you together to have a talk with you. The country you inhabit no longer belongs to Mexico, but to a mighty nation whose territory extends from the great ocean you have all seen or heard of, to another great ocean thousands of miles toward the rising sun.... Our armies are now in Mexico, and will soon conquer the whole country. But you have nothing to fear from us, if you do what is right...if you are faithful to your new rulers.... I hope you will alter your habits, and be industrious and frugal, and give up all the low vices which you prac-

tice.... We shall watch over you, and give you true liberty; but beware of
sedition, lawlessness, and all other crimes, for the army which shields can
assuredly punish, and it will reach you in your most retired hiding places.

General Kearney moved easily into New Mexico, and Santa Fe was
taken without battle. An American staff officer described the reaction of
the Mexican population to the U.S. army's entrance into the capital city:

Our march into the city...was extremely warlike, with drawn sabres,
and daggers in every look.... As the American flag was raised, and the
cannon boomed its glorious national salute from the hill, the pent-up
emotions of many of the women could be suppressed no longer...as the
wail of grief arose above the din of our horses' tread, and reached our
ears from the depth of the gloomy-looking buildings on every hand.

That was in August. In December, Mexicans in Taos, New Mexico,
rebelled against American rule. The revolt was put down and arrests were
made. But many of the rebels fled and carried on sporadic attacks, killing a
number of Americans, then hiding in the mountains. The American army
pursued, and in a final desperate battle, in which six to seven hundred rebels
were engaged, 150 were killed, and it seemed the rebellion was now over.

In Los Angeles, too, there was a revolt. Mexicans forced the American
garrison there to surrender in September 1846. The United States did not
retake Los Angeles until January, after a bloody battle.

General Taylor had moved across the Rio Grande, occupied Matamoros, and now moved southward through Mexico. But his volunteers
became more unruly on Mexican territory. Mexican villages were pillaged
by drunken troops. Cases of rape began to multiply.

As the soldiers moved up the Rio Grande to Camargo, the heat
became unbearable, the water impure, and sickness grew—diarrhea,
dysentery, and other maladies—until a thousand were dead. At first the
dead were buried to the sounds of the "Dead March" played by a military
band. Then the number of dead was too great, and formal military funer-
als ceased. Southward to Monterey and another battle, where men and
horses died in agony, and one officer described the ground as "slippery
with...foam and blood."

The U.S. Navy bombarded Vera Cruz in an indiscriminate killing of
civilians. One of the navy's shells hit the post office, another a surgical
hospital. In two days, thirteen hundred shells were fired into the city, until
it surrendered. A reporter for the *New Orleans Delta* wrote: "The Mexicans variously estimate their loss at from 500 to 1000 killed and wounded,

but all agree that the loss among the soldiery is comparatively small and the destruction among the women and children is very great."

Colonel Hitchcock, coming into the city, wrote: "I shall never forget the horrible fire of our mortars...going with dreadful certainty...often in the centre of private dwellings—it was awful. I shudder to think of it." Still, Hitchcock, the dutiful soldier, wrote for General Scott "a sort of address to the Mexican people" which was then printed in English and Spanish by the tens of thousands saying "we have not a particle of ill-will towards you...we are here for no earthly purpose except the hope of obtaining a peace."

It was a war of the American elite against the Mexican elite, each side exhorting, using, killing its own population as well as the other. The Mexican commander Santa Anna had crushed rebellion after rebellion, his troops also raping and plundering after victory. When Col. Hitchcock and Gen. Winfield Scott moved into Santa Anna's estate, they found its walls full of ornate paintings. But half his army was dead or wounded.

General Scott moved toward the last battle—for Mexico City—with ten thousand soldiers. They were not anxious for battle. Three days' march from Mexico City, at Jalapa, seven of his eleven regiments evaporated, their enlistment times up, the reality of battle and disease too much for them.

On the outskirts of Mexico City, at Churubusco, Mexican and American armies clashed for three hours and thousands died on both sides. Among the Mexicans taken prisoner were sixty-nine U.S. Army deserters.

As often in war, battles were fought without point. After one such engagement near Mexico City, with terrible casualties, a marine lieutenant blamed Gen. Scott: "He had originated it in error and caused it to be fought, with inadequate forces, for an object that had no existence."

In the final battle for Mexico City, Anglo-American troops took the height of Chapultepec and entered the city of 200,000 people, General Santa Anna having moved northward. This was September 1847. A Mexican merchant wrote to a friend about the bombardment of the city: "In some cases whole blocks were destroyed and a great number of men, women and children killed and wounded."

General Santa Anna fled to Huamantla, where another battle was fought, and he had to flee again. An American infantry lieutenant wrote to his parents what happened after an officer named Walker was killed in battle:

General Lane...told us to "avenge the death of the gallant Walker.... Grog shops were broken open first, and then, maddened with liquor, every species of outrage was committed. Old women and girls were stripped of their clothing—and many suffered still greater outrages. Men were shot by dozens...their property, churches, stores and dwelling houses ransacked.... It made me for the first time ashamed of my country.

One Pennsylvania volunteer, stationed at Matamoros late in the war, wrote:

We are under very strict discipline here. Some of our officers are very good men but the balance of them are very tyrannical and brutal toward the men.... [T]onight on drill an officer laid a soldier's skull open with his sword.... But the time may come and that soon when officers and men will stand on equal footing.... A soldier's life is very disgusting.

On the night of August 15, 1847, volunteer regiments from Virginia, Mississippi, and North Carolina rebelled in northern Mexico against Col. Robert Treat Paine. Paine killed a mutineer, but two of his lieutenants refused to help him quell the mutiny. The rebels were ultimately exonerated in an attempt to keep the peace.

Desertion grew. In March 1847 the army reported over a thousand deserters. The total number of deserters during the war was 9,207 (5,331 regulars and 3,876 volunteers). Those who did not desert became harder and harder to manage. General Cushing referred to sixty-five such men in the First Regiment of the Massachusetts Infantry as "incorrigibly mutinous and insubordinate."

The glory of the victory was for the president and the generals, not the deserters, the dead, the wounded. The Massachusetts Volunteers had started with 630 men. They came home with three hundred dead, mostly from disease, and at the reception dinner on their return their commander, General Cushing, was hissed by his men.

As the veterans returned home, speculators immediately showed up to buy the land warrants given by the government. Many of the soldiers, desperate for money, sold their 160 acres for less than fifty dollars.

Mexico surrendered. There were calls among Americans to take all of Mexico. The Treaty of Guadalupe Hidalgo, signed February 1848, just took half. The Texas boundary was set at the Rio Grande; New Mexico and California were ceded. The United States paid Mexico $15 million, which led the *Whig Intelligencer* to conclude that "we take nothing by conquest.... Thank God."

Exercises

1. When did Mexico achieve independence from Spain?
    When did Texas become independent from Mexico?
    When did Texas become a state of the United States?
    When did the Mexican-American War begin?

2. Before President Polk's term, which river had the U.S. government recognized as the border between Mexico and Texas? Which river did Texas claim as its border with Mexico? Which river did Polk choose as the border? How did Polk's choice of the border allow the United States to provoke a war with Mexico?

3. What were the arguments that the news media used to support a war with Mexico?

4. What were Colonel Hitchcock's private thoughts concerning the war with Mexico? Why might he have not shared those thoughts with fellow officers and enlisted men?

5. By 1848, did Congressman Lincoln end up supporting the war?

6. Walt Whitman wrote that Mexico must be soundly punished. What did Mexico do that persuaded Whitman to demand that Mexico be "crushed"?

7. What role did race play in both the promotion of and opposition to the war?

8. The *New York Herald* believed that, in conquering Mexico, the United States would "civilize" it. What exactly do you think the *Herald* meant by "civilize"? What data lead you to your hypothesis?

    a. building factories and transform farmers into workers

    b. convert Mexican Catholics into Protestants

    c. teach the Mexican better table manners

    d. importing slavery-based plantations

e. dividing Mexican provinces into states subjected to the rules laid down by the U.S. Constitution (those rules are as follows: each state has a constitutional convention to create a state constitution that must be submitted and accepted by the U.S. Congress before the state is admitted to the Union—can elect and send representatives to Congress)

f. having Mexicans of mixed Spanish/Indian descent ruled by Anglo-Saxon Protestants whose government would be more efficient and less corrupt than the Mexican government was in 1845

9. Who were the opponents of the war? How did they manifest (in word and deed) their opposition to the war? To what degree were their tactics effective? How could they have been more effective (what were the obstacles in the way of their success)?

10. How can the division over the Mexican-American War (1846–48) be seen as a prelude to the Civil War (1861–65)?

11. Apart from an increase in pay, why might an Irish-American soldier desert the U.S. Army and join the Mexican army?

12. Why did many of the American soldiers wish to stop fighting?

13. How strong was the Mexican/Indian resistance to U.S. military advances at each of the following points of contact: Santa Fe, Taos, Los Angeles, Camargo, Vera Cruz, Churubusca, Mexico City, Huatmantla? To what can you attribute the degree of strength or weakness of the resistance?

14. What evidence does Zinn provide to determine how widespread desertion was among American soldiers?

15. Many soldiers signed up to go to war in hopes of acquiring land. Why then did these same soldiers sell their hard-won 160-acre land warrants to land speculators?

16. What percentage of Mexico did the United States take/buy/acquire in the Treaty of Guadalupe Hidalgo? Was this a better or worse bargain than the Louisiana Purchase?

17. *Draw a map* that includes the following: the Mexican Cession; the state borders of California, Colorado, Nevada, Utah, New Mexico, Arizona, and Texas; Mexico; the Rio Grande; the Nueces River; Washington, D.C.; the Louisiana Purchase; the Oregon Territory; the cities of Santa Fe, Taos, Los Angeles, Vera Cruz, and Mexico City.

18. *Debate Resolution:* The United States did not provoke a war with Mexico over minor issues.

Chapter 9

Slavery Without Submission, Emancipation Without Freedom

The United States government's support of slavery was based on an overpowering practicality. In 1790, a thousand tons of cotton were being produced every year in the South. By 1860, it was a million tons. In the same period, 500,000 slaves grew to 4 million. A system harried by slave rebellions and conspiracies (Gabriel Prosser, 1800; Denmark Vesey, 1822; Nat Turner, 1831) developed a network of controls in the southern states, backed by the laws, courts, armed forces, and race prejudice of the nation's political leaders.

It would take either a full-scale slave rebellion or a full-scale war to end such a deeply entrenched system. If a rebellion, it might get out of hand, and turn its ferocity beyond slavery to the most successful system of capitalist enrichment in the world. If a war, those who made the war would organize its consequences. Hence, it was Abraham Lincoln who freed the slaves, not John Brown. In 1859, John Brown was hanged, with federal complicity, for attempting to do by small-scale violence what Lincoln would do by large-scale violence several years later—end slavery.

With slavery abolished by order of the government—true, a government pushed hard to do so, by blacks, free and slave, and by white abolitionists—its end could be orchestrated so as to set limits to emancipation. Liberation from the top would go only so far as the interests of the dominant groups permitted. If carried further by the momentum of war, the rhetoric of a crusade, it could be pulled back to a safer position. Thus, while the ending of slavery led to a reconstruction of national politics and

129

economics, it was not a radical reconstruction, but a safe one—in fact, a profitable one.

The plantation system, based on tobacco growing in Virginia, North Carolina, and Kentucky, and rice in South Carolina, expanded into lush new cotton lands in Georgia, Alabama, Mississippi—and needed more slaves. But slave importation became illegal in 1808. Therefore, "from the beginning, the law went unenforced," says John Hope Franklin (*From Slavery to Freedom*). "The long, unprotected coast, the certain markets, and the prospects of huge profits were too much for the American merchants and they yielded to the temptation...." He estimates that perhaps 250,000 slaves were imported illegally before the Civil War.

How can slavery be described? Perhaps not at all by those who have not experienced it. The 1932 edition of a best-selling textbook by two northern liberal historians saw slavery as perhaps the Negro's "necessary transition to civilization." Economists or cliometricians (statistical historians) have tried to assess slavery by estimating how much money was spent on slaves for food and medical care. But can this describe the reality of slavery as it was to a human being who lived inside it? Are the *conditions* of slavery as important as the *existence* of slavery?

John Little, a former slave, wrote:

> They say slaves are happy, because they laugh, and are merry. I myself and three or four others, have received two hundred lashes in the day, and had our feet in fetters; yet, at night, we would sing and dance, and make others laugh at the rattling of our chains. Happy men we must have been! We did it to keep down trouble, and to keep our hearts from being completely broken: that is as true as the gospel! Just look at it,—must not we have been very happy? Yet I have done it myself—I have cut capers in chains.

A record of deaths kept in a plantation journal (now in the University of North Carolina Archives) lists the ages and cause of death of all those who died on the plantation between 1850 and 1855. Of the thirty-two who died in that period, only four reached the age of sixty, four reached the age of fifty, seven died in their forties, seven died in their twenties or thirties, and nine died before they were five years old.

But can statistics record what it meant for families to be torn apart, when a master, for profit, sold a husband or a wife, a son or a daughter? In 1858, a slave named Abream Scriven was sold by his master, and wrote to his wife: "Give my love to my father and mother and tell them good Bye for me, and if we Shall not meet in this world I hope to meet in heaven."

Slave revolts in the United States were not as frequent or as large-scale as those in the Caribbean islands or in South America. Probably the largest slave revolt in the United States took place near New Orleans in 1811. Four to five hundred slaves gathered after a rising at the plantation of a Major Andry. Armed with cane knives, axes, and clubs, they wounded Andry, killed his son, and began marching from plantation to plantation, their numbers growing. They were attacked by U.S. army and militia forces; sixty-six were killed on the spot, and sixteen were tried and shot by a firing squad.

The conspiracy of Denmark Vesey, himself a free Negro, was thwarted before it could be carried out in 1822. The plan was to burn Charleston, South Carolina, then the sixth-largest city in the nation, and to initiate a general revolt of slaves in the area. Several witnesses said thousands of blacks were implicated in one way or another. Blacks had made about 250 pike heads and bayonets and over three hundred daggers, according to Herbert Aptheker's account. But the plan was betrayed, and thirty-five blacks, including Vesey, were hanged. The trial record itself, published in Charleston, was ordered destroyed soon after publication, as too dangerous for slaves to see.

In Southampton County, Virginia, in the summer of 1831, a slave named Nat Turner, claiming religious visions, gathered about seventy slaves, who went on a rampage from plantation to plantation, murdering at least fifty-five men, women, and children. They gathered supporters, but were captured as their ammunition ran out. Turner and perhaps eighteen others were hanged.

This threw the slaveholding South into a panic, and then into a determined effort to bolster the security of the slave system. After that, Virginia kept a militia force of 101,000, almost 10 percent of its total population. Rebellion, though rare, was a constant fear among slave owners.

Eugene Genovese, in his comprehensive study of slavery, *Roll, Jordan, Roll*, sees a record of "simultaneous accommodation and resistance to slavery." The resistance included stealing property, sabotage and slowness, killing overseers and masters, burning down plantation buildings, running away. Even the accommodation "breathed a critical spirit and disguised subversive actions."

Running away was much more realistic than armed insurrection. During the 1850s about a thousand slaves a year escaped into the North, Canada, and Mexico. Thousands ran away for short periods. And this despite the terror facing the runaway. The dogs used in tracking fugitives "bit, tore, mutilated, and if not pulled off in time, killed their prey," Genovese says.

Harriet Tubman, born into slavery, her head injured by an overseer when she was fifteen, made her way to freedom alone as a young woman, then became the most famous conductor on the Underground Railroad. She made nineteen dangerous trips back and forth, often disguised, escorting more than three hundred slaves to freedom, always carrying a pistol, telling the fugitives, "You'll be free or die." She expressed her philosophy: "There was one of two things I had a right to, liberty or death; if I could not have one, I would have the other; for no man should take me alive...."

One form of resistance was not to work so hard. W. E. B. Du Bois wrote, in *The Gift of Black Folk*:

> As a tropical product with a sensuous receptivity to the beauty of the world, he was not as easily reduced to be the mechanical draft-horse which the northern European laborer became.... [T]hus he was easily accused of laziness and driven as a slave when in truth he brought to modern manual labor a renewed valuation of life.

The instances where poor whites helped slaves were not frequent, but sufficient to show the need for setting one group against the other. Genovese says:

> The slaveholders...suspected that non-slaveholders would encourage slave disobedience and even rebellion, not so much out of sympathy for the blacks as out of hatred for the rich planters and resentment of their own poverty. White men sometimes were linked to slave insurrectionary plots, and each such incident rekindled fears.

This helps explain the stern police measures against whites who fraternized with blacks. In return, blacks helped whites in need. One black runaway told of a slave woman who had received fifty lashes of the whip for giving food to a white neighbor who was poor and sick.

When the Brunswick canal was built in Georgia, the black slaves and white Irish workers were segregated, the excuse being that they would do violence against one another. That may well have been true, but Fanny Kemble, the famous actress and wife of a planter, wrote in her journal:

> But the Irish are not only quarrelers, and rioters, and fighters, and drinkers, and despisers of niggers—they are a passionate, impulsive, warm-hearted, generous people.... [T]hey might actually take to sympathy with the slaves, and I leave you to judge of the possible consequences. You perceive, I am sure, that they can by no means be allowed to work together on the Brunswick Canal.

The need for slave control led to an ingenious device, paying poor whites—themselves so troublesome for two hundred years of southern history—to be overseers of black labor and therefore buffers for black hatred.

Religion was used by plantation owners for control.

As for black preachers, as Genovese puts it, "they had to speak a language defiant enough to hold the high-spirited among their flock but neither so inflammatory as to rouse them to battles they could not win nor so ominous as to arouse the ire of ruling powers." Practicality decided: "The slave communities counseled a strategy of patience, of acceptance of what could not be helped, of a dogged effort to keep the black community alive and healthy...."

It was once thought that slavery had destroyed the black family. But interviews with ex-slaves, done in the 1930s by the Federal Writers Project of the New Deal for the Library of Congress, told a different story, which George Rawick summarizes (*From Sundown to Sunup*): "The slave community acted like a generalized extended kinship system in which all adults looked after all children and there was little division between 'my children for whom I'm responsible' and 'your children for whom you're responsible.'...It was part and parcel, as we shall see, of the social process out of which came black pride, black identity, black culture, the black community, and black rebellion in America."

Old letters and records dug out by historian Herbert Gutman (*The Black Family in Slavery and Freedom*) show the stubborn resistance of the slave family to pressures of disintegration. A woman wrote to her son from whom she had been separated for twenty years: "I long to see you in my old age.... Now my dear son I pray you to come and see your dear old Mother.... I love you Cato you love your Mother—You are my only son...."

And a man wrote to his wife, sold away from him with their children: "Send me some of the children's hair in a separate paper with their names on the paper.... I had rather anything to had happened to me most than ever to have been parted from you and the children.... Laura I do love you the same...."

Also insisting on the strength of blacks even under slavery, Lawrence Levine (*Black Culture and Black Consciousness*) gives a picture of a rich culture among slaves, a complex mixture of adaptation and rebellion, through the creativity of stories and songs:

> We raise de wheat,
> Dey gib us de corn;
> We bake de bread,
> Dey gib us de crust,
> We sif de meal,
> Dey gib us de huss;
> We peel de meat,
> Dey gib us de skin;
> And dat's de way
> Dey take us in....

Spirituals often had double meanings. The lyrics "O Canaan, sweet Canaan, I am bound for the land of Canaan" often meant that slaves meant to get to the North, their Canaan. During the Civil War, slaves began to make up new spirituals with bolder messages: "Before I'd be a slave, I'd be buried in my grave, and go home to my Lord and be saved." And the spiritual "Many Thousand Go":

> No more peck o' corn for me, no more, no more,
> No more driver's lash for me, no more, no more....

While southern slaves held on, free blacks in the North (there were about 130,000 in 1830, about 200,000 in 1850) agitated for the abolition of slavery. In 1829, David Walker, son of a slave, but born free in North Carolina, moved to Boston, where he sold old clothes. The pamphlet he wrote and printed, *Walker's Appeal*, became widely known. It infuriated southern slaveholders; Georgia offered a reward of $10,000 to anyone who would deliver Walker alive, and $1,000 to anyone who would kill him. It is not hard to understand why when you read his *Appeal*. Blacks must fight for their freedom, he said:

> Let our enemies go on with their butcheries, and at once fill up their cup.
> Never make an attempt to gain our freedom or natural right...until you
> see your way clear—when that hour arrives and you move, be not afraid
> or dismayed.... God has been pleased to give us two eyes, two hands,
> two feet, and some sense in our heads as well as they. They have no more
> right to hold us in slavery than we have to hold them.... "Every dog
> must have its day," the American's is coming to an end.

One summer day in 1830, David Walker was found dead near the doorway of his shop in Boston.

Some born in slavery acted out the unfulfilled desire of millions. Frederick Douglass, a slave, sent to Baltimore to work as a servant and as a laborer in the shipyard, somehow learned to read and write, and at twenty-one, in the year 1838, escaped to the North, where he became the most famous black man of his time, as a lecturer, newspaper editor, and writer. In his autobiography, *Narrative of the Life of Frederick Douglass*, he recalled his first childhood thoughts about his condition:

> Why am I a slave? Why are some people slaves, and others masters? Was there ever a time when this was not so? How did the relation commence?
>
> Once, however, engaged in the inquiry, I was not very long in finding out the true solution of the matter. It was not color, but crime, not God, but man, that afforded the true explanation of the existence of slavery; nor was I long in finding out another important truth, viz: what man can make, man can unmake....
>
> I distinctly remember being, even then, most strongly impressed with the idea of being a free man some day. This cheering assurance was an inborn dream of my human nature—a constant menace to slavery—and one which all the powers of slavery were unable to silence or extinguish.

The Fugitive Slave Act passed in 1850 was a concession to the southern states in return for the admission of the Mexican war territories (California, especially) into the Union as nonslave states. The act made it easy for slave owners to recapture ex-slaves or simply to pick up blacks they claimed had run away. Northern blacks organized resistance to the Fugitive Slave Act, denouncing President Fillmore, who signed it, and Sen. Daniel Webster, who supported it. One of these was J. W. Loguen, son of a slave mother and her white owner. He had escaped to freedom on his master's horse, gone to college, and was now a minister in Syracuse, New York. He spoke to a meeting in that city in 1850:

> The time has come to change the tones of submission into tones of defiance—and to tell Mr. Fillmore and Mr. Webster, if they propose to execute this measure upon us, to send on their blood-hounds.... I received my freedom from Heaven, and with it came the command to defend my title to it.... I don't respect this law—I don't fear it—I won't obey it! It outlaws me, and I outlaw it....

The following year, in Syracuse, a runaway slave named Jerry was captured and put on trial. A crowd used crowbars and a battering ram to break into the courthouse, defying marshals with drawn guns, and set Jerry free.

Loguen made his home in Syracuse a major station on the Underground Railroad. It was said that he helped fifteen hundred slaves on their way to Canada. His memoir of slavery came to the attention of his former owner, and she wrote to him, asking him either to return or to send her $1,000 in compensation. Loguen's reply to her was printed in the abolitionist newspaper, *The Liberator:*

> Mrs. Sarah Logue.... You say you have offers to buy me, and that you shall sell me if I do not send you $1000, and in the same breath and almost in the same sentence, you say, "You know we raised you as we did our own children." Woman, did you raise your own children for the market? Did you raise them for the whipping post? Did you raise them to be driven off, bound to a coffle in chains?...Shame on you!...
>
> Have you got to learn that human rights are mutual and reciprocal, and if you take my liberty and life, you forfeit your own liberty and life? Before God and high heaven, is there a law for one man which is not a law for every other man?
>
> If you or any other speculator on my body and rights, wish to know how I regard my rights, they need but come here, and lay their hands on me to enslave me....
>
> Yours, etc. J. W. Loguen

Frederick Douglass knew that the shame of slavery was not just the South's, that the whole nation was complicit in it. On the Fourth of July, 1852, he gave an Independence Day address:

> Fellow Citizens: What to the American slave is your Fourth of July? I answer, a day that reveals to him more than all other days of the year, the gross injustice and cruelty to which he is the constant victim. To him your celebration is a sham; your boasted liberty an unholy license; your national greatness, swelling vanity; your sounds of rejoicing are empty and heartless; your denunciation of tyrants, brass-fronted impudence; your shouts of liberty and equality, hollow mockery; your prayers and hymns, your sermons and thanksgivings, with all your religious parade and solemnity, are to him mere bombast, fraud, deception, impiety, and hypocrisy—a thin veil to cover up crimes which would disgrace a nation of savages. There is not a nation of the earth guilty of practices more shocking and bloody than are the people of these United States at this very hour.

Ten years after Nat Turner's rebellion, there was no sign of black insurrection in the South. But that year, 1841, one incident took place which kept alive the idea of rebellion. Slaves being transported on a ship, the *Creole*, overpowered the crew, killed one of them, and sailed into the British West Indies (where slavery had been abolished in 1833). England refused to return the slaves (there was much agitation in England against American slavery), and this led to angry talk in Congress of war with England, encouraged by Secretary of State Daniel Webster. The *Colored People's Press* denounced Webster's "bullying position," and, recalling the Revolutionary War and the War of 1812, wrote: "If war be declared... Will we fight in defense of a government which denies us the most precious right of citizenship?..."

As the tension grew, North and South, blacks became more militant. Frederick Douglass spoke in 1853:

> Let me give you a word of the philosophy of reforms. The whole history of the progress of human liberty shows that all concessions yet made to her august claims have been born of struggle.... If there is no struggle there is no progress.... Power concedes nothing without a demand. It never did and it never will....

How ever-present was slavery in the minds of northern Negroes in the decades before the Civil War is shown by black children in a Cincinnati school, a private school financed by Negroes. The children were responding to the question "What do you think *most* about?" Only five answers remain in the records, and all refer to slavery. A seven-year-old child wrote: "I am sorrow to hear that the boat...went down with 200 poor slaves from up the river. Oh how sorrow I am to hear that, it grieves my heart so that I could faint in one minute."

White abolitionists did courageous and pioneering work, on the lecture platform, in newspapers, in the Underground Railroad. Black abolitionists, less publicized, were the backbone of the antislavery movement. Before Garrison published his famous *Liberator* in Boston in 1831, the first national convention of Negroes had been held, David Walker had already written his *Appeal*, and the black abolitionist magazine *Freedom's Journal* had appeared. Of *The Liberator*'s first twenty-five subscribers, most were black.

Blacks had to struggle constantly with the unconscious racism of white abolitionists. They also had to insist on their own independent voice. Douglass wrote for *The Liberator*, but in 1847 started his own newspaper in Rochester, the *North Star*, which led to a break with Garrison. In 1854, a conference of Negroes declared: "...it is emphatically our battle; no one else can fight it for us.... Our relations to the Anti-Slavery movement must be and are changed. Instead of depending upon it we must lead it."

Certain black women faced the triple hurdle—of being abolitionists in a slave society, of being black among white reformers, and of being women in a reform movement dominated by men. When Sojourner Truth rose to speak in 1853 in New York City at the Fourth National Woman's Rights Convention, it all came together. There was a hostile mob in the hall shouting, jeering, threatening. She said: "I know that it feels a kind o' hissin' and ticklin' like to see a colored woman get up and tell you about things, and Woman's Rights.... I am sittin' among you to watch; and every once and awhile I will come out and tell you what time of night it is...."

After Nat Turner's violent uprising and Virginia's bloody repression, the security system inside the South became tighter. Perhaps only an outsider could hope to launch a rebellion. It was such a person, a white man of ferocious courage and determination, John Brown, whose wild scheme it was to seize the federal arsenal at Harpers Ferry, Virginia, and then set off a revolt of slaves through the South.

Harriet Tubman, five feet tall, a veteran of countless secret missions piloting blacks out of slavery, was involved with John Brown and his plans. But sickness prevented her from joining him. Frederick Douglass too had met with Brown. He argued against the plan from the standpoint of its chances of success, but he admired the ailing man of sixty, tall, gaunt, white-haired.

Douglass was right; the plan would not work. The local militia, joined by a hundred marines under the command of Robert E. Lee, surrounded the insurgents. Although his men were dead or captured, John Brown refused to surrender: he barricaded himself in a small brick building near the gate of the armory. The troops battered down a door; a marine lieutenant moved in and struck Brown with his sword. Wounded, sick, he was interrogated. W. E. B. Du Bois, in his book *John Brown*, writes:

> Picture the situation: An old and blood-bespattered man, half-dead from the wounds inflicted but a few hours before; a man lying in the cold and dirt, without sleep for fifty-five nerve-wrecking hours, without food for nearly as long, with the dead bodies of his two sons almost before his eyes, the piled corpses of his seven slain comrades near and afar, a wife and a bereaved family listening in vain, and a Lost Cause, the dream of a lifetime, lying dead in his heart....

Lying there, interrogated by the governor of Virginia, Brown said: "You had better—all you people at the South—prepare yourselves for a settlement of this question.... You may dispose of me very easily—I am nearly disposed of now, but this question is still to be settled,—this Negro question, I mean; the end of that is not yet."

Ralph Waldo Emerson, not an activist himself, said of the execution of John Brown: "He will make the gallows holy as the cross."

Of the twenty-two men in John Brown's striking force, five were black. Two of these were killed on the spot, one escaped, and two were hanged by the authorities. Before his execution, John Copeland wrote to his parents: "Remember that if I must die I die in trying to liberate a few of my poor and oppressed people from my condition of servitude which God in his Holy Writ has hurled his most bitter denunciations against.... I am not terrified by the gallows."

John Brown was executed by the state of Virginia with the approval of the national government. It was the national government that, while weakly enforcing the law ending the slave trade, sternly enforced the laws providing for the return of fugitives to slavery. It was the national government that, in Andrew Jackson's administration, collaborated with the South to keep abolitionist literature out of the mails in the southern states. It was the Supreme Court of the United States that declared in 1857 that the slave Dred Scott could not sue for his freedom because he was not a person, but property.

Such a government would never accept an end to slavery by rebellion. It would end slavery only under conditions controlled by whites, and only when required by the political and economic needs of the business elite of the North. It was Abraham Lincoln who combined perfectly the needs of business, the political ambition of the new Republican party, and the rhetoric of humanitarianism. He would keep the abolition of slavery not at the top of his list of priorities, but close enough to the top so it could be pushed there temporarily by abolitionist pressures and by practical political advantage.

Lincoln could skillfully blend the interests of the very rich and the interests of the black at a moment in history when these interests met. And he could link these two with a growing section of Americans, the white, up-and-coming, economically ambitious, politically active middle class. As Richard Hofstadter puts it:

> Thoroughly middle class in his ideas, he spoke for those millions of Americans who had begun their lives as hired workers—as farm hands, clerks, teachers, mechanics, flatboat men, and rail-splitters—and had passed into the ranks of landed farmers, prosperous grocers, lawyers, merchants, physicians and politicians.

Lincoln could argue with lucidity and passion against slavery on moral grounds, while acting cautiously in practical politics. He believed "that the institution of slavery is founded on injustice and bad policy, but that the promulgation of abolition doctrines tends to increase rather than abate its evils."

Lincoln refused to denounce the Fugitive Slave Law publicly. He wrote to a friend: "I confess I hate to see the poor creatures hunted down... but I bite my lips and keep quiet." And when he did propose, in 1849, as a congressman, a resolution to abolish slavery in the District of Columbia, he accompanied this with a section requiring local authorities to arrest and return fugitive slaves coming into Washington. (This led Wendell Phillips, the Boston abolitionist, to refer to him years later as "that slavehound from Illinois.") He opposed slavery, but could not see blacks as equals, so a constant theme in his approach was to free the slaves and to send them back to Africa.

In his 1858 campaign in Illinois for the Senate against Stephen Douglas, Lincoln spoke differently depending on the views of his listeners (and also perhaps depending on how close it was to the election). Speaking in northern Illinois in July (in Chicago), he said:

> Let us discard all this quibbling about this man and the other man, this race and that race and the other race being inferior, and therefore they must be placed in an inferior position. Let us discard all these things, and unite as one people throughout this land, until we shall once more stand up declaring that all men are created equal.

Two months later in Charleston, in southern Illinois, Lincoln told his audience:

> I will say, then, that I am not, nor ever have been, in favor of bringing about in any way the social and political equality of the white and black races [applause]; that I am not, nor ever have been, in favor of making voters or jurors of negroes, nor of qualifying them to hold office, nor to intermarry with white people....
>
> And inasmuch as they cannot so live, while they do remain together there must be the position of superior and inferior, and I as much as any other man am in favor of having the superior position assigned to the white race.

Behind the secession of the South from the Union, after Lincoln was elected president in the fall of 1860 as candidate of the new Republican party, was a long series of policy clashes between South and North. The northern elite wanted economic expansion—free land, free labor, a free market, a high protective tariff for manufacturers, a bank of the United

States. The slave interests opposed all that; they saw Lincoln and the Republicans as making continuation of their pleasant and prosperous way of life impossible in the future.

So, when Lincoln was elected, seven southern states seceded from the Union. Lincoln initiated hostilities by trying to repossess the federal base at Fort Sumter, South Carolina, and four more states seceded. The Confederacy was formed; the Civil War was on.

Lincoln's first inaugural address, in March 1861, was conciliatory: "I have no purpose, directly or indirectly, to interfere with the institution of slavery in the States where it exists. I believe I have no lawful right to do so, and I have no inclination to do so." And with the war four months on, when Gen. John C. Frémont in Missouri declared martial law and said slaves of owners resisting the United States were to be free, Lincoln countermanded this order. He was anxious to hold in the Union the slave states of Maryland, Kentucky, Missouri, and Delaware.

It was only as the war grew more bitter, the casualties mounted, desperation to win heightened, and the criticism of the abolitionists threatened to unravel the tattered coalition behind Lincoln that he began to act against slavery. Hofstadter puts it this way: "Like a delicate barometer, he recorded the trend of pressures, and as the Radical pressure increased he moved toward the left."

Racism in the North was as entrenched as slavery in the South, and it would take the war to shake both. New York blacks could not vote unless they owned $250 in property (a qualification not applied to whites). A proposal to abolish this, put on the ballot in 1860, was defeated two to one.

Wendell Phillips, with all his criticism of Lincoln, recognized the possibilities in his election. Speaking at the Tremont Temple in Boston the day after the election, Phillips said:

> If the telegraph speaks truth, for the first time in our history the slave has chosen a President of the United States.... Not an Abolitionist, hardly an antislavery man, Mr. Lincoln consents to represent an antislavery idea. A pawn on the political chessboard, his value is in his position; with fair effort, we may soon change him for knight, bishop or queen, and sweep the board. [Applause.]

The spirit of Congress, even after the war began, was shown in a resolution it passed in the summer of 1861, with only a few dissenting votes: "...this war is not waged...for any purpose of...over-throwing or interfering with the rights of established institutions of those states, but...to preserve the Union."

The abolitionists stepped up their campaign. Emancipation petitions poured into Congress in 1861 and 1862. In May of that year, Wendell Phillips said: "Abraham Lincoln may not wish it; he cannot prevent it.... [T]he negro is the pebble in the cog-wheel, and the machine cannot go on until you get him out."

In July of 1862 Congress passed a Confiscation Act, which enabled the freeing of slaves of those fighting the Union. But this was not enforced by the Union generals, and Lincoln ignored the nonenforcement. Horace Greeley, editor of the *New York Tribune*, wrote an open letter to Lincoln warning him that his supporters were "sorely disappointed and deeply pained.... We require of you, as the first servant of the Republic, charged especially and preeminently with this duty, that you EXECUTE THE LAWS.... We think you are strangely and disastrously remiss...with regard to the emancipating provisions of the new Confiscation Act.... We think you are unduly influenced by the councils...of certain politicians hailing from the Border Slave States."

Greeley appealed to the practical need of winning the war. "We must have scouts, guides, spies, cooks, teamsters, diggers and choppers from the blacks of the South, whether we allow them to fight for us or not.... I entreat you to render a hearty and unequivocal obedience to the law of the land."

Lincoln replied to Greeley:

Dear Sir: ...I have not meant to leave any one in doubt.... My paramount object in this struggle is to save the Union, and is not either to save or destroy Slavery. If I could save the Union without freeing any slave, I would do it; and if I could save it by freeing all the slaves, I would do it.... I have here stated my purpose according to my view of official duty, and I intend no modification of my oft-expressed personal wish that all men, everywhere, could be free.

When in September 1862 Lincoln issued his preliminary Emancipation Proclamation, it was a military move, giving the South four months to stop rebelling, threatening to emancipate their slaves if they continued to fight, promising to leave slavery untouched in states that came over to the North.

Thus, when the Emancipation Proclamation was issued January 1, 1863, it declared slaves free in those areas still fighting against the Union (which it listed very carefully), and said nothing about slaves behind Union lines.

Limited as it was, the Emancipation Proclamation spurred antislavery forces. By the summer of 1864, 400,000 signatures asking for legislation to end slavery had been gathered and sent to Congress, something unprecedented in the history of the country. That April, the Senate had adopted the Thirteenth Amendment, declaring an end to slavery, and in January 1865, the House of Representatives followed.

With the proclamation, the Union army was open to blacks. And the more blacks entered the war, the more it appeared a war for their liberation. The more whites had to sacrifice, the more resentment there was, particularly among poor whites in the North, who were drafted by a law that allowed the rich to buy their way out of the draft for $300. And so the draft riots of 1863 took place, uprisings of angry whites in northern cities, their targets not the rich, far away, but the blacks, near at hand.

It was an orgy of death and violence. A black man in Detroit described what he saw: a mob, with kegs of beer on wagons, armed with clubs and bricks, marching through the city, attacking black men, women, children. He heard one man say: "If we are got to be killed up for Negroes then we will kill every one in this town."

The Civil War was one of the bloodiest in human history up to that time: 600,000 dead on both sides, in a population of 30 million—the equivalent, in the United States of 1990, with a population of 250 million, of 5 million dead. As the battles became more intense, as the bodies piled up, as war fatigue grew, and hundreds of thousands of slaves were deserting the plantations, 4 million blacks in the South became a great potential force for whichever side would use them.

Du Bois, in *Black Reconstruction*, pointed this out: "It was this plain alternative that brought Lee's sudden surrender. Either the South must make terms with its slaves, free them, use them to fight the North...or they could surrender to the North with the assumption that the North after the war must help them to defend slavery, as it had before. Black women played an important part in the war, especially toward the end. Sojourner Truth became recruiter of black troops for the Union army, as did Josephine St. Pierre Ruffin of Boston. Harriet Tubman raided plantations, leading black and white troops, and in one expedition freed 750 slaves.

It has been said that black acceptance of slavery is proved by the fact that during the Civil War, when there were opportunities for escape, most slaves stayed on the plantation. In fact, half a million ran away—about one in five, a high proportion when one considers that there was great difficulty in knowing where to go and how to live.

In 1865, a South Carolina planter wrote to the *New York Tribune*:

> ...the conduct of the Negro in the late crisis of our affairs has convinced me that we were all laboring under a delusion.... I believed that these people were content, happy, and attached to their masters. But events and reflection have caused me to change these positions.... If they were content, happy and attached to their masters, why did they desert him in the moment of his need and flock to an enemy, whom they did not know; and thus left their perhaps really good masters whom they did know from infancy?

The war produced no general rising of slaves, but in parts of Mississippi, Arkansas, and Kentucky, slaves destroyed plantations or took them over. Two hundred thousand blacks joined the army and navy, and thirty-eight thousand were killed. Historian James McPherson says: "Without their help, the North could not have won the war as soon as it did, and perhaps it could not have won at all."

What happened to blacks in the Union army and in the northern cities during the war gave some hint of how limited the emancipation would be, even with full victory over the Confederacy. Off-duty black soldiers were attacked in northern cities, as in Zanesville, Ohio, in February 1864, where cries were heard to "kill the nigger." Black soldiers were used for the heaviest and dirtiest work, digging trenches, hauling logs and cannon, loading ammunition, digging wells for white regiments. White privates received $13 a month; Negro privates received $10 a month. Finally, in June of 1864, Congress passed a law granting equal pay to Negro soldiers.

After a number of military defeats, the Confederate secretary of war, Judah Benjamin, wrote in late 1864 to a newspaper editor in Charleston: "It is well known that General Lee...is strongly in favor of our using the negroes for defense, and emancipating them, if necessary, for that purpose...." One general, indignant, wrote: "If slaves will make good soldiers, our whole theory of slavery is wrong."

By early 1865, the pressure had mounted, and in March, President Davis of the Confederacy signed a "Negro Soldier Law" authorizing the enlistment of slaves as soldiers, to be freed by consent of their owners and their state governments. But before it had any significant effect, the war was over.

Former slaves, interviewed by the Federal Writers Project in the thirties, recalled the war's end. Susie Melton:

I was a young gal, about ten years old, and we done heard that Lincoln gonna turn the niggers free.... Was wintertime and mighty cold that night, but everybody commenced getting ready to leave. Didn't care nothin' about missus—was going to the Union lines. And all that night the niggers danced and sang right out in the cold. Next morning at day break we all started out with blankets and clothes and pots and pans and chickens piled on our backs.... And as the sun come up over the trees, the niggers started to singing:

> Sun, you be here and I'll be gone
> Sun, you be here and I'll be gone
> Sun, you be here and I'll be gone

Anna Woods recalled:

We wasn't there in Texas long when the soldiers marched in to tell us that we were free.... I remembers one woman. She jumped on a barrel and she shouted. She jumped off and she shouted. She jumped back on again and shouted some more. She kept that up for a long time, just jumping on a barrel and back off again.

Annie Mae Weathers said:

I remember hearing my pa say that when somebody came and hollered, "You niggers is free at last," say he just dropped his hoe and said in a queer voice, "Thank God for that."

The Federal Writers Project recorded an ex-slave named Fannie Berry:

Niggers shoutin' and clappin' hands and singin'! Chillun runnin' all over the place beatin' time and yellin'! Everybody happy. Sho' did some celebratin'. Run to the kitchen and shout in the window: "Mammy, don't you cook no more. You's free! You's free!"

Many Negroes understood that their status after the war, whatever their situation legally, would depend on whether they owned the land they worked on or would be forced to be semislaves for others.

Abandoned plantations, however, were leased to former planters, and to white men of the North. As one colored newspaper said: "The slaves were made serfs and chained to the soil.... Such was the boasted freedom acquired by the colored man at the hands of the Yankee."

Under congressional policy approved by Lincoln, the property confiscated during the war under the Confiscation Act of July 1862 would revert to the heirs of the Confederate owners. Dr. John Rock, a black physician in

Boston, spoke at a meeting: "It is the slave who ought to be compensated. The property of the South is by right the property of the slave...."

In the South Carolina Sea Islands, out of 16,000 acres up for sale in March of 1863, freedmen who pooled their money were able to buy 2,000 acres, the rest being bought by northern investors and speculators. A freedman on the islands dictated a letter to a former teacher: "My Dear Young Missus: Do, my missus, tell Linkum dat we wants land—dis bery land dat is rich wid de sweat ob de face and de blood ob we back.... We could a bin buy all we want, but dey make de lots too big, and cut we out."

Ex-slave Thomas Hall told the Federal Writers Project: "Lincoln got the praise for freeing us, but did he do it? He gave us freedom without giving us any chance to live to ourselve and we still had to depend on the southern white man for work, food, and clothing, and he held us out of necessity and want in a state of servitude but little better than slavery."

The American government had set out to fight the slave states in 1861, not to end slavery, but to retain the enormous national territory and market and resources. Yet, victory required a crusade, and the momentum of that crusade brought new forces into national politics: more blacks determined to make their freedom mean something; more whites—whether Freedman's Bureau officials, or teachers in the Sea Islands, or "carpetbaggers" with various mixtures of humanitarianism and personal ambition—concerned with racial equality.

There was also the powerful interest of the Republican party in maintaining control over the national government, with the prospect of southern black votes to accomplish this. Northern businessmen, seeing Republican policies as beneficial to them, went along for a while.

The result was that brief period after the Civil War in which southern Negroes voted, elected blacks to state legislatures and to Congress, introduced free and racially mixed public education to the South. A legal framework was constructed. The Thirteenth Amendment outlawed slavery: "Neither slavery nor involuntary servitude, except as a punishment for crime whereof the party shall have been duly convicted, shall exist within the United States, or any place subject to their jurisdiction." The Fourteenth Amendment repudiated the prewar Dred Scott decision by declaring that "all persons born or naturalized in the United States" were citizens. It also seemed to make a powerful statement for racial equality, severely limiting "states' rights":

> No State shall make or enforce any law which shall abridge the privi-
> leges or immunities of citizens of the United States; nor shall any State

deprive any person of life, liberty, or property, without due process of law; nor deny to any person within its jurisdiction the equal protection of the laws.

The Fifteenth Amendment said: "The right of citizens of the United States to vote shall not be denied or abridged by the United States or by any State on account of race, color, or previous condition of servitude."

Congress passed a number of laws in the late 1860s and early 1870s in the same spirit—laws making it a crime to deprive Negroes of their rights, requiring federal officials to enforce those rights, giving Negroes the right to enter contracts and buy property without discrimination. And the Civil Rights Act of 1875 outlawed the exclusion of Negroes from hotels, theaters, railroads, and other public accommodations.

With these laws, with the Union army in the South as protection, and a civilian army of officials in the Freedman's Bureau to help them, southern Negroes came forward, voted, formed political organizations, and expressed themselves forcefully on issues important to them.

They were hampered in this for several years by Andrew Johnson, the vice president under Lincoln, who became president when Lincoln was assassinated at the close of the war. Johnson vetoed bills to help Negroes; he made it easy for Confederate states to come back into the Union without guaranteeing equal rights to blacks. During his presidency, these returned southern states enacted "black codes," which made the freed slaves like serfs, still working the plantations.

Andrew Johnson clashed with senators and congressmen who, in some cases for reasons of justice, in others out of political calculation, supported equal rights and voting for the freedman. These members of Congress succeeded in impeaching Johnson in 1868, using as an excuse that he had violated some minor statute, but the Senate fell one vote short of the two-thirds required to remove him from office. In the presidential election of that year, Republican Ulysses Grant was elected, winning by 300,000 votes, with 700,000 Negroes voting, and so Johnson was out as an obstacle. Now the southern states could come back into the Union only by approving the new constitutional amendments.

Whatever northern politicians were doing to help their cause, southern blacks were determined to make the most of their freedom, in spite of their lack of land and resources. They began immediately asserting their independence of whites, forming their own churches, becoming politically active, strengthening their family ties, trying to educate their children.

Black voting in the period after 1869 resulted in two Negro members of the U.S. Senate (Hiram Revels and Blanche Bruce, both from Mississippi) and twenty congressmen. This list would dwindle rapidly after 1876; the last black left Congress in 1901.

Negroes were now elected to southern state legislatures, although in all these they were a minority except in the lower house of the South Carolina legislature. A great propaganda campaign was undertaken North and South (one which lasted well into the twentieth century, in the history textbooks of American schools) to show that blacks were inept, lazy, corrupt, and ruinous to the governments of the South when they were in office. Undoubtedly there was corruption, but one could hardly claim that blacks had invented political conniving, especially in the bizarre climate of financial finagling North and South after the Civil War.

It was true that the public debt of South Carolina, $7 million in 1865, went up to $29 million in 1873, but the new legislature introduced free public schools into the state for the first time. Not only were seventy thousand Negro children going to school by 1876 where none had gone before, but fifty thousand white children were going to school where only twenty thousand had attended in 1860.

A Columbia University scholar of the twentieth century, John Burgess, referred to Black Reconstruction as follows:

> In place of government by the most intelligent and virtuous part of the people for the benefit of the governed, here was government by the most ignorant and vicious part of the population.... A black skin means membership in a race of men which has never of itself succeeded in subjecting passion to reason; has never, therefore, created civilization of any kind.

One has to measure against those words the black leaders in the postwar South. For instance, Henry MacNeal Turner, who had escaped from peonage on a South Carolina plantation at the age of fifteen, taught himself to read and write, read law books while a messenger in a lawyer's office in Baltimore, and medical books while a handyman in a Baltimore medical school, served as chaplain to a Negro regiment, and then was elected to the first postwar legislature of Georgia.

In 1868, the Georgia legislature voted to expel all its Negro members—two senators, twenty-five representatives—and Turner spoke to the Georgia House of Representatives (a black woman graduate student at Atlanta University later brought his speech to light):

> Mr. Speaker: ...I am here to demand my rights, and to hurl thunderbolts at the men who would dare to cross the threshold of my manhood....

> The scene presented in this House, today, is one unparalleled.... Never, in the history of the world, has a man been arraigned before a body clothed with legislative, judicial or executive functions, charged with the offense of being of a darker hue than his fellowmen....
>
> The great question, sir is this: Am I a man? If I am such, I claim the rights of a man....
>
> Why, sir, we have worked in your fields, and garnered your harvests, for two hundred and fifty years! And what do we ask of you in return? Do we ask you for compensation for the sweat our fathers bore for you—for the tears you have caused, and the hearts you have broken, and the lives you have curtailed, and the blood you have spilled? Do we ask retaliation? We ask it not. We are willing to let the dead past bury its dead; but we ask you now for our RIGHTS....

Frances Ellen Watkins Harper, born free in Baltimore, self-supporting from the age of thirteen, working as a nursemaid, later as an abolitionist lecturer, reader of her own poetry, spoke all through the southern states after the war. She was a feminist, participant in the 1866 Woman's Rights Convention, and founder of the National Association of Colored Women. In the 1890s she wrote the first novel published by a black woman: *Iola Leroy, or Shadows Uplifted.*

Through all the struggles to gain equal rights for blacks, certain black women spoke out on their special situation. Sojourner Truth, at a meeting of the American Equal Rights Association, said:

> There is a great stir about colored men getting their rights, but not a word about the colored women; and if colored men get their rights, and not colored women theirs, you see the colored men will be masters over the women, and it will be just as bad as it was before. So I am for keeping the thing going while things are stirring; because if we wait till it is still, it will take a great while to get it going again....
>
> I am above eighty years old; it is about time for me to be going. I have been forty years a slave and forty years free, and would be here forty years more to have equal rights for all...

The constitutional amendments were passed, the laws for racial equality were passed, and the black man began to vote and to hold office. But so long as the Negro remained dependent on privileged whites for work, for the necessities of life, his vote could be bought or taken away by threat of force. Thus, laws calling for equal treatment became meaningless. While Union troops—including colored troops—remained in the

South, this process was delayed. But the balance of military powers began to change.

The southern white oligarchy used its economic power to organize the Ku Klux Klan and other terrorist groups. Northern politicians began to weigh the advantage of the political support of impoverished blacks—maintained in voting and office only by force—against the more stable situation of a South returned to white supremacy, accepting Republican dominance and business legislation. It was only a matter of time before blacks would be reduced once again to conditions not far from slavery.

Violence began almost immediately with the end of the war. In Memphis, Tennessee, in May of 1866, whites on a rampage of murder killed forty-six Negroes, most of them veterans of the Union army, as well as two white sympathizers. Five Negro women were raped. Ninety homes, twelve schools, and four churches were burned. In New Orleans, in the summer of 1866, another riot against blacks killed thirty-five Negroes and three whites.

The violence mounted through the late 1860s and early 1870s as the Ku Klux Klan organized raids, lynchings, beatings, burnings. For Kentucky alone, between 1867 and 1871, the National Archives lists 116 acts of violence. A sampling:

> 1. A mob visited Harrodsburg in Mercer County to take from jail a man name Robertson Nov. 14, 1867....
> 5. Sam Davis hung by a mob in Harrodsburg, May 28, 1868.
> 6. Wm. Pierce hung by a mob in Christian July 12, 1868.
> 7. Geo. Roger hung by a mob in Bradsfordville Martin County July 11, 1868....
> 10. Silas Woodford age sixty badly beaten by disguised mob....
> 109. Negro killed by Ku Klux Klan in Hay county January 14, 1871.

As white violence rose in the 1870s, the national government, even under President Grant, became less enthusiastic about defending blacks, and certainly not prepared to arm them. The Supreme Court played its gyroscopic role of pulling the other branches of government back to more conservative directions when they went too far. It began interpreting the Fourteenth Amendment—passed presumably for racial equality—in a way that made it impotent for this purpose.

In 1883, the Civil Rights Act of 1875, outlawing discrimination against Negroes using public facilities, was nullified by the Supreme Court, which said: "Individual invasion of individual rights is not the subject-matter of the amendment." The Fourteenth Amendment, it said, was aimed at state action only. "No state shall..."

A remarkable dissent was written by Supreme Court Justice John Harlan, himself a former slave owner in Kentucky, who said there was constitutional justification for banning private discrimination. He noted that the Thirteenth Amendment, which banned slavery, applied to individual plantation owners, not just the state. He then argued that discrimination was a badge of slavery and similarly outlawable. He pointed also to the first clause of the Fourteenth Amendment, saying that anyone born in the United States was a citizen, and to the clause in Article 4, Section 2, saying "the citizens of each State shall be entitled to all privileges and immunities of citizens in the several States."

Harlan was fighting a force greater than logic or justice; the mood of the Court reflected a new coalition of northern industrialists and southern businessmen-planters. The culmination of this mood came in the decision of 1896, *Plessy v. Ferguson*, when the Court ruled that a railroad could segregate black and white if the segregated facilities were equal. Harlan again dissented: "Our Constitution is color-blind...."

It was the year 1877 that spelled out clearly and dramatically what was happening. When the year opened, the presidential election of the past November was in bitter dispute. The Democratic candidate, Samuel Tilden, had 184 electoral votes and needed one more to be elected: his popular vote was greater by 250,000. The Republican candidate, Rutherford Hayes, had 166 electoral votes. Three states not yet counted had a total of 19 electoral votes; if Hayes could get all of those, he would have 185 and be president. This is what his managers proceeded to arrange. They made concessions to the Democratic party and the white South, including an agreement to remove Union troops from the South, the last military obstacle to the reestablishment of white supremacy there.

Northern political and economic interests needed powerful allies and stability in the face of national crisis. The country had been in economic depression since 1873, and by 1877 farmers and workers were beginning to rebel. As C. Vann Woodward puts it in his history of the 1877 Compromise, *Reunion and Reaction*:

> It was a depression year, the worst year of the severest depression yet experienced. In the East labor and the unemployed were in a bitter and violent temper.... Out West a tide of agrarian radicalism was rising.... From both East and West came threats against the elaborate structure of protective tariffs, national banks, railroad subsidies and monetary arrangements upon which the new economic order was founded.

It was a time for reconciliation between southern and northern elites. Woodward asks: "[C]ould the South be induced to combine with the Northern conservatives and become a prop instead of a menace to the new capitalist order?"

With billions of dollars' worth of slaves gone, the wealth of the old South was wiped out. They now looked to the national government for help: credit, subsidies, flood control projects. Woodward says: "By means of appropriations, subsidies, grants, and bonds such as Congress had so lavishly showered upon capitalist enterprise in the North, the South might yet mend its fortunes—or at any rate the fortunes of a privileged elite."

And so the deal was made. The proper committee was set up by both houses of Congress to decide where the electoral votes would go. The decision was: they belonged to Hayes, and he was now president. As Woodward sums it up:

> The Compromise of 1877 did not restore the old order in the South.... It did assure the dominant whites political autonomy and non-intervention in matters of race policy and promised them a share in the blessings of the new economic order. In return, the South became, in effect, a satellite of the dominant region....

The importance of the new capitalism in overturning what black power existed in the postwar South is affirmed by Horace Mann Bond's study of Alabama Reconstruction. It was an age of coal and power, and northern Alabama had both. "The bankers in Philadelphia and New York, and even in London and Paris, had known this for almost two decades. The only thing lacking was transportation." And so, in the mid-1870s, Bond notes, northern bankers began appearing in the directories of southern railroad lines. J. P. Morgan appears by 1875 as director for several lines in Alabama and Georgia.

In the year 1886, Henry Grady, an editor of the *Atlanta Constitution*, spoke at a dinner in New York. In the audience were J. P. Morgan, H. M. Flagler (an associate of John D. Rockefeller), Russell Sage, and Charles Tiffany. His talk was called "The New South" and his theme was: Let bygones be bygones; let us have a new era of peace and prosperity.

That same month, an article in the *New York Daily Tribune* told of "the leading coal and iron men of the South" visiting New York and leaving "thoroughly satisfied." The reason:

> The time for which they have been waiting for nearly twenty years, when Northern capitalists would be convinced not only of the safety but

of the immense profits to be gained from the investment of their money in developing the fabulously rich coal and iron resources of Alabama, Tennessee, and Georgia, has come at last.

The North, it must be recalled, did not have to undergo a revolution in its thinking to accept the subordination of the Negro. When the Civil War ended, nineteen of the twenty-four northern states did not allow blacks to vote.

By 1900, all the southern states, in new constitutions and new statutes, had written into law the disfranchisement and segregation of Negroes, and a *New York Times* editorial said: "Northern men...no longer denounce the suppression of the Negro vote.... The necessity of it under the supreme law of self-preservation is candidly recognized."

Those Negro leaders most accepted in white society, like the educator Booker T. Washington, a one-time White House guest of Theodore Roosevelt, urged Negro political passivity. Invited by the white organizers of the Cotton States and International Exposition in Atlanta in 1895 to speak, Washington urged the southern Negro to "cast down your bucket where you are"—that is, to stay in the South, to be farmers, mechanics, domestics, perhaps even to attain to the professions.

He urged white employers to hire Negroes rather than immigrants of "strange tongue and habits." Negroes, "without strikes and labor wars," were the "most patient, faithful, law-abiding and unresentful people that the world has seen." He said: "The wisest among my race understand that the agitation of questions of social equality is the extremest folly."

Perhaps Washington saw this as a necessary tactic of survival in a time of hangings and burnings of Negroes throughout the South. It was a low point for black people in America. Thomas Fortune, a young black editor of the *New York Globe*, testified before a Senate committee in 1883 about the situation of the Negro in the United States. He spoke of "widespread poverty," of government betrayal, of desperate Negro attempts to educate themselves.

The average wage of Negro farm laborers in the South was about fifty cents a day, Fortune said. He was usually paid in "orders," not money, which he could use only at a store controlled by the planter, "a system of fraud."

Fortune spoke of "the penitentiary system of the South, with its infamous chain-gang... the object being to terrorize the blacks and furnish victims for contractors, who purchase the labor of these wretches from the State for a song.... The white man who shoots a negro always goes free, while the negro who steals a hog is sent to the chain-gang for ten years."

Many Negroes fled. About six thousand black people left Texas, Louisiana, and Mississippi and migrated to Kansas to escape violence and poverty. "We have found no leader to trust but God overhead of us," one said. Those who remained in the South began to organize in self-defense all through the 1880s, in the face of over a hundred lynchings a year.

There were black leaders who thought Booker T. Washington wrong in advocating caution and moderation. John Hope, a young black man in Georgia, who heard Washington's Cotton Exposition speech, told students at a Negro college in Nashville, Tennessee: "If we are not striving for equality, in heaven's name for what are we living? I regard it as cowardly and dishonest for any of our colored men to tell white people or colored people that we are not struggling for equality...."

Another black man, who came to teach at Atlanta University, W. E. B. Du Bois, saw the late-nineteenth-century betrayal of the Negro as part of a larger happening in the United States, something happening not only to poor blacks but to poor whites. In *Black Reconstruction*, he saw this new capitalism as part of a process of exploitation and bribery taking place in all the "civilized" countries of the world: "Home labor in cultured lands, appeased and misled by a ballot whose power the dictatorship of vast capital strictly curtailed, was bribed by high wage and political office to unite in an exploitation of white, yellow, brown and black labor, in lesser lands...."

Was Du Bois right—that in that growth of American capitalism, before and after the Civil War, whites as well as blacks were in some sense becoming slaves?

Exercises

1. On what basis did the U.S. government support slavery?

2. What actions did the U.S. government take to support slavery? Do these actions support Zinn's assertion on p. 139 that "Such a government would never accept an end to slavery by rebellion"? Why would the white elite want to determine when and how slavery would end?

3. Page 130: "Are the *conditions* of slavery as important as the *existence* of slavery?" Why does Zinn ask this question?

4. Why would someone dance and laugh the evening of the morning he received two hundred lashes?

5. Was resistance to slavery more, as much, or less, effective than rebellion? Explain.

6. How were the following used as methods of controlling not only the slave population but poor whites as well?
    * force
    * segregation
    * religion

   What is the evidence that it was dangerous to slave masters to allow poor whites and blacks to fraternize?

7. How did slaves manage to maintain a community? Why did they work so hard to do so?

8. How can you account for Harriet Tubman's success?
    a. She had no fear.
    b. She was a fanatic.
    c. She was lucky.
    d. She had lots of help.
    e. She wore a disguise.
    f. She was smart enough to get out and not return.
    g. She carried a revolver.

   Does Zinn give you enough information to answer this question? If yes, what is the data he provides? If not, what information do you need (what questions do you still need answers to) in order to answer this question with any degree of satisfaction?

9. Why was there a price on David Walker's head?

10. Why might Frederick Douglass have been "the most famous black man of his time"?

11. What was J. W. Loguen's argument against the Fugitive Slave Act of 1850?

12. What does Sarah Logue's proposal and Loguen's response reveal about how slave owners justified slavery?

13. Why would the United States even talk about going to war with England over the Creole?

14. How did the racism of white abolitionists reveal itself? How could a white person be both an abolitionist and a racist? Why would a racist be an abolitionist? (Was the institution of slavery undermining the free labor philosophy that allowed the northern elite to justify economic inequality of the factory system?)

15. What was the "the triple hurdle" that Sojourner Truth had to overcome?

16. How old was John Brown at the time he led the raid on Harpers Ferry? What did he hope to accomplish?

17. How does the picture of John Brown below compare to the one that Zinn paints? The incident described below takes place in Kansas, in 1856, two years before Brown's raid on Harpers Ferry. John Brown had recently declared "that something must be done to show these barbarians that we too have rights." They were headed for Pottawatomie Creek with broad swords.

> ...for the lanky Ohio farmer who proposed to meddle with the peculiar institution lived with strange fever-haunted dreams and felt an overwhelming compulsion to act on them. He was a rover, a ne'er-do-well, wholly ineffectual in everything he did save that he had the knack of drawing an entire nation after him on the road to unreasoning violence....
>
> They had taken up arms two or three days earlier, along with other men, in a dimly legal free-state militia company, to go to the defense of Lawrence [Kansas]...they got there too late, and all of the company but Brown and his chosen seven disbanded and went home. But Brown was obsessed....
>
> John Brown and his band [four of which were his sons] went stumping along through the night. They were in proslavery land

now, and any man they saw would be an enemy. They came to one lonely cabin, saw lamplight gleaming under the door, and pounded for admittance. There was a noise as if someone were cocking a gun and sliding the muzzle through a chink in the logs, and the men slipped away from there—it was not precisely open combat that they were looking for. They went on, and after a time they came to a cabin occupied by a family named Doyle.

The Doyles were poor whites from Tennessee. They had come to Kansas recently, and although they believed in slavery…they did not like to lie too close to it; it appears that they had migrated in order to get away from it. Brown hammered on the door. It was opened, and he ordered Doyle and Doyle's two grown sons to come outside. The three men obeyed, the door closed behind them, and Brown's band led the three away from the cabin. Then there were quick muffled sounds, brief cries, silence and stillness and darkness, and Brown and his followers went off down the road. In the morning the bodies of the three Doyles were found lying on the ground, fearfully mangled. They had been hacked to death with the [broad swords]…. The father had been shot in the head.

Bruce Catton,
This Hallowed Ground, New York,
Simon and Shuster, 1961,
pp. 10–11.

18. Lincoln was able to speak to both sides of the slavery debate. Why did he feel compelled to speak to both sides, given his personal solution to the problem of slavery in America?

19. How did the northern elite's plans for economic expansion force the South into radical opposition?

20. According to Zinn, "Lincoln initiated hostilities by trying to repossess the federal base at Fort Sumter."

   a. Look at three or four other sources to compare the details of the Battle of Fort Sumter with Zinn's interpretation.

   b. Compare Lincoln's maneuvers surrounding the Fort Sumter battle with Polk's maneuvers in starting the Mexican-American War. What might you conclude from such a comparison?

21. Lincoln's goal in waging war on the South was to "preserve the Union" by subjugating the South of the northern capital's control. What series of events altered Lincoln's rhetoric to include emancipation as a goal of the war?

22. How was the Emancipation Proclamation a military tactic?

23. What evidence supports the thesis that the North could not have won without the help of American blacks?

24. After the South surrendered unconditionally, how did Congress dispose of the land confiscated during the war? Of what significance was this decision? (For example, what did it reveal about the congressional majority's belief about the future status of blacks in the United States?)

25. Given the data from Zinn, how would you characterize (good, bad, messy, progressive, regressive) the period of Reconstruction (1863–1877)? In your characterization, include a description of the role of the U.S. government and the southern states, the status of the freed slaves, and the actions of white racists.

26. In 1868, was the Georgia legislature successful in expelling its black members?

27. Why does Zinn choose to tell us about Frances Ellen Watkins Harper? What is the point?

28. Why does Zinn think that laws calling for equal treatment of blacks and whites were meaningless in practice? What other reforms would have had to accompany such laws for the laws to be meaningful in Zinn's eyes? Why? Do you agree?

29. What caused Republicans to abandon their defense of black rights? Discuss economic as well as political reasons.

30. In 1883, the Supreme Court declared the Civil Rights Act of 1875 unconstitutional. What was the majority argument? What was Justice Harlan's dissenting argument?

31. How does Horace Mann Bond's study of Alabama Reconstruction reveal that the ultimate result of the Civil War was to reduce the South to colonial status? [To help define "colonial status," one might think the relationship between Britain and her American colonies was as defined by the Navigation Acts. These acts were passed by the English Parliament starting in 1665.]

32. The editorial board of the *New York Times* wrote in 1900: "Northern men...no longer denounce the suppression of the Negro vote.... The necessity of it under the supreme law of self-preservation is candidly recognized" (page 153). Why would allowing white southerners to deny blacks the right and ability to vote (often by violent means, including murder) contribute to the self-preservation of "northern men"?

33. How did blacks respond to the end of the U.S. government's military protection of black civil rights?

34. *Draw a map* that identifies the following: those states that voted for Lincoln, Douglas, Breckinridge, and Bell in the election of 1860.

35. *Debate Resolution:* The Civil War was fought to end slavery.

36. *Draw a map* for the year 1854 that includes the following: slave and free states; free territories; territories open to slavery as determined by the Kansas-Nebraska Act of 1854; territories open to slavery as determined by the Compromise of 1850; the Missouri Compromise (1820) line.

Chapter 10

The Other Civil War

The stories of class struggle in the nineteenth century are not usually found in textbooks on United States history. That struggle is most often obscured by the pretense of intense conflict between the major political parties, although both parties have represented the same dominant classes of the nation.

Andrew Jackson, who was elected president in 1828 and served for two terms, said he spoke for "the humble members of society—the farmer, mechanics and laborers." He certainly did not speak for the Indians being pushed off their lands, or for the slaves. But the tensions aroused by the developing factory system, the growing immigration, required that the government develop a mass base of support among whites. The myth of "Jacksonian Democracy" was designed to do just that.

It was the new politics of ambiguity—speaking for the lower and middle classes to get their support in times of rapid growth and potential turmoil. To give people a choice between two different parties and allow them, in a period of rebellion, to choose the slightly more democratic one was an ingenious mode of control.

The Jacksonian idea was to achieve stability and control by winning to the Democratic party "the middling interest, and especially...the substantial yeomanry of the country" by "prudent, judicious, well-considered reform." That is, reform that would not yield too much. These were the words of Robert Rantoul, a reformer, corporation lawyer, and Jacksonian Democrat. It was a forecast of the successful appeal of the Democratic party—and at times the Republican party—in the twentieth century.

America was developing with enormous speed and excitement. In 1790, fewer than a million Americans lived in cities; in 1840 the figure was 11 million. New York had 130,000 people in 1820, a million by 1860. And while the traveler Alexis de Tocqueville had expressed astonishment at "the general equality of condition among the people," his observation was not in accord with the facts.

In Philadelphia, working-class families lived fifty-five to a tenement, usually one room per family, with no garbage removal, no toilets, no fresh air or water. There was fresh water newly pumped from the Schuylkill River, but it was going to the homes of the rich.

In New York you could see the poor lying in the streets with the garbage. There were no sewers in the slums, and filthy water drained into yards and alleys, into the cellars where the poorest of the poor lived, bringing with it a typhoid epidemic in 1837, typhus in 1842. In the cholera epidemic of 1832, the rich fled the city; the poor stayed and died.

These poor could not be counted on as political allies of the government. But they were there—like slaves, or Indians—invisible ordinarily, a menace if they rose. There were more solid citizens, however, who might give steady support to the system—better-paid workers, landowning farmers. Also, there was the new urban white-collar worker, born in the rising commerce of the time, who would be wooed enough and paid enough to consider himself a member of the bourgeois class and to give support to that class in times of crisis.

The opening of the West was being helped by turnpikes, canals, railroads, the telegraph. Farms were becoming mechanized. Iron plows cut plowing time in half; by the 1850s John Deere Company was turning out ten thousand plows a year. Cyrus McCormick was making a thousand mechanical reapers a year in his factory in Chicago. A man with a sickle could cut half an acre of wheat in a day; with a reaper he could cut ten acres.

In an economic system not rationally planned for human need, but developing fitfully, chaotically out of the profit motive, there seemed to be no way to avoid recurrent booms and slumps. There was a depression in 1837, another in 1853. One way to achieve stability was to decrease competition, organize the businesses, move toward monopoly. In the mid-1850s, price agreements and mergers became frequent: the New York Central Railroad was a merger of many railroads. The American Brass Association was formed "to meet ruinous competition," it said. The Hampton County Cotton Spinners Association was organized to control prices, and so was the American Iron Association.

With industry requiring large amounts of capital, risks had to be minimized. State legislatures gave charters to corporations giving them legal rights to conduct business and raise money, without imperiling the personal fortunes of the owners and managers. Between 1790 and 1860, twenty-three hundred corporations were chartered.

The federal government, starting with Alexander Hamilton and the first Congress, had given vital help to the business interests, and this was now done on a much larger scale.

Railroad men traveled to Washington and to state capitals armed with money, shares of stock, free railroad passes. Between 1850 and 1857 they got 25 million acres of public land, free of charge, and millions of dollars in bonds—loans—from the state legislatures. In Wisconsin in 1856, the LaCrosse and Milwaukee Railroad got a million acres free by distributing about $900,000 in stocks and bonds to fifty-nine assemblymen, thirteen senators, and the governor. Two years later the railroad was bankrupt and the bonds were worthless.

In the East, mill owners had become powerful, and organized. By 1850, fifteen Boston families called the "Associates" controlled 20 percent of the cotton spindleage in the United States, 39 percent of insurance capital in Massachusetts, 40 percent of banking resources in Boston.

On the eve of the Civil War it was money and profit, not the movement against slavery, that was uppermost in the priorities of the men who ran the country. As Thomas Cochran and William Miller (*The Age of Enterprise*) put it:

> Webster was the hero of the North—not Emerson, Parker, Garrison, or Phillips; Webster the tariff man, the land speculator, the corporation lawyer, politician for the Boston Associates, inheritor of Hamilton's coronet. "The great object of government" said he "is the protection of property at home, and respect and renown abroad." For these he preached union; for these he surrendered the fugitive slave.

They wrote of the Boston rich:

> Living sumptuously on Beacon Hill, admired by their neighbors for their philanthropy and their patronage of art and culture, these men traded in State Street while overseers ran their factories, managers directed their railroads, agents sold their water power and real estate.

Ralph Waldo Emerson described Boston in those years: "There is a certain poor-smell in all the streets, in Beacon Street and Mount Vernon, as well as in the lawyers' offices, and the wharves, and the same meanness and sterility, and leave-all-hope-behind, as one finds in a boot manufacturer's premises." The preacher Theodore Parker told his congregation: "Money is this day the strongest power of the nation."

The attempts at political stability, at economic control, did not quite work. The new industrialism, the crowded cities, the long hours in the factories, the sudden economic crises leading to high prices and lost jobs, the lack of food and water, the freezing winters, the hot tenements in the summer, the epidemics of disease, the deaths of children—these led to sporadic reactions from the poor. Sometimes there were spontaneous, unorganized uprisings against the rich. Sometimes the anger was deflected into racial hatred for blacks, religious warfare against Catholics, nativist fury against immigrants. Sometimes it was organized into demonstrations and strikes.

The full extent of the working-class consciousness of those years—as of any years—is lost in history, but fragments remain and make us wonder how much of this always existed underneath the very practical silence of working people. In 1827 an "Address...before the Mechanics and Working Classes...of Philadelphia" was recorded, written by an "Unlettered Mechanic," probably a young shoemaker:

> We find ourselves oppressed on every hand—we labor hard in producing all the comforts of life for the enjoyment of others, while we ourselves obtain but a scanty portion, and even that in the present state of society depends on the will of employers.

Frances Wright of Scotland, an early feminist and utopian socialist, was invited by Philadelphia workingmen to speak on the Fourth of July, 1829, to one of the first citywide associations of labor unions in the United States. She asked if the Revolution had been fought "to crush down the sons and daughters of your country's industry under...neglect, poverty, vice, starvation, and disease...." She wondered if the new technology was not lowering the value of human labor, making people appendages to machines, crippling the minds and bodies of child laborers.

Later that year, George Henry Evans, a printer, editor of the *Workingman's Advocate*, wrote "The Working Men's Declaration of Independence." Among its list of "facts" submitted to "candid and impartial" fellow citizens:

> 1. The laws for levying taxes are...operating most oppressively on one class of society....
> 3. The laws for private incorporation are all partial...favoring one class of society to the expense of the other....

6. The laws...have deprived nine tenths of the members of the body politics, who are not wealthy, of the equal means to enjoy "life, liberty, and the pursuit of happiness."...The lien law in favor of the landlords against tenants...is one illustration among innumerable others.

Evans believed that "all on arriving at adult age are entitled to equal property."

A citywide "Trades' Union" in Boston in 1834, including mechanics from Charlestown and women shoe binders from Lynn, referred to the Declaration of Independence:

We hold...that laws which have a tendency to raise any peculiar class above their fellow citizens, by granting special privileges, are contrary to and in defiance of those primary principles....

Our public system of Education, which so liberally endows those seminaries of learning, which...are only accessible to the wealthy, while our common schools...are so illy provided for.... Thus even in childhood the poor are apt to think themselves inferior....

Episodes of insurrection of that time have gone unrecorded in traditional histories. Such was the riot in Baltimore in the summer of 1835, when the Bank of Maryland collapsed and its depositors lost their savings. Convinced that a great fraud had taken place, a crowd gathered and began breaking the windows of officials associated with the bank. When the rioters destroyed a house, the militia attacked, killing some twenty people, wounding a hundred. The next evening, other houses were attacked.

During those years, trade unions were forming. The courts called them conspiracies to restrain trade and therefore illegal. A New York judge, levying fines against "a conspiracy" of tailors, said: "In this favored land of law and liberty, the road to advancement is open to all.... Every American knows that...he needs no artificial combination for his protection. They are of foreign origin and I am led to believe mainly upheld by foreigners."

A handbill was then circulated throughout the city:

THE RICH AGAINST THE POOR!

Judge Edwards, the tool of the aristocracy, against the people! Mechanics and working men! A deadly blow has been struck at your liberty!...They have established the precedent that workingmen have no right to regulate the price of labor, or, in other words, the rich are the only judges of the wants of the poor man.

At City Hall Park, twenty-seven thousand people gathered to denounce the court decision, and elected a Committee of Correspondence which organized, three months later, a convention of Mechanics, Farmers, and Working Men, elected by farmers and working people in various towns in New York State. The convention met in Utica, drew up a Declaration of Independence from existing political parties, and established an Equal Rights party.

Although they ran their own candidates for office, there was no great confidence in the ballot as a way of achieving change. One of the great orators of the movement, Seth Luther, told a Fourth of July rally: "We will try the ballot box first. If that will not effect our righteous purpose, the next and last resort is the cartridge box."

The crisis of 1837 led to rallies and meetings in many cities. The banks had suspended specie payments—refusing to pay hard money for the bank notes they had issued. Working people, already hard-pressed to buy food, found that the prices of flour, pork, coal became impossibly high. In Philadelphia, twenty thousand people assembled, and someone wrote to President Van Buren describing it:

> This afternoon, the largest public meeting I ever saw assembled in Independence Square. It was called by placards posted through the city yesterday and last night. It was projected and carried on entirely by the working classes; without consultation or cooperation with any of those who usually take the lead in such matters. The officers and speakers were of those classes.... It was directed against the banks.

In New York, members of the Equal Rights party (often called the Locofocos) announced a meeting: "Bread, Meat, Rent, and Fuel! Their prices must come down! The people will meet in the Park, rain or shine, at 4 o'clock, p.m. on Monday afternoon.... All friends of humanity determined to resist monopolists and extortioners are invited to attend." The *Commercial Register*, a New York newspaper, reported on the meeting and what followed:

> At 4 o'clock, a concourse of several thousands had convened in front of the City Hall.... One of these orators...directed the popular vengeance against Mr. Eli Hart. "Fellow citizens!" he exclaimed, "Mr. Hart has now 53,000 barrels of flour in his store; let us go and offer him eight dollars a barrel, and if he does not take it..."
>
> A large body of the meeting moved off in the direction of Mr. Hart's store.... Barrels of flour, by dozens, fifties and hundreds were tumbled into the street from the doors, and thrown in rapid succession

from the windows.... About one thousand bushels of wheat, and four or five hundred barrels of flour, were thus wantonly and foolishly as well as wickedly destroyed. The most active of the destructionists were foreigners, but there were probably five hundred or a thousand others, standing by and abetting their incendiary labors.

Amidst the falling and bursting of the barrels and sacks of wheat, numbers of women were engaged, like the crones who strip the dead in battle, filling the boxes and baskets with which they were provided, and their aprons, with flour, and making off with it....

Night had now closed upon the scene, but the work of destruction did not cease until strong bodies of police arrived, followed, soon afterward, by detachments of troops....

This was the Flour Riot of 1837. During the crisis of that year, 50,000 persons (one-third of the working class) were without work in New York City alone, and 200,000 (of a population of 500,000) were living, as one observer put it, "in utter and hopeless distress."

There is no complete record of the meetings, riots, actions, organized and disorganized, violent and nonviolent, which took place in the mid-nineteenth century, as the country grew, as the cities became crowded, with working conditions bad, living conditions intolerable, with the economy in the hands of bankers, speculators, landlords, merchants.

In 1835, fifty different trades organized unions in Philadelphia, and there was a successful general strike of laborers, factory workers, bookbinders, jewelers, coal heavers, butchers, cabinet workers—for the ten-hour day.

Weavers in Philadelphia in the early 1840s—mostly Irish immigrants working at home for employers—struck for higher wages, attacked the homes of those refusing to strike, and destroyed their work. A sheriff's posse tried to arrest some strikers, but it was broken up by four hundred weavers armed with muskets and sticks.

Soon, however, antagonism developed between these Irish Catholic weavers and native-born Protestant skilled workers over issues of religion. In May 1844 there were Protestant-Catholic riots in Kensington, a suburb of Philadelphia. Middle-class politicians soon led each group into a different political party (the nativists into the American Republican party, the Irish into the Democratic party), party politics and religion now substituting for class conflict.

The result of all this, says David Montgomery, historian of the Kensington Riots, was the fragmentation of the Philadelphia working class. It "thereby created for historians the illusion of a society lacking in class conflict," while in reality the class conflicts of nineteenth-century America "were as fierce as any known to the industrial world."

The immigrants from Ireland, fleeing starvation there when the potato crop failed, were coming to America now, packed into old sailing ships. The stories of these ships differ only in detail from the accounts of the ships that earlier brought black slaves and later German, Italian, and Russian immigrants. This is a contemporary account of one ship arriving from Ireland in May 1847, detained at Grosse Isle on the Canadian border:

> Who can imagine the horrors of even the shortest passage in an emigrant ship crowded beyond its utmost capacity of stowage with unhappy beings of all ages, with fever raging in their midst...the crew sullen or brutal from very desperation, or paralyzed with terror of the plague—the miserable passengers in different stages of the disease; many dying, some dead;...the wails of children, the ravings of the delirious, the cries and groans of those in mortal agony!

How could these new Irish immigrants, themselves poor and despised, become sympathizers with the black slaves? Indeed, most working-class activists at this time ignored the plight of blacks. Ely Moore, a New York trade union leader elected to Congress, argued in the House of Representatives against receiving abolitionist petitions. Racist hostility became an easy substitute for class frustration.

On the other hand, a white shoemaker wrote in 1848 in the *Awl*, the newspaper of Lynn shoe factory workers:

> ...we are nothing but a standing army that keeps three million of our brethren in bondage.... Living under the shade of Bunker Hill monument, demanding in the name of humanity, our right, and withholding those rights from others because their skin is black! Is it any wonder that God in his righteous anger has punished us by forcing us to drink the bitter cup of degradation.

Another economic crisis came in 1857. The boom in railroads and manufacturing, the surge of immigration, the increased speculation in stocks and bonds, the stealing, corruption, manipulation, led to wild expansion and then crash. By October of that year, 200,000 were unemployed, and thousands of recent immigrants crowded into the eastern ports, hoping to work their way back to Europe.

In Newark, New Jersey, a rally of several thousand demanded the city give work to the unemployed. And in New York, fifteen thousand people met at Tompkins Square in downtown Manhattan. From there they marched to Wall Street and paraded around the Stock Exchange shouting: "We want work!" That summer, riots occurred in the slum areas of New York. A mob of five hundred attacked the police one day with pistols and bricks. There were parades of the unemployed, demanding bread and work, looting shops. In November, a crowd occupied City Hall, and the U.S. marines were brought in to drive them out.

Of the country's work force of 6 million in 1850, half a million were women: 330,000 worked as domestics; 55,000 were teachers. Of the 181,000 women in factories, half worked in textile mills.

They organized. Women struck by themselves for the first time in 1825. They were the United Tailoresses of New York, demanding higher wages. In 1828, the first strike of mill women on their own took place in Dover, New Hampshire, when several hundred women paraded with banners and flags. They were forced to return to the mill, their demands unmet, and their leaders were fired and blacklisted.

In Exeter, New Hampshire, women mill workers went on strike ("turned out," in the language of that day) because the overseer was setting the clocks back to get more time from them. Their strike succeeded in exacting a promise from the company that the overseers would set their watches right.

The "Lowell system," in which young girls would go to work in the mills and live in dormitories supervised by matrons, at first seemed beneficent, sociable, a welcome escape from household drudgery or domestic service. Lowell, Massachusetts, was the first town created for the textile mill industry; it was named after the wealthy and influential Lowell family. But the dormitories became prisonlike, controlled by rules and regulations. The supper (served after the women had risen at four in the morning and worked until seven thirty in the evening) often consisted merely of bread and gravy.

So the Lowell girls organized. They started their own newspapers. They protested against the weaving rooms, which were poorly lit, badly ventilated, impossibly hot in the summer, damp and cold in the winter. The young women organized a Factory Girls' Association, and fifteen hundred went on strike in 1836 against a raise in boardinghouse charges. Harriet Hanson was an eleven-year-old girl working in the mill. She later recalled:

> ...when the girls in my room stood irresolute, uncertain what to do...I, who began to think they would not go out, after all their talk, became impatient, and started on ahead, saying, with childish bravado, "I don't care what you do, *I* am going to turn out, whether anyone else does or

not," and I marched out, and was followed by the others. As I looked back at the long line that followed me, I was more proud than I have ever been since....

The strikers marched through the streets of Lowell, singing. They held out a month, but then their money ran out, they were evicted from the boardinghouses, and many of them went back to work. The leaders were fired, including Harriet Hanson's widowed mother, a matron in the boardinghouse, who was blamed for her child's going out on strike.

Resistance continued. Meanwhile, the girls tried to hold on to thoughts about fresh air, the country, a less harried way of life. One of them recalled: "In sweet June weather I would lean far out of the window, and try not to hear the unceasing clash of sound inside."

In 1835, twenty mills went on strike to reduce the workday from thirteen and a half hours to eleven hours, to get cash wages instead of company scrip, and to end fines for lateness. Fifteen hundred children and parents went out on strike, and it lasted six weeks. Strikebreakers were brought in, and some workers went back to work, but the strikers did win a twelve-hour day and nine hours on Saturday. That year and the next, there were 140 strikes in the eastern part of the United States.

The crisis that followed the 1837 panic stimulated the formation in 1845 of the Female Labor Reform Association in Lowell, which sent thousands of petitions to the Massachusetts legislature asking for a ten-hour day. But a legislative committee reported: "Your committee returned fully satisfied that the order, decorum, and general appearance of things in and around the mills could not be improved by any suggestion of theirs or by any act of the legislature." In the late 1840s, the New England farm women who worked in the mills began to leave them, as more and more Irish immigrants took their place.

In Paterson, New Jersey, the first of a series of mill strikes was started by children. When the company suddenly put off their dinner hour from noon to 1:00 P.M., the children marched off the job, their parents cheering them on. They were joined by other working people in the town—carpenters, masons, machinists—who turned the strike into a ten-hour-day struggle. After a week, however, with the threat of bringing in militia, the children returned to work, and their leaders were fired. Soon after, trying to prevent more trouble, the company restored the noon dinner hour.

It was the shoemakers of Lynn, Massachusetts, a factory town northeast of Boston, who started the largest strike to take place in the United States before the Civil War. Lynn had pioneered in the use of sewing machines in factories, replacing shoemaker artisans. The factory workers in Lynn, who began to organize in the 1830s, later started a militant newspaper, the *Awl*. In 1844, four years before Marx and Engels's *Communist Manifesto* appeared, the *Awl* wrote:

> The division of society into the producing and the non-producing classes, and the fact of the unequal distribution of value between the two, introduces us at once to another distinction—that of capital and labor.... labor now becomes a commodity.... [C]apital and labor stand opposed.

The economic crisis of 1857 brought the shoe business to a halt, and many workers in Lynn lost their jobs. There was already anger at machine stitching replacing shoemakers. Prices were up, wages were repeatedly cut, and by the fall of 1859 men were earning three dollars a week and women were earning one dollar a week, working sixteen hours a day.

In early 1860, three thousand shoemakers met in the Lyceum Hall in Lynn and began a strike on Washington's Birthday. In a week, strikes had begun in all the shoe towns of New England, with Mechanics Associations in twenty-five towns and twenty thousand shoeworkers on strike. Newspapers called it "The Revolution at the North," "The Rebellion Among the Workmen of New England," "Beginning of the Conflict Between Capital and Labor."

One thousand women and five thousand men marched through the streets of Lynn in a blizzard, carrying banners and American flags. A huge Ladies' Procession was organized, the women marching through streets high with snowdrifts, carrying signs: "American Ladies Will Not Be Slaves." Ten days after that, a procession of ten thousand striking workers, including delegations from Salem, Marblehead, and other towns, men and women, marched through Lynn, in what was the greatest demonstration of labor to take place in New England up to that time.

Police from Boston and militia were sent in to make sure strikers did not interfere with shipments of shoes to be finished out of the state. The strike processions went on, while city grocers and provisions dealers provided food for the strikers. The strike continued through March with morale high, but by April it was losing force. The manufacturers offered higher wages to bring the strikers back into the factories, but without recognizing the unions, so that workers still had to face the employer as individuals.

Their class spirit was fierce but, in the view of Alan Dawley, who studied the Lynn strike (*Class and Community,*) electoral politics drained the energies of the resisters into the channels of the system.

Class-consciousness was overwhelmed during the Civil War, both North and South, by military and political unity in the crisis of war. That unity was weaned by rhetoric and enforced by arms. It was a war proclaimed as a war for liberty, but working people would be attacked by soldiers if they dared to strike, Indians would be massacred in Colorado by the U.S. Army, and those daring to criticize Lincoln's policies would be put in jail without trial—perhaps thirty thousand political prisoners.

Still, there were signs, in both the North and South, of dissent from that unity—anger of poor against rich, rebellion against the dominant political and economic forces.

In the North, the war brought high prices for food and the necessities of life. Employers made excess profits while wages were kept low. There were strikes all over the country during the war. The headline in *Fincher's Trade Review* of November 21, 1863, "THE REVOLUTION IN NEW YORK," was an exaggeration, but the list of labor activities that followed it is impressive evidence of the hidden resentments of the poor during the war.

> The upheaval of the laboring masses in New York has startled the capitalists of that city and vicinity....
>
> The workmen on the iron clads are yet holding out against the contractors....
>
> The glass cutters demand 15 percent to present wages.
>
> Imperfect as we confess our list to be, there is enough to convince the reader that the social revolution now working its way through the land must succeed, if workingmen are only true to each other.
>
> The stage drivers, to the number of 800, are on a strike....
>
> The workingmen of Boston are not behind.... In addition to the strike at the Charlestown Navy Yard....
>
> The riggers are on a strike....
>
> At this writing it is rumored, says the *Boston Post*, that a general strike is contemplated among the workmen in the iron establishments at South Boston, and other parts of the city.

The war brought many women into shops and factories. In New York City, girls sewed umbrellas from six in the morning to midnight, earning three dollars a week, and there was a strike of women umbrella workers in New York and Brooklyn. In Providence, Rhode Island, a Ladies Cigar Makers Union was organized.

All together, by 1864, about 200,000 workers, men and women, were in trade unions, forming national unions in some of the trades, putting out labor newspapers.

Union troops were used to break strikes. Federal soldiers were sent to Cold Springs, New York, to end a strike at a gun works where workers wanted a wage increase. Striking machinists and tailors in St. Louis were forced back to work by the army.

White workers of the North were not enthusiastic about a war that seemed to be fought for the black slave, or for the capitalist, for anyone but them. They worked in semislave conditions themselves. They thought the war was profiting the new class of millionaires.

The Irish working people of New York, recent immigrants, poor, looked upon with contempt by native Americans, could hardly find sympathy for the black population of the city who competed with them for jobs as longshoremen, barbers, waiters, domestic servants. Blacks, pushed out of these jobs, often were used to break strikes. Then came the war, the draft, the chance of death. And the Conscription Act of 1863 provided that the rich could avoid military service: they could pay three hundred dollars or buy a substitute.

When recruiting for the army began in July 1863, a mob in New York wrecked the main recruiting station. Then, for three days, crowds of white workers marched through the city, destroying buildings, factories, streetcar lines, homes. The draft riots were complex—antiblack, antirich, anti-Republican. From an assault on draft headquarters, the rioters went on to attacks on wealthy homes, then to the murder of blacks. They set the city's colored orphan asylum on fire. They shot, burned, and hanged blacks they found in the streets. Many people were thrown into the rivers to drown.

On the fourth day, Union troops returning from the Battle of Gettysburg came into the city and stopped the rioting. Perhaps four hundred people were killed, perhaps a thousand. No exact figures have ever been given, but the number of lives lost was greater than in any other incident of domestic violence in American history.

There were antidraft riots—not so prolonged or bloody—in other northern cities: Newark, Troy, Boston, Toledo, Evansville. In Boston the dead were Irish workers attacking an armory, who were fired on by soldiers.

In the South, beneath the apparent unity of the white Confederacy, there was also conflict. Most whites—two-thirds of them—did not own slaves. A few thousand families made up the plantation elite.

Millions of southern whites were poor farmers, living in shacks or abandoned outhouses. Just before the Civil War, in Jackson, Mississippi, slaves working in a cotton factory received twenty cents a day for board, and white workers at the same factory received thirty cents.

Behind the rebel battle yells and the legendary spirit of the Confederate army, there was much reluctance to fight. The conscription law of the Confederacy too provided that the rich could avoid service. Did Confederate soldiers begin to suspect they were fighting for the privileges of an elite they could never belong to? In April 1863, there was a bread riot in Richmond. That summer, draft riots occurred in various southern cities. In September, a bread riot in Mobile, Alabama. Georgia Lee Tatum, in her study *Disloyalty in the Confederacy*, writes: "Before the end of the war, there was much disaffection in every state, and many of the disloyal had formed into bands—in some states into well-organized, active societies."

The Civil War was one of the first instances of modern warfare: deadly artillery shells, Gatling guns, bayonet charges—combining the indiscriminate killing of mechanized war with hand-to-hand combat. In one charge before Petersburg, Virginia, a regiment of 850 Maine soldiers lost 632 men in half an hour. It was a vast butchery, 623,000 dead on both sides, and 471,000 wounded—over a million dead and wounded in a country whose population was 30 million.

No wonder that desertions grew among southern soldiers as the war went on. As for the Union army, by the end of the war, 200,000 had deserted.

Still, 600,000 had volunteered for the Confederacy in 1861, and many in the Union army were volunteers. The psychology of patriotism, the lure of adventure, the aura of moral crusade created by political leaders, worked effectively to dim class resentments against the rich and powerful,and turn much of the anger against "the enemy." As Edmund Wilson put it in *Patriotic Gore* (written after World War II):

> We have seen, in our most recent wars, how a divided and arguing public opinion may be converted overnight into a national near-unanimity, an obedient flood of energy which will carry the young to destruction and overpower any effort to stem it.

Under the deafening noise of the war, Congress was passing and Lincoln was signing into law a whole series of acts to give business interests what they wanted, and what the agrarian South had blocked before secession. The Republican platform of 1860 had been a clear appeal to businessmen. Now Congress in 1861 passed the Morrill Tariff. This made foreign goods more expensive, allowed American manufacturers to raise their prices, and forced American consumers to pay more.

The following year a Homestead Act was passed. It gave 160 acres of western land, unoccupied and publicly owned, to anyone who would cultivate it for five years. Anyone willing to pay $1.25 an acre could buy a homestead. Few ordinary people had the $200 necessary to do this; speculators moved in and bought up much of the land. Homestead land added up to 50 million acres. But during the Civil War, over 100 million acres were given by Congress and the president to various railroads, free of charge. Congress also set up a national bank, putting the government into partnership with the banking interests, guaranteeing their profits.

With strikes spreading, employers pressed Congress for help. The Contract Labor Law of 1864 made it possible for companies to sign contracts with foreign workers whenever the workers pledged to give twelve months of their wages to pay the cost of emigration. This gave the employers during the Civil War not only very cheap labor, but strikebreakers.

In the thirty years leading up to the Civil War, the law was increasingly interpreted in the courts to suit the capitalist development of the country. Mill owners were given the legal right to destroy other people's property by flood to carry on their business. The law of "eminent domain" was used to take farmers' land and give it to canal companies or railroad companies as subsidies.

It was a time when the law did not even pretend to protect working people—as it would in the next century. Health and safety laws were either nonexistent or unenforced. In Lawrence, Massachusetts, in 1860, on a winter day, the Pemberton Mill collapsed, with nine hundred workers inside, mostly women. Eighty-eight died, and although there was evidence that the structure had never been adequate to support the heavy machinery inside, and that this was known to the construction engineer, a jury found "no evidence of criminal intent."

Morton Horwitz (*The Transformation of American Law*) sums up what happened in the courts of law by the time of the Civil War:

> By the middle of the nineteenth century the legal system had been reshaped to the advantage of men of commerce and industry at the expense of farmers, workers, consumers, and other less powerful groups within the society.... [I]t actively promoted a legal redistribution of wealth against the weakest groups in the society.

In premodern times, the maldistribution of wealth was accomplished by simple force. In modern times, exploitation is disguised—it is accomplished by law, which has the look of neutrality and fairness.

With the war over, the urgency of national unity slackened and ordinary people could turn more to their daily lives, their problems of survival. The disbanded armies now were in the streets, looking for work.

The cities to which the soldiers returned were death traps of typhus, tuberculosis, hunger, and fire. In New York, 100,000 people lived in the cellars of the slums; 12,000 women worked in houses of prostitution to keep from starving; the garbage, lying two feet deep in the streets, was alive with rats. In Philadelphia, while the rich got fresh water from the Schuylkill River, everyone else drank from the Delaware, into which 13 million gallons of sewage were dumped every day. In the Great Chicago Fire in 1871, the tenements fell so fast, one after another, that people said it sounded like an earthquake.

A movement for the eight-hour day began among working people after the war, helped by the formation of the first national federation of unions, the National Labor Union. A three-month strike of 100,000 workers in New York won the eight-hour day, and at a victory celebration in June 1872, 150,000 workers paraded through the city.

Women, brought into industry during the war, organized unions: cigarmakers, tailoresses, umbrella sewers, capmakers, printers, laundresses, shoeworkers. They formed the Daughters of St. Crispin, and succeeded in getting the Cigarmakers Union and the National Typographical Union to admit women for the first time.

The dangers of mill work intensified efforts to organize. Work often went on around the clock. At a mill in Providence, Rhode Island, fire broke out one night in 1866. There was panic among the six hundred workers, mostly women, and many jumped to their deaths from upper-story windows.

In Fall River, Massachusetts, women weavers formed a union independent of the men weavers. They refused to take a 10 percent wage cut that the men had accepted, struck against three mills, won the men's support, and brought to a halt 3,500 looms and 156,000 spindles, with 3,200 workers on strike. But their children needed food; they had to return to work, signing an "iron-clad oath" (later called a "yellow-dog contract") not to join a union.

Black workers at this time found the National Labor Union reluctant to organize them. So they formed their own unions and carried on their own strikes—like the levee workers in Mobile, Alabama, in 1867, Negro longshoremen in Charleston, dockworkers in Savannah. This probably stimulated the National Labor Union, at its 1869 convention, to resolve to organize women and Negroes, declaring that it recognized "neither color nor sex on the question of the rights of labor." A journalist wrote about the remarkable signs of racial unity at this convention:

When a native Mississippian and an ex-confederate officer, in addressing a convention, refers to a colored delegate who has preceded him as
"the gentleman from Georgia"...when an ardent and Democratic parti-
san (from New York at that) declares with a rich Irish brogue that he
asks for himself no privilege as a mechanic or as a citizen that he is not
willing to concede to every other man, white or black...then one may
indeed be warranted in asserting that time works curious changes....

Most unions, however, still kept Negroes out, or asked them to form
their own locals.

The National Labor Union began to expend more and more of its
energy on political issues, especially currency reform, a demand for the
issuance of paper money: greenbacks. As it became less an organizer of
labor struggles, and more a lobbyist with Congress, concerned with voting, it lost vitality.

Reform laws were being passed for the first time, and hopes were
high. The Pennsylvania legislature in 1869 passed a mine safety act providing for the "regulation and ventilation of mines, and for the protection
of the lives of the miners." It calmed anger but accomplished little.

In 1873, another economic crisis devastated the nation. The crisis was
built into a system that was chaotic in its nature, in which only the very
rich were secure. It was a system of periodic crisis—1837, 1857, 1873 (and
later: 1893, 1907, 1919, 1929)—that wiped out small businesses and
brought cold, hunger, and death to working people while the fortunes of
the Astors, Vanderbilts, Rockefellers, Morgans, kept growing through
war and peace, crisis and recovery. During the 1873 crisis, Andrew
Carnegie was capturing the steel market, John D. Rockefeller was wiping
out his competitors in oil.

"LABOR DEPRESSION IN BROOKLYN" was the headline in the
New York Herald in November 1873. It listed closings and layoffs: a felt-
skirt factory, a picture-frame factory, a glass-cutting establishment, a
steelworks factory. And women's trades: milliners, dressmakers, shoe-
binders.

The depression continued through the 1870s. During the first three
months of 1874, ninety thousand workers, almost half of them women,
had to sleep in police stations in New York. All over the country, people
were evicted from their homes. Many roamed the cities looking for food.
Desperate workers tried to get to Europe or to South America. In 1878, the
SS *Metropolis*, filled with laborers, left the United States for South America
and sank with all aboard.

Mass meetings and demonstrations of the unemployed took place all over the country. Unemployed councils were set up. A meeting in New York at Cooper Institute in late 1873 drew a huge crowd, overflowing into the streets. The meeting asked that before bills became law they should be approved by a public vote, that no individual should own more than $30,000; they asked for an eight-hour day.

In Chicago, twenty thousand unemployed marched through the streets to City Hall asking for "bread for the needy, clothing for the naked, and houses for the homeless." Actions like this resulted in some relief for about ten thousand families.

In January 1874, in New York City, a huge parade of workers, kept by the police from approaching City Hall, went to Tompkins Square, and there were told by the police they couldn't have the meeting. They stayed, and the police attacked. One newspaper reported: "Police clubs rose and fell. Women and children ran screaming in all directions. Many of them were trampled underfoot in the stampede for the gates. In the street bystanders were ridden down and mercilessly clubbed by mounted officers."

It was a time when employers brought in recent immigrants—desperate for work, different from the strikers in language and culture—to break strikes. Italians were imported into the bituminous coal area around Pittsburgh in 1874 to replace striking miners. This led to the killing of three Italians, to trials in which jurors of the community exonerated the strikers, and to bitter feelings between Italians and other organized workers.

The centennial year of 1876—one hundred years after the Declaration of Independence—brought forth a number of new declarations. Whites and blacks, separately, expressed their disillusionment. A "Negro Declaration of Independence" denounced the Republican party on which they had once depended to gain full freedom, and proposed independent political action by colored voters. And the Workingmen's party of Illinois, at a July 4 celebration organized by German socialists in Chicago, said in its Declaration of Independence:

> The present system has enabled capitalists to make laws in their own interests to the injury and oppression of the workers.
>
> It has made the name Democracy, for which our forefathers fought and died, a mockery and a shadow, by giving to property an unproportionate amount of representation and control over Legislation.
>
> It has enabled capitalists...to secure government aid, inland grants and money loans, to selfish railroad corporations, who, by monopoliz-

ing the means of transportation are enabled to swindle both the producer and the consumer....

It has presented to the world the absurd spectacle of a deadly civil war for the abolition of negro slavery while the majority of the white population, those who have created all the wealth of the nation, are compelled to suffer under a bondage infinitely more galling and humiliating....

We, therefore, the representatives of the workers of Chicago, in mass meeting assembled, do solemnly publish and declare...

That we are absolved from all allegiance to the existing political parties of this country, and that as free and independent producers we shall endeavor to acquire the full power to make our own laws, manage our own production, and govern ourselves.

In the year 1877, the country was in the depths of the depression. That summer, in the hot cities where poor families lived in cellars and drank infested water, the children became sick in large numbers. The *New York Times* wrote: "...already the cry of the dying children begins to be heard.... Soon, to judge from the past, there will be a thousand deaths of infants per week in the city." That first week in July, in Baltimore, where all liquid sewage ran through the streets, 139 babies died.

That year there came a series of tumultuous strikes by railroad workers in a dozen cities; they shook the nation as no labor conflict in its history had done.

It began with wage cuts on railroad after railroad, in tense situations of already low wages ($1.75 a day for brakemen working twelve hours), scheming and profiteering by the railroad companies, deaths and injuries among the workers—loss of hands, feet, fingers, the crushing of men between cars.

At the Baltimore & Ohio station in Martinsburg, West Virginia, workers determined to fight the wage cut went on strike, uncoupled the engines, ran them into the roundhouse, and announced no more trains would leave Martinsburg until the 10 percent cut was canceled.

Six hundred freight trains now jammed the yards at Martinsburg. The West Virginia governor applied to newly elected President Rutherford Hayes for federal troops. Much of the U.S. Army was tied up in Indian battles in the West. Congress had not appropriated money for the army yet, but J. P. Morgan, August Belmont, and other bankers now offered to lend money to pay army officers (but not enlisted men). Federal troops arrived in Martinsburg, and the freight cars began to move.

In Baltimore, a crowd of thousands sympathetic to the railroad strikers surrounded the armory of the National Guard. The crowd hurled rocks, and the soldiers came out, firing. The streets now became the scene of a moving, bloody battle. When the evening was over, ten men or boys were dead, more badly wounded, one soldier wounded. Half of the 120 troops quit and the rest went on to the train depot, where a crowd of two hundred smashed the engine of a passenger train, tore up tracks, and engaged the militia again in a running battle.

By now, fifteen thousand people surrounded the depot. Soon, three passenger cars, the station platform, and a locomotive were on fire. The governor asked for federal troops, and Hayes responded. Five hundred soldiers arrived and Baltimore quieted down.

The rebellion of the railroad workers now spread. Joseph Dacus, then editor of the St. Louis *Republican*, reported:

> Strikes were occurring almost every hour. The great State of Pennsylvania was in an uproar; New Jersey was afflicted by a paralyzing dread; New York was mustering an army of militia; Ohio was shaken from Lake Erie to the Ohio River; Indiana rested in a dreadful suspense. Illinois, and especially its great metropolis, Chicago, apparently hung on the verge of a vortex of confusion and tumult. St. Louis had already felt the effect of the premonitory shocks of the uprising....

The strike spread to Pittsburgh and the Pennsylvania Railroad. Railroad and local officials decided that the Pittsburgh militia would not kill their fellow townsmen, and urged that Philadelphia troops be called in. By now two thousand cars were idle in Pittsburgh. The Philadelphia troops came and began to clear the track. Rocks flew. Gunfire was exchanged between crowd and troops. At least ten people were killed, all workingmen, most of them not railroaders.

Now the whole city rose in anger. A crowd surrounded the troops, who moved into a roundhouse. Railroad cars were set afire, buildings began to burn, and finally the roundhouse itself, the troops marching out of it to safety. There was more gunfire, the Union Depot was set afire, thousands looted the freight cars. A huge grain elevator and a small section of the city went up in flames. In a few days, twenty-four people had been killed (including four soldiers). Seventy-nine buildings had been burned to the ground. Something like a general strike was developing in Pittsburgh: mill workers, car workers, miners, laborers, and the employees at the Carnegie steel plant.

The entire National Guard of Pennsylvania, nine thousand men, was called out. But many of the companies couldn't move, as strikers in other towns held up traffic. In Lebanon, Pennsylvania, one National Guard company mutinied and marched through an excited town. In Altoona, troops surrounded by rioters, immobilized by sabotaged engines, surrendered, stacked arms, fraternized with the crowd, and then were allowed to go home, to the accompaniment of singing by a quartet in an all-Negro militia company.

In Reading, Pennsylvania, the railroad was two months behind in paying wages, and two thousand people gathered. Men who had blackened their faces with coal dust set about methodically tearing up tracks, jamming switches, derailing cars, setting fire to cabooses and also to a railroad bridge.

A National Guard company arrived. The crowd threw stones, fired pistols. The soldiers fired into the crowd. Six men were killed. The crowd grew angrier, more menacing. A contingent of soldiers announced it would not fire, one soldier saying he would rather put a bullet through the president of Philadelphia & Reading Coal & Iron.

Meanwhile the leaders of the big railway brotherhoods, the Order of Railway Conductors, the Brotherhood of Locomotive Firemen, the Brotherhood of Engineers, disavowed the strike. There was talk in the press of "communistic ideas...widely entertained...by the workmen employed in mines and factories and by the railroads."

There was a Workingmen's party, with several thousand members in Chicago. Most of its members were immigrants from Germany and Bohemia. In the midst of the railroad strikes, that summer of 1877, it called a rally. Six thousand people came and demanded nationalization of the railroads. Albert Parsons gave a fiery speech. He was from Alabama, had fought in the Confederacy during the Civil War, married a brown-skinned woman of Spanish and Indian blood, worked as a typesetter, and was one of the best English-speaking orators the Workingmen's party had.

The next day, a crowd of young people, not especially connected with the rally of the evening before, began moving through the railroad yards, closed down the freights, went to the factories, called out the mill workers, the stockyard workers, the crewmen on the Lake Michigan ships, closed down the brickyards and lumberyards. That day also, Albert Parsons was fired from his job with the *Chicago Times* and declared blacklisted.

The police attacked the crowds. The press reported: "The sound of clubs falling on skulls was sickening for the first minute, until one grew accustomed to it. A rioter dropped at every whack, it seemed, for the ground was covered with them." Two companies of U.S. infantry arrived, joining National Guardsmen and Civil War veterans. Police fired into a surging crowd, and three men were killed.

The next day, an armed crowd of five thousand fought the police. The police fired again and again, and when it was over, and the dead were counted, they were, as usual, workingmen and boys, eighteen of them, their skulls smashed by clubs, their vital organs pierced by gunfire.

The one city where the Workingmen's party clearly led the rebellion was St. Louis, a city of flour mills, foundries, packing houses, machine shops, breweries, and railroads. Here, as elsewhere, there were wage cuts on the railroads. And here there were perhaps a thousand members of the Workingmen's party, many of them bakers, coopers, cabinetmakers, cigarmakers, brewery workers. The party was organized in four sections, by nationality: German, English, French, Bohemian.

All four sections took a ferry across the Mississippi to join a mass meeting of railroad men in East St. Louis. Railroaders in East St. Louis declared themselves on strike. The mayor of East St. Louis was a European immigrant, himself an active revolutionist as a youth, and railroad men's votes dominated the city.

In St. Louis, itself, the Workingmen's party called a mass meeting to which five thousand people came. They called for nationalization of the railroads, mines, and all industry.

At one of those meetings a black man spoke for those who worked on the steamboats and levees. He asked: "Will you stand to us regardless of color?" The crowd shouted back: "We will!"

Handbills calling for a general strike were soon all over the city. There was a march of four hundred Negro steamboat men and roustabouts along the river, six hundred factory workers carrying a banner: "No Monopoly— Workingmen's Rights." A great procession moved through the city, ending with a rally of ten thousand people listening to communist speakers.

In New York, several thousand gathered at Tompkins Square. The tone of the meeting was moderate, speaking of "a political revolution through the ballot box." And: "If you will unite, we may have here within five years a socialistic republic...." It was a peaceful meeting. It adjourned. The last words heard from the platform were: "Whatever we poor men may not have, we have free speech, and no one can take it from us." Then the police charged, using their clubs.

In St. Louis, as elsewhere, the momentum of the crowds, the meetings, the enthusiasm, could not be sustained. As they diminished, the police, militia, and federal troops moved in and the strike leaders were arrested, then fired from their jobs with the railroad.

When the great railroad strikes of 1877 were over, a hundred people were dead, a thousand people had gone to jail, 100,000 workers had gone on strike, and the strikes had roused into action countless unemployed in the cities. More than half the freight on the nation's 75,000 miles of track had stopped running at the height of the strikes.

The railroads made some concessions, withdrew some wage cuts, but also strengthened their "Coal and Iron Police." In a number of large cities, National Guard armories were built, with loopholes for guns.

In 1877, the same year blacks learned they did not have enough strength to make real the promise of equality in the Civil War, working people learned they were not united enough, not powerful enough, to defeat the combination of private capital and government power. But there was more to come.

Exercises

1. Make and fill in a graph like the one below to illustrate the rise in the total population of Americans living in cities from 1790–1840.

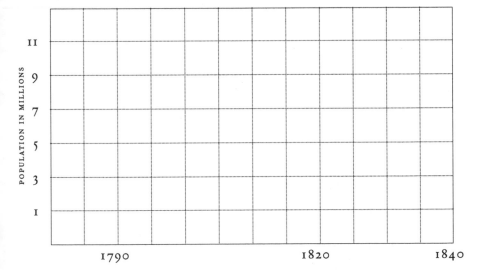

2. What factors contributed to the growth of monopolies before the Civil War?
    What are some examples of monopolies formed in the 1850s?

3. What role did the federal and state governments play in the creation of monopolies?

4. Define "working-class consciousness." Use the following documents to help you.

    * 1827 "Address...before the Mechanics and Working Classes...of Philadelphia"
    * 1829 Frances Wright's speech on July 4th
    * 1829 George Henry Evans's "The Working Men's Declaration of Independence"
    * 1834 Boston "Trades Union" document

5. The following questions refer to the time between c. 1830 and c. 1855.
    a. What were the different *forms* through which working people manifested their opposition to their political and economic position? Give *specific examples* to illustrate each form or type of opposition. (Types/forms can include any of the following: pamphlets/ newspapers; demonstrations; strikes; organizations; meetings; riots; protests; debates; petitions; formation of political parties; creation of new political arms of existing parties or splinter groups).
    b. Of the above examples, which were ineffective and why? Which were effective? What effect did the form of protest have?

6. What do workers want (refer to questions a–l below)? Were the demands/requests of workers reasonable? If so, why did management object to these demands/requests? Why might managers/owners be led to believe that the incidents referred to in the questions below might represent a conspiracy? How might one argue that they did not represent a conspiracy?

a. Why did a crowd destroy the houses of bank officials in Maryland in 1835?

b. Why did the New York Tailors object to Judge Edwards's decision regarding the right of the Tailors to form a union?

c. What did the New York Locofocos want in 1837?

d. What did the trade unions in Philadelphia want in 1835?

e. What did the Irish weavers of Philadelphia want in the early 1840s?

f. What did several thousand people in Newark, New Jersey, want in 1857?

g. What did the United Tailoresses want in 1825?

h. What did the women mill workers in Exeter, New Hampshire, want in 1828?

i. What did the Lowell Girls want?

j. What did the Female Labor Reform Association of Lowell want in 1845?

k. What did the Paterson children want?

l. What did the shoemakers of Lynn, Massachusetts, want?

7. Did the Civil War (1861–1865) effectively end the growing division between capital and labor? Explain.

8. Why were there draft riots in 1863?

9. During the Civil War, northern congressmen, without the representatives from the seceded states, were able to pass legislation favorable to northern business interests. How do each of the following pieces of legislation favor the northern/western economic system (manufacturing/commerce/wage labor) over the southern system (plantation-agricultural/raw materials/slave labor):

a. Morrill Tariff (1861)

b. Homestead Act (1862)

c. Contract Labor Law (1864)

10. How did judges interpret the law in favor of those businessmen who wished to expand at the expense of others?

11. After the Civil War (post-1865), were the conditions of the urban poor the same, worse, or better than they had been before the Civil War (pre-1861)?

12. What types of work opened up to women as a result of the Civil War?

13. Why did the men of the National Labor Union vote to include blacks and women among their numbers in 1869?

14. After the Civil War (post-1865), local trade unions joined together into national organizations. How did the tactics of labor change as a result of this transformation?

15. What evidence does Zinn provide to illustrate the fact that economic crisis made workers adopt more radical tactics than they had used during periods of economic growth? Why would this happen?

16. How did the railroad strike of 1877 differ from other strikes described in this chapter? How was it similar? Did it represent a new stage in American labor history?

17. What does the title of this chapter mean? What is "The Other Civil War"?

18. *Debate Resolution:* Owners and government officials were not solely responsible for the violence that erupted surrounding labor disputes.

Chapter 11

Robber Barons and Rebels

In the year 1877, the signals were given for the rest of the century: the blacks would be put back; the strikes of white workers would not be tolerated; the industrial and political elites of North and South would take hold of the country and organize the greatest march of economic growth in human history. They would do it with the aid of, and at the expense of, black labor, white labor, Chinese labor, European immigrant labor, female labor, rewarding workers differently by race, sex, national origin, and social class, in such a way as to create separate levels of oppression—a skillful terracing to stabilize the pyramid of wealth.

[handwritten margin note: every one would contrib]

Between the Civil War and 1900, steam and electricity replaced human muscle, iron replaced wood, and steel replaced iron (before the Bessemer process, iron was hardened into steel at the rate of three to five tons a day; now the same amount could be processed in fifteen minutes). Machines could now drive steel tools. Oil could lubricate machines and light homes, streets, factories. People and goods could move by railroad, propelled by steam along steel rails; by 1900 there were 193,000 miles of railroad. The telephone, the typewriter, and the adding machine speeded up the work of business.

Machines changed farming. Before the Civil War it took 61 hours of labor to produce an acre of wheat. By 1900, it took 3 hours, 19 minutes. Manufactured ice enabled the transport of food over long distances, and the industry of meatpacking was born.

Steam drove textile mill spindles; it drove sewing machines. It came

↑impact on
↓economic/
social

from coal. Pneumatic drills now drilled deeper into the earth for coal. In 1860, 14 million tons of coal were mined; by 1884 it was 100 million tons. More coal meant more steel, because coal furnaces converted iron into steel; by 1880 a million tons of steel were being produced; by 1910, 25 million tons. By now electricity was beginning to replace steam. Electrical wire needed copper, of which 30,000 tons were produced in 1880; 500,000 tons by 1910.

humans played a part too.

To accomplish all this required ingenious inventors of new processes and new machines, clever organizers and administrators of the new corporations, a country rich with land and minerals, and a huge supply of human beings to do the back-breaking, unhealthful, and dangerous work. Immigrants would come from Europe and China to make the new labor force. Farmers unable to buy the new machinery or pay the new railroad rates would move to the cities. Between 1860 and 1914, New York grew from 850,000 to 4 million, Chicago from 110,000 to 2 million, Philadelphia from 650,000 to 1.5 million.

In some cases the inventor himself became the organizer of businesses—like Thomas Edison, inventor of electrical devices. In other cases, the businessman compiled other people's inventions, like Gustavus Swift, a Chicago butcher who put together the ice-cooled railway car with the ice-cooled warehouse to make the first national meatpacking company in 1885. James Duke used a new cigarette-rolling machine that could roll, paste, and cut tubes of tobacco into 100,000 cigarettes a day; in 1890 he combined the four biggest cigarette producers to form the American Tobacco Company.

Most people of $ came from it

While some multimillionaires started in poverty, most did not. A study of the origins of 303 textile, railroad, and steel executives of the 1870s showed that 90 percent came from middle- or upper-class families. The Horatio Alger stories of "rags to riches" were true for a few men, but mostly a myth, and a useful myth for control.

Most of the fortune building was done legally, with the collaboration of the government and the courts. Sometimes the collaboration had to be paid for. Thomas Edison promised New Jersey politicians $1,000 each in return for favorable legislation. Daniel Drew and Jay Gould spent $1 million to bribe the New York legislature to legalize their issue of $8 million in "watered stock" (stock not representing real value) on the Erie Railroad.

The first transcontinental railroad was built with blood, sweat, politics, and thievery, out of the meeting of the Union Pacific and Central Pacific railroads. The Central Pacific started on the West Coast going east;

bribing & lying...

it spent $200,000 in Washington on bribes to get 9 million acres of free land and $24 million in bonds, and paid $79 million, an overpayment of $36 million, to a construction company which really was its own. The construction was done by three thousand Irish and ten thousand Chinese, over a period of four years, working for one or two dollars a day.

The Union Pacific started in Nebraska going west. It had been given 12 million acres of free land and $27 million in government bonds. It created the Credit Mobilier company and gave them $94 million for construction when the actual cost was $44 million. Shares were sold cheaply to congressmen to prevent investigation. This was at the suggestion of Massachusetts Congressman Oakes Ames, a shovel manufacturer and director of Credit Mobilier, who said: "There is no difficulty in getting men to look after their own property." The Union Pacific used twenty thousand workers —war veterans and Irish immigrants, who laid five miles of track a day and died by the hundreds in the heat, the cold, and the battles with Indians opposing the invasion of their territory.

Both railroads used longer, twisting routes to get subsidies from towns they went through. In 1869, amid music and speeches, the two crooked lines met in Utah.

The wild fraud on the railroads led to more control of railroad finances by bankers, who wanted more stability. By the 1890s, most of the country's railway mileage was concentrated in six huge systems. Four of these were completely or partially controlled by the House of Morgan, and two others by the bankers Kuhn, Loeb, and Company.

There was a human cost to this exciting story of financial ingenuity. In the year 1889, records of the Interstate Commerce Commission showed that 22,000 railroad workers were killed or injured.

J. P. Morgan had started before the war, as the son of a banker who began selling stocks for the railroads for good commissions. During the Civil War he bought 5,000 rifles for $3.50 each from an army arsenal, and sold them to a general in the field for $22 each. The rifles were defective and would shoot off the thumbs of the soldiers using them. A congressional committee noted this in the small print of an obscure report, but a federal judge upheld the deal as the fulfillment of a valid legal contract.

Morgan had escaped military service in the Civil War by paying $300 to a substitute. So did John D. Rockefeller, Andrew Carnegie, Philip Armour, Jay Gould, and James Mellon. Mellon's father had written to him that "a man may be a patriot without risking his own life or sacrificing his health. There are plenty of lives less valuable."

WOW

While making his fortune, Morgan brought rationality and organization to the national economy. He kept the system stable. He said: "We do not want financial convulsions and have one thing one day and another thing another day." He linked railroads to one another, all of them to banks, banks to insurance companies. By 1900, he controlled 100,000 miles of railroad, half the country's mileage.

John D. Rockefeller started as a bookkeeper in Cleveland, became a merchant, accumulated money, and decided that, in the new industry of oil, who controlled the oil refineries controlled the industry. He bought his first oil refinery in 1862, and by 1870 set up Standard Oil Company of Ohio, made secret agreements with railroads to ship his oil with them if they gave him rebates—discounts—on their prices, and thus drove competitors out of business. One independent refiner said: "If we did not sell out.... we would be crushed out.... There was only one buyer on the market and we had to sell at their terms."

Andrew Carnegie was a telegraph clerk at seventeen, then secretary to the head of the Pennsylvania Railroad, then broker in Wall Street selling railroad bonds for huge commissions, and was soon a millionaire. He went to London in 1872, saw the new Bessemer method of producing steel, and returned to the United States to build a million-dollar steel plant. Foreign competition was kept out by a high tariff conveniently set by Congress. By 1900 he was making $40 million a year, and that year, at a dinner party, he agreed to sell his steel company to J. P. Morgan. He scribbled the price on a note: $492,000,000.

Morgan then formed the U.S. Steel Corporation, combining Carnegie's corporation with others, and took a fee of $150 million for arranging the consolidation. How could dividends be paid to all those stockholders and bondholders? By making sure Congress passed tariffs keeping out foreign steel; by closing off competition and maintaining the price at $28 a ton; and by working 200,000 men twelve hours a day for wages that barely kept their families alive.

And so it went, in industry after industry—shrewd, efficient businessmen building empires, choking out competition, maintaining high prices, keeping wages low, using government subsidies. These industries were the first beneficiaries of the "welfare state." By the turn of the century, American Telephone and Telegraph had a monopoly of the nation's telephone system, International Harvester made 85 percent of all farm machinery, and in every other industry resources became concentrated, controlled.

The banks had interests in so many of these monopolies as to create an interlocking network of powerful corporation directors, each of whom sat on the boards of many other corporations. According to a Senate report of the early twentieth century, Morgan at his peak sat on the board of forty-eight corporations; Rockefeller, thirty-seven corporations.

Meanwhile, the government of the United States was behaving almost exactly as Karl Marx described a capitalist state: pretending neutrality to maintain order, but serving the interests of the rich. Not that the rich agreed among themselves; they had disputes over policies. But the purpose of the state was to settle upper-class disputes peacefully, control lower-class rebellion, and adopt policies that would further the long-range stability of the system. The arrangement between Democrats and Republicans to elect Rutherford Hayes in 1877 set the tone. Whether Democrats or Republicans won, national policy would not change in any important way.

When Grover Cleveland, a Democrat, ran for President in 1884, the general impression in the country was that he opposed the power of monopolies and corporations, and that the Republican party, whose candidate was James Blaine, stood for the wealthy. But when Cleveland defeated Blaine, Jay Gould wired him: "I feel...that the vast business interests of the country will be entirely safe in your hands." And he was right.

Cleveland himself assured industrialists that his election should not frighten them: "No harm shall come to any business interest as the result of administrative policy so long as I am President ...a transfer of executive control from one party to another does not mean any serious disturbance of existing conditions."

The presidential election had avoided real issues. It took the usual form of election campaigns, concealing the basic similarity of the parties by dwelling on personalities, gossip, trivialities. Henry Adams, an astute literary commentator on that era, wrote to a friend about the election:

> We are here plunged in politics funnier than words can express. Very great issues are involved.... But the amusing thing is that no one talks about real interests. By common consent they agree to let these alone.... Instead of this the press is engaged in a most amusing dispute whether Mr. Cleveland had an illegitimate child and did or did not live with more than one mistress.

In 1887, with a huge surplus in the treasury, Cleveland vetoed a bill appropriating $100,000 to give relief to Texas farmers to help them buy seed grain during a drought. He said: "Federal aid in such cases...encourages the expectation of paternal care on the part of the government and weakens the sturdiness of our national character." But that same year,

Cleveland used his gold surplus to pay off wealthy bondholders at $28 above the $100 value of each bond—a gift of $45 million.

The chief reform of the Cleveland administration gives away the secret of reform legislation in America. The Interstate Commerce Act of 1887 was supposed to regulate the railroads on behalf of the consumers. But Richard Olney, a lawyer for the Boston & Maine and other railroads, and soon to be Cleveland's attorney general, told railroad officials who complained about the Interstate Commerce Commission that it would not be wise to abolish the commission "from a railroad point of view." He explained:

> The Commission…is or can be made, of great use to the railroads. It satisfies the popular clamor for a government supervision of railroads, at the same time that that supervision is almost entirely nominal…. The part of wisdom is not to destroy the Commission, but to utilize it.

Republican Benjamin Harrison, who succeeded Cleveland as president from 1889 to 1893, had been a lawyer for the railroads and had commanded a company of soldiers during the strike of 1877. Harrison's term also saw a gesture toward reform. The Sherman Anti-Trust Act, passed in 1890, made it illegal to form a "combination or conspiracy" to restrain trade in interstate or foreign commerce. Senator John Sherman, author of the act, explained the need to conciliate the critics of monopoly: "You must heed their appeal or be ready for the socialist, the communist, the nihilist. Society is now disturbed by forces never felt before…."

Cleveland, elected again in 1892, facing the agitation in the country caused by the panic and depression of 1893, used troops to break up "Coxey's Army," a demonstration of unemployed men who had come to Washington, and again to break up the national strike on the railroads the following year.

Meanwhile, the Supreme Court, despite its look of somber, black-robed fairness, was doing its bit for the ruling elite. How could it be independent, with its members chosen by the president and ratified by the Senate? How could it be neutral between rich and poor when its members were often former wealthy lawyers, and almost always came from the upper class? Early in the nineteenth century the Court laid the legal basis for a nationally regulated economy by establishing federal control over interstate commerce, and the legal basis for corporate capitalism by making the contract sacred.

In 1895 the Court interpreted the Sherman Anti-Trust Act so as to make it harmless.

Very soon after the Fourteenth Amendment became law, the Supreme Court began to demolish it as a protection for blacks, and to develop it as a protection for corporations. In 1886, the Court did away with 230 state laws that had been passed to regulate corporations. It declared that corporations were "persons" and their money was property protected by the due process clause of the Fourteenth Amendment. Of the Fourteenth Amendment cases brought before the Supreme Court between 1890 and 1910, nineteen dealt with the Negro, 288 dealt with corporations.

In 1893, Supreme Court Justice David J. Brewer, addressing the New York State Bar Association, said: "It is the unvarying law that the wealth of the community will be in the hands of the few...."

This was not just a whim of the 1880s and 1890s—it went back to the Founding Fathers, who had learned their law in the era of *Blackstone's Commentaries*, which said: "So great is the regard of the law for private property, that it will not authorize the least violation of it; no, not even for the common good of the whole community."

Control in modern times requires more than force, more than law. It requires that a population dangerously concentrated in cities and factories, whose lives are filled with cause for rebellion, be taught that all is right as it is. And so, the schools, the churches, the popular literature taught that to be rich was a sign of superiority, to be poor a sign of personal failure, and that the only way upward for a poor person was to climb into the ranks of the rich by extraordinary effort and extraordinary luck.

The rich, giving part of their enormous earnings to educational institutions, became known as philanthropists. Rockefeller was a donor to colleges all over the country and helped found the University of Chicago. Huntington, of the Central Pacific, gave money to two Negro colleges, Hampton Institute and Tuskegee Institute. Carnegie gave money to colleges and to public libraries. Johns Hopkins University was founded by a millionaire merchant, and millionaires Cornelius Vanderbilt, Ezra Cornell, James Duke, and Leland Stanford created universities in their own names.

These educational institutions did not encourage dissent; they trained the middlemen in the American system—the teachers, doctors, lawyers, administrators, engineers, technicians, politicians—those who would be paid to keep the system going, to be loyal buffers against trouble.

In the meantime, the spread of public school education enabled the learning of writing, reading, and arithmetic for a whole generation of workers, skilled and semiskilled, who would be the literate labor force of the new industrial age. It was important that these people learn obedience to authority. A journalist observer of the schools in the 1890s wrote: "The unkindly spirit of the teacher is strikingly apparent; the pupils, being completely subjugated to her will, are silent and motionless, the spiritual atmosphere of the classroom is damp and chilly."

This continued into the twentieth century, when William Bagley's *Classroom Management* became a standard teacher training text, reprinted thirty times. Bagley said: "One who studies educational theory aright can see in the mechanical routine of the classroom the educative forces that are slowly transforming the child from a little savage into a creature of law and order, fit for the life of civilized society."

It was in the middle and late nineteenth century that high schools developed as aids to the industrial system, that history was widely required in the curriculum to foster patriotism. Loyalty oaths, teacher certification, and the requirement of citizenship were introduced to control both the educational and the political quality of teachers. Also, in the latter part of the century, school officials—not teachers—were given control over textbooks. Laws passed by the states barred certain kinds of textbooks. Idaho and Montana, for instance, forbade textbooks propagating "political" doctrines.

Against this gigantic organization of knowledge and education for orthodoxy and obedience, there arose a literature of dissent and protest, which had to make its way from reader to reader against great obstacles. Henry George, a self-educated workingman from a poor Philadelphia family, who became a newspaperman and an economist, wrote a book that was published in 1879 and sold millions of copies, not only in the United States, but all over the world. His book *Progress and Poverty* argued that the basis of wealth was land, that this was becoming monopolized, and that a single tax on land, abolishing all others, would bring enough revenue to solve the problem of poverty and equalize wealth in the nation.

A different kind of challenge to the economic and social system was given by Edward Bellamy, a lawyer and writer from western Massachusetts, who wrote, in simple, intriguing language, a novel called *Looking Backward*, in which the author falls asleep and wakes up in the year 2000, to find a socialistic society in which people work and live cooperatively. *Looking Backward*, which described socialism vividly, lovingly, sold a million copies in a few years, and over a hundred groups were organized around the country to try to make the dream come true.

It seemed that despite the strenuous efforts of government, business, the church, the schools, to control their thinking, millions of Americans were ready to consider harsh criticism of the existing system, to contemplate other possible ways of living. They were helped in this by the great movements of workers and farmers that swept the country in the 1880s and 1890s. These movements went beyond the scattered strikes and tenants' struggles of the period 1830–1877. They were nationwide movements, more threatening than before to the ruling elite, more dangerously suggestive. It was a time when revolutionary organizations existed in major American cities, and revolutionary talk was in the air.

In the 1880s and 1890s, immigrants were pouring in from Europe at a faster rate than before. They all went through the harrowing ocean voyage of the poor. Now there were not so many Irish and German immigrants as Italians, Russians, Jews, Greeks—people from southern and eastern Europe, even more alien to native-born Anglo-Saxons than the earlier newcomers.

The immigration of these different ethnic groups contributed to the fragmentation of the working class. The Irish, still recalling the hatred against them when they arrived, began to get jobs with the new political machines that wanted their vote. Those who became policemen encountered the new Jewish immigrants. On July 30, 1902, New York's Jewish community held a mass funeral for an important rabbi, and a riot took place, led by Irish who resented Jews coming into their neighborhood.

There was desperate economic competition among the newcomers. By 1880, Chinese immigrants, brought in by the railroads to do the back-breaking labor at pitiful wages, numbered 75,000 in California, almost one-tenth of the population. They became the objects of continuous violence. The novelist Bret Harte wrote an obituary for a Chinese man named Wan Lee: "Dead, my revered friends, dead. Stoned to death in the streets of San Francisco, in the year of grace 1869 by a mob of halfgrown boys and Christian school children."

In Rock Springs, Wyoming, in the summer of 1885, whites attacked five hundred Chinese miners, massacring twenty-eight of them in cold blood.

A traffic in immigrant child laborers developed, either by contract with desperate parents in the home country or by kidnapping. The children were then supervised by "padrones" in a form of slavery, sometimes sent out as beggar musicians. Droves of them roamed the streets of New York and Philadelphia.

As the immigrants became naturalized citizens, they were brought into the American two-party system, invited to be loyal to one party or the other, their political energy thus siphoned into elections. An article in *L'Italia*, in November 1894, called for Italians to support the Republican party. Irish and Jewish leaders backed the Democrats.

There were 5.5 million immigrants in the 1880s, 4 million in the 1890s, creating a labor surplus that kept wages down. The immigrants were more controllable, more helpless than native workers; they were culturally displaced, at odds with one another, therefore useful as strikebreakers. Often their children worked, intensifying the problem of an oversized labor force and joblessness; in 1880 there were 1,118,000 children under sixteen (one out of six) at work in the United States.

Women immigrants became servants, prostitutes, housewives, factory workers, and sometimes rebels.

In 1884, women's assemblies of textile workers and hatmakers went on strike. The following year in New York, cloak and shirt makers, men and women (holding separate meetings but acting together), went on strike. The *New York World* called it "a revolt for bread and butter." They won higher wages and shorter hours.

That winter in Yonkers, a few women carpet weavers were fired for joining the Knights of Labor, and in the cold of February, twenty-five hundred women walked out and picketed the mill. The police attacked the picket line and arrested them, but a jury found them not guilty. A great dinner was held by working people in New York to honor them, with two thousand delegates from unions all over the city. The strike lasted six months, and the women won some of their demands, getting back their jobs, but without recognition of their union.

What was astonishing in so many of these struggles was not that the strikers did not win all that they wanted, but that, against such great odds, they dared to resist, and were not destroyed.

Perhaps it was the recognition that day-to-day combat was not enough, that fundamental change was needed, which stimulated the growth of revolutionary movements at this time. In 1883, an anarchist congress took place in Pittsburgh. It drew up a manifesto: "...All laws are directed against the working people.... The workers can therefore expect no help from any capitalistic party in their struggle against the existing system. They must achieve their liberation by their own efforts."

The manifesto asked "equal rights for all without distinction to sex or race." It quoted the *Communist Manifesto*: "Workmen of all lands, unite! You have nothing to lose but your chains; you have a world to win!"

In Chicago, the new International Working People's Association connected to the First International in Europe, had five thousand members, published newspapers in five languages, organized mass demonstrations and parades, and through its leadership in strikes was a powerful influence in the twenty-two unions that made up the Central Labor Union of Chicago. There were differences in theory among all these revolutionary groups, but the theorists were often brought together by the practical needs of labor struggles, and there were many in the mid-1880s.

By the spring of 1886, the movement for an eight-hour day had grown. On May 1, the American Federation of Labor, now five years old, called for nationwide strikes wherever the eight-hour day was refused. Terence Powderly, head of the Knights of Labor, opposed the strike, saying that employers and employees must first be educated on the eight-hour day, but assemblies of the Knights made plans to strike. The grand chief of the Brotherhood of Locomotive Engineers opposed the eight-hour day, saying "two hours less work means two hours more loafing about the corners and two hours more for drink," but railroad workers did not agree and supported the eight-hour movement.

So, 350,000 workers in 11,562 establishments all over the country went out on strike. In Detroit, 11,000 workers marched in an eight-hour parade. In New York, 25,000 formed a torchlight procession along Broadway. In Chicago, 40,000 struck, and 45,000 were granted a shorter working day to prevent them from striking. Every railroad in Chicago stopped running, and most of the industries in Chicago were paralyzed. The stockyards were closed down.

A "Citizens' Committee" of businessmen met daily to map strategy in Chicago. The state militia had been called out, the police were ready, and the *Chicago Mail* on May 1 asked that Albert Parsons and August Spies, the anarchist leaders of the International Working People's Association, be watched. "Keep them in view. Hold them personally responsible for any trouble that occurs. Make an example of them if trouble occurs."

Under the leadership of Parsons and Spies, the Central Labor Union, with twenty-two unions, had adopted a fiery resolution in the fall of 1885:

> Be it Resolved, That we urgently call upon the wage-earning class to arm itself in order to be able to put forth against their exploiters such an argument which alone can be effective: Violence, and further be it Resolved, that notwithstanding that we expect very little from the introduction of the eight-hour day, we firmly promise to assist our more backward brethren in this class struggle with all means and power at our disposal, so long as they will continue to show an open and resolute

front to our common oppressors, the aristocratic vagabonds and exploiters. Our war-cry is "Death to the foes of the human race."

On May 3, a series of events took place which were to put Parsons and Spies in exactly the position that the *Chicago Mail* had suggested ("Make an example of them if trouble occurs"). That day, in front of the McCormick Harvester Works, where strikers and sympathizers fought scabs, the police fired into a crowd of strikers running from the scene, wounded many of them, and killed four. Spies, enraged, went to the printing shop of the *Arbeiter-Zeitung* and printed a circular in both English and German:

> Revenge!
> Workingmen, to Arms!!!
> ...You have for years endured the most abject humiliations;...you have worked yourself to death...your Children you have sacrificed to the factory lord—in short: you have been miserable and obedient slaves all these years: Why? To satisfy the insatiable greed, to fill the coffers of your lazy thieving master? When you ask them now to lessen your burdens, he sends his bloodhounds out to shoot you, kill you!
> ...To arms we call you, to arms!

A meeting was called for Haymarket Square on the evening of May 4, and about three thousand persons assembled. It was a quiet meeting, and as storm clouds gathered and the hour grew late, the crowd dwindled to a few hundred. A detachment of 180 policemen showed up, advanced on the speakers' platform, ordered the crowd to disperse. The speaker said the meeting was almost over. A bomb then exploded in the midst of the police, wounding sixty-six policemen, of whom seven later died. The police fired into the crowd, killing several people, wounding two hundred.

With no evidence on who threw the bomb, the police arrested eight anarchist leaders in Chicago. The *Chicago Journal* said: "Justice should be prompt in dealing with the arrested anarchists. The law regarding accessories to crime in this State is so plain that their trials will be short." Illinois law said that anyone inciting a murder was guilty of that murder. The evidence against the eight anarchists was their ideas, their literature; none had been at Haymarket that day except Fielden, who was speaking when the bomb exploded. A jury found them guilty, and they were sentenced to death. Their appeals were denied; the U.S. Supreme Court said it had no jurisdiction.

The event aroused international excitement. Meetings took place in

France, Holland, Russia, Italy, Spain. In London a meeting of protest was sponsored by George Bernard Shaw, William Morris, and Peter Kropotkin, among others. Shaw had responded in his characteristic way to the turning down of an appeal by the eight members of the Illinois Supreme Court: "If the world must lose eight of its people, it can better afford to lose the eight members of the Illinois Supreme Court."

A year after the trial, four of the convicted anarchists—Albert Parsons, a printer; August Spies, an upholsterer; Adolph Fischer, and George Engel—were hanged. Louis Lingg, a twenty-one-year-old carpenter, blew himself up in his cell by exploding a dynamite tube in his mouth. Three remained in prison.

The executions aroused people all over the country. There was a funeral march of twenty-five thousand in Chicago.

While the immedite result was a suppression of the radical movement, the long-term effect was to keep alive the class anger of many, to inspire others—especially young people of that generation—to action in revolutionary causes. Sixty thousand signed petitions to the new governor of Illinois, John Peter Altgeld, who investigated the facts, denounced what had happened, and pardoned the three remaining prisoners. Year after year, all over the country, memorial meetings for the Haymarket martyrs were held; it is impossible to know the number of individuals whose political awakening—as with Emma Goldman and Alexander Berkman, long-time revolutionary stalwarts of the next generation—came from the Haymarket Affair.

Some of the energy of resentment in late 1886 was poured into the electoral campaign for mayor of New York that fall. Trade unions formed an Independent Labor party and nominated for mayor Henry George, the radical economist, whose *Progress and Poverty* had been read by tens of thousands of workers.

The Democrats nominated an iron manufacturer, Abram Hewitt, and the Republicans nominated Theodore Roosevelt. In a campaign of coercion and bribery, Hewitt was elected with 41 percent of the vote, George came second with more votes than Roosevelt. Roosevelt third with 27 percent of the vote. The *New York World* saw this as a signal:

> The deep-voiced protest conveyed in the 67,000 votes for Henry George against the combined power of both political parties, of Wall Street and the business interests, and of the public press should be a warning to the community to heed the demands of Labor so far as they are just and reasonable....

In other cities in the country too, labor candidates ran, electing a mayor in Milwaukee, and various local officials in Fort Worth, Texas; Eaton, Ohio; and Leadville, Colorado.

It seemed that the weight of Haymarket had not crushed the labor movement. The year 1886 became known to contemporaries as "the year of the great uprising of labor." From 1881 to 1885, strikes had averaged about 500 each year, involving perhaps 150,000 workers each year. In 1886 there were over 1,400 strikes, involving 500,000 workers. John Commons, in his *History of the Labor Movement in the United States*, saw in that:

> the signs of a great movement by the class of the unskilled, which had finally risen in rebellion.... The movement bore in every way the aspect of a social war. A frenzied hatred of labour for capital was shown in every important strike.... Extreme bitterness toward capital manifested itself in all the actions of the Knights of Labor, and wherever the leaders undertook to hold it within bounds, they were generally discarded by their followers....

Even among southern blacks, where all the military, political, and economic force of the southern states, with the acquiescence of the national government, was concentrated on keeping them docile and working, there were sporadic rebellions. In the cotton fields, blacks were dispersed in their work, but in the sugar fields, work was done in gangs, so there was opportunity for organized action.

By 1886, the Knights of Labor was organizing in the sugar fields. The black workers, unable to feed and clothe their families on their wages, often paid in store scrip, asked a dollar a day. The following year, in the fall, close to ten thousand sugar laborers went on strike, 90 percent of them Negroes and members of the Knights. The militia arrived and gun battles began.

Violence erupted in the town of Thibodaux, Louisiana, where hundreds of strikers, evicted from their plantation shacks, gathered, penniless and ragged, carrying their bed clothing and babies. Their refusal to work threatened the entire sugar crop, and martial law was declared in Thibodaux. Henry and George Cox, two Negro brothers, leaders in the Knights of Labor, were arrested, locked up, then taken from their cells, and never heard from again. On the night of November 22, shooting broke out, each side claiming the other was at fault; by noon the next day, thirty Negroes were dead or dying, and hundreds wounded. Two whites were wounded. A Negro newspaper in New Orleans wrote:

...Lame men and blind women shot; children and hoary-headed grand-sires ruthlessly swept down! The Negroes offered no resistance; they could not, as the killing was unexpected. Those of them not killed took to the woods, a majority of them finding refuge in this city.... Citizens of the United States killed by a mob directed by a State judge.... Laboring men seeking an advance in wages, treated as if they were dogs!...

Native-born poor whites were not doing well either. In the South, they were tenant farmers rather than landowners. In the southern cities, they were tenants, not homeowners. And the slums of the southern cities were among the worst, poor whites living like the blacks, on unpaved dirt streets "choked up with garbage, filth and mud," according to a report of one state board of health.

In the year 1891, miners of the Tennessee Coal Mine Company were asked to sign an "iron-clad contract": pledging no strikes, agreeing to get paid in scrip, and giving up the right to check the weight of the coal they mined (they were paid by the weight). They refused to sign and were evicted from their houses. Convicts were brought in to replace them.

On the night of October 31, 1891, a thousand armed miners took control of the mine area, set five hundred convicts free, and burned down the stockades in which the convicts were kept. The companies surrendered, agreeing not to use convicts, not to require the "iron-clad contract," and to let the miners check on the weight of the coal they mined.

The following year, there were more insurrections in Tennessee. Miners overpowered guards of the Tennessee Coal and Iron Company, burned the stockades, shipped the convicts to Nashville. Other unions in Tennessee came to their aid. An observer reported back to the Chattanooga Federation of Trades: "The entire district is as one over the main proposition, 'the convicts must go.' I counted 840 rifles on Monday as the miners passed.... Whites and Negroes are standing shoulder to shoulder."

That same year, in New Orleans, forty-two union locals, with over twenty thousand members, mostly white but including some blacks (there was one black on the strike committee), called a general strike, involving half the population of the city. Work in New Orleans came to a stop. After three days—with strikebreakers brought in, martial law, and the threat of militia—the strike ended with a compromise, gaining hours and wages but without recognition of the unions as bargaining agents.

The year 1892 saw strike struggles all over the country: besides the general strike in New Orleans and the coal miners' strike in Tennessee, there was a railroad switchmen's strike in Buffalo, New York, and a copper miners' strike in Coeur d'Alene, Idaho. The Coeur d'Alene strike was marked by gun battles between strikers and strikebreakers, and many deaths.

In early 1892, the Carnegie Steel plant at Homestead, Pennsylvania, just outside of Pittsburgh, was being managed by Henry Clay Frick while Carnegie was in Europe. Frick decided to reduce the workers' wages and break their union. He built a fence three miles long and twelve feet high around the steelworks and topped it with barbed wire, adding peepholes for rifles. When the workers did not accept the pay cut, Frick laid off the entire work force. The Pinkerton detective agency was hired to protect strikebreakers.

On the night of July 5, 1892, hundreds of Pinkerton guards boarded barges five miles down the river from Homestead and moved toward the plant, where ten thousand strikers and sympathizers waited. The crowd warned the Pinkertons not to step off the barge. A striker lay down on the gangplank, and when a Pinkerton man tried to shove him aside, he fired, wounding the detective in the thigh. In the gunfire that followed on both sides, seven workers were killed.

The Pinkertons had to retreat onto the barges. They were attacked from all sides, voted to surrender, and then were beaten by the enraged crowd. There were dead on both sides. For the next several days the strikers were in command of the area. Now the state went into action: the governor brought in the militia, armed with the latest rifles and Gatling guns, to protect the import of strikebreakers.

Strike leaders were charged with murder; 160 other strikers were tried for other crimes. All were acquitted by friendly juries. The strike held for four months, but the plant was producing steel with strikebreakers who were brought in, often in locked trains, not knowing their destination, not knowing a strike was on. The strikers, with no resources left, agreed to return to work, their leaders blacklisted.

In the midst of the Homestead strike, a young anarchist from New York named Alexander Berkman, in a plan prepared by anarchist friends in New York, including his lover Emma Goldman, came to Pittsburgh and entered the office of Henry Clay Frick, determined to kill him. Berkman's aim was poor; he wounded Frick and was overwhelmed, then was tried and found guilty of attempted murder.

He served fourteen years in the state penitentiary. His *Prison Memoirs of an Anarchist* gave a graphic description of the assassination attempt and of his years in prison, when he changed his mind about the usefulness of assassinations but remained a dedicated revolutionary. Emma Goldman's autobiography, *Living My Life*, conveys the anger, the sense of injustice, the desire for a new kind of life, that grew among the young radicals of that day.

The year 1893 saw the biggest economic crisis in the country's history. After several decades of wild industrial growth, financial manipulation, uncontrolled speculation and profiteering, it all collapsed: 642 banks failed and 16,000 businesses closed down. Out of the labor force of 15 million, 3 million were unemployed. No state government voted relief, but mass demonstrations all over the country forced city governments to set up soup kitchens and give people work on streets or parks.

In New York City, in Union Square, Emma Goldman addressed a huge meeting of the unemployed and urged those whose children needed food to go into the stores and take it. She was arrested for "inciting to riot" and sentenced to two years in prison. In Chicago, it was estimated that 200,000 people were without work, the floors and stairways of City Hall and the police stations packed every night with homeless men trying to sleep.

The depression lasted for years and brought a wave of strikes throughout the country. The largest of these was the nationwide strike of railroad workers in 1894 that began at the Pullman Company in Illinois, just outside of Chicago.

Railroad work was one of the most dangerous jobs in America; over two thousand railroad workers were being killed each year, and thirty thousand injured. The *Locomotive Firemen's Magazine* said: "It comes to this: while railroad managers reduce their force and require men to do double duty, involving loss of rest and sleep...the accidents are chargeable to the greed of the corporation."

It was the Depression of 1893 that propelled Eugene Debs into a lifetime of action for unionism and socialism. He had worked on the railroads for four years until he was nineteen, but left when a friend was killed after falling under a locomotive. He read Edward Bellamy's *Looking Backward*; it deeply affected him.

In the midst of the economic crisis of 1893, a small group of railroad workers, including Debs, formed the American Railway Union, to unite all railway workers. Debs said: "It has been my life's desire to unify railroad employees and to eliminate the aristocracy of labor...and organize them so all will be on an equality...."

Debs wanted to include everyone, but blacks were kept out; at a convention in 1894, the provision in the constitution barring blacks was affirmed by a vote of 112 to 100. Later, Debs thought this might have had a crucial effect on the outcome of the Pullman strike, for black workers were in no mood to cooperate with the strikers.

In June 1894, workers at the Pullman Palace Car Company went on strike. They received immediate support from other unions in the Chicago area. The Pullman strikers appealed to a convention of the American Railway Union for support:

> Mr. President and Brothers of the American Railway Union. We struck at Pullman because we were without hope. We joined the American Railway Union because it gave us a glimmer of hope. Twenty thousand souls, men, women and little ones, have their eyes turned toward this convention today, straining eagerly through dark despondency for a glimmer of the heaven-sent message you alone can give us on this earth....
>
> You all must know that the proximate cause of our strike was the discharge of two members of our grievance committee.... Five reductions in wages.... Pullman, both the man and the town, is an ulcer on the body politic. He owns the houses, the schoolhouses, and churches of God in the town he gave his once humble name....

The American Railway Union responded. It asked its members all over the country not to handle Pullman cars. Since virtually all passenger trains had Pullman cars, this amounted to a boycott of all trains—a nationwide strike. Soon all traffic on the twenty-four railroad lines leading out of Chicago had come to a halt. Workers derailed freight cars, blocked tracks, pulled engineers off trains if they refused to cooperate.

The General Managers Association, representing the railroad owners, agreed to pay two thousand deputies, sent in to break the strike. But the strike went on. The attorney general of the United States, Richard Olney, a former railroad lawyer, now got a court injunction against blocking trains, on the legal ground that the federal mails were being interfered with. When the strikers ignored the injunction, President Cleveland ordered federal troops to Chicago. On July 6, hundreds of cars were burned by strikers.

The following day, the state militia moved in. A crowd of five thousand gathered. Rocks were thrown at the militia, and the command was given to fire. The *Chicago Times* reported:

> The command to charge was given.... From that moment only bayonets were used.... A dozen men in the front line of rioters received bayonet wounds.... The police were not inclined to be merciful, and driving the mob against the barbed wires clubbed it unmercifully.... The ground

over which the fight had occurred was like a battlefield. The men shot by the troops and police lay about like logs....

In Chicago that day, thirteen people were killed, fifty-three seriously wounded, seven hundred arrested. Before the strike was over, perhaps thirty-four were dead. With fourteen thousand police, militia, troops in Chicago, the strike was crushed. Debs was arrested for contempt of court, for violating the injunction that said he could not do or say anything to carry on the strike.

Debs, in court, denied he was a socialist. But during his six months in prison, he studied socialism and talked to fellow prisoners who were socialists. Later he wrote: "I was to be baptized in Socialism in the roar of conflict...in the gleam of every bayonet and the flash of every rifle the class struggle was revealed...."

Two years after he came out of prison, Debs wrote in the *Railway Times*: "The issue is Socialism versus Capitalism. I am for Socialism because I am for humanity. We have been cursed with the reign of gold long enough. Money constitutes no proper basis of civilization. The time has come to regenerate society—we are on the eve of a universal change."

Thus, the eighties and nineties saw bursts of labor insurrection, more organized than the spontaneous strikes of 1877. There were now revolutionary movements influencing labor struggles, the ideas of socialism affecting labor leaders. Radical literature was appearing, speaking of fundamental changes, of new possibilities for living.

In this same period, those who worked on the land—farmers, North and South, black and white—were going far beyond the scattered tenant protests of the pre–Civil War years and creating the greatest movement of agrarian rebellion the country had ever seen.

Behind the despair so often registered in the farm country literature of that day, there must have been visions, from time to time, of a different way to live, as in a Hamlin Garland novel, *A Spoil of Office*, where the heroine speaks at a farmers' picnic:

> I see a time when the farmer will not need to live in a cabin on a lonely farm. I see the farmers coming together in groups. I see them with time to read, and time to visit with their fellows. I see them enjoying lectures in beautiful halls, erected in every village. I see them gather like the Saxons of old upon the green at evening to sing and dance. I see cities rising near them with schools, and churches, and concert halls and theaters. I see a day when the farmer will no longer be a drudge and his wife a bond

slave, but happy men and women who will go singing to their pleasant tasks upon their fruitful farms.

Between 1860 and 1910, the U.S. Army, wiping out the Indian villages on the Great Plains, paved the way for the railroads to move in and take the best land. Then the farmers came for what was left. From 1860 to 1900 the population of the United States grew from 31 million to 75 million. The crowded cities of the East needed food, and the number of farms grew from 2 million to 6 million.

Farming became mechanized—steel plows, mowing machines, reapers, harvesters, improved cotton gins for pulling the fibers away from the seed, and, by the turn of the century, giant combines that cut the grain, threshed it, and put it in bags. In 1830 a bushel of wheat had taken three hours to produce. By 1900, it took ten minutes. Specialization developed by region: cotton and tobacco in the South, wheat and corn in the Midwest.

Land cost money, and machines cost money—so farmers had to borrow, hoping that the prices of their harvests would stay high, so they could pay the bank for the loan, the railroad for transportation, the grain merchant for handling their grain, the storage elevator for storing it. But they found the prices for their produce going down, and the prices of transportation and loans going up, because the individual farmer could not control the price of his grain, while the monopolist railroad and the monopolist banker could charge what they liked.

The farmers who could not pay saw their homes and land taken away. They became tenants. By 1880, 25 percent of all farms were rented by tenants, and the number kept rising. Many did not even have money to rent and became farm laborers; by 1900 there were 4.5 million farm laborers in the country. It was the fate that awaited every farmer who couldn't pay his debts.

Could the squeezed and desperate farmer turn to the government for help?

The government was helping the bankers and hurting the farmers; it kept the amount of money—based on the gold supply—steady, while the population rose, so there was less and less money in circulation. The farmer had to pay off his debts in dollars that were harder to get. The bankers, getting the loans back, were getting dollars worth more than when they loaned them out—a kind of interest on top of interest. That is why so much of the talk of farmers' movements in those days had to do with putting more money in circulation—by printing greenbacks (paper money for which there was no gold in the treasury) or by making silver a basis for issuing money.

It was in the South that the crop-lien system was most brutal. By this system the farmer would get the things he needed from the merchant: the use of the cotton gin at harvest time, whatever supplies were necessary. He didn't have money to pay, so the merchant would get a lien—a mortgage on his crop—on which the farmer might pay 25 percent interest. The farmer would owe more money every year until finally his farm was taken away and he became a tenant.

In the depths of the 1877 depression, a group of white farmers gathered together on a farm in Texas and formed the first "Farmers Alliance." In a few years, it was across the state. By 1886, 100,000 farmers had joined in two thousand suballiances. They began to offer alternatives to the old system: join the Alliance and form cooperatives; buy things together and get lower prices. They began putting their cotton together and selling it cooperatively—they called it "bulking."

In some states a Grange movement developed; it managed to get laws passed to help farmers. But the Grange, as one of its newspapers put it, "is essentially conservative...." It was a time of crisis, and the Grange was doing too little. It lost members, while the Farmers Alliance kept growing.

From the beginning, the Farmers Alliance showed sympathy with the growing labor movement. When Knights of Labor men went on strike against a steamship line in Galveston, Texas, a group of Alliance people in Texas passed a resolution:

Whereas we see the unjust encroachments that the capitalists are making upon all the different departments of labor...we extend to the Knights of Labor our hearty sympathy in their manly struggle against monopolistic oppression and...we propose to stand by the Knights.

In the summer of 1886, in the town of Cleburne, Texas, near Dallas, the Alliance gathered and drew up the first document of the Populist movement, asking "such legislation as shall secure to our people freedom from the onerous and shameful abuses that the industrial classes are now suffering at the hands of arrogant capitalists and powerful corporations." They called for a national conference of all labor organizations and proposed regulation of railroad rates, heavy taxation of land held only for speculative purposes, and an increase in the money supply.

The Alliance kept growing. By early 1887, it had 200,000 members in three thousand suballiances. By 1892 farmer lecturers had gone into forty-three states and reached 2 million farm families. It was a drive based on the idea of cooperation, of farmers creating their own culture, their own political parties.

Organizers from Texas came to Georgia to form alliances, and in three years Georgia had 100,000 members in 134 of the 137 counties. In Tennessee, there were soon 125,000 members and 3,600 suballiances in 92 of the state's 96 counties. The Alliance moved into Mississippi "like a cyclone," someone said, and into Louisiana and North Carolina. Then northward into Kansas and the Dakotas, where thirty-five cooperative warehouses were set up.

Now there were 400,000 members in the National Farmers Alliance. And the conditions spurring the Alliance onward got worse. Corn that had brought $.45 a bushel in 1870 brought $.10 a bushel in 1889. In the South the situation was worse than anywhere—90 percent of the farmers lived on credit.

There was one victory along the way. Farmers were being charged too much for jute bags (to put cotton in), which were controlled by a trust. The Alliance farmers organized a boycott of jute, made their own bags out of cotton, and forced the jute manufacturers to start selling their bags at $.05 a yard instead of $.14.

There were Alliance experiments. In the Dakotas, a great cooperative insurance plan for farmers insured them against loss of their crops. Where the big insurance companies had asked $.50 an acre, the cooperative asked $.25 or less. It issued thirty thousand policies, covering 2 million acres.

The complexity of Populist belief was shown in one of its important leaders in Texas, Charles Macune. He was a radical in economics (antitrust, anticapitalist), a conservative in politics (against a new party independent of the Democrats), and a racist. Macune came forward with a plan that was to become central to the Populist platform—the "sub-Treasury" plan. The government would have its own warehouses where farmers would store produce and get certificates from this sub-Treasury. These would be greenbacks, and thus much more currency would be made available, not dependent on gold or silver, but based on the amount of farm produce.

Macune's sub-Treasury plan depended on the government. And since it would not be taken up by the two major parties, it meant (against Macune's own beliefs) organizing a third party. The Alliance went to work. In 1890 thirty-eight Alliance people were elected to Congress. In the South, the Alliance elected governors in Georgia and Texas. It took over the Democratic party in Georgia and won three-fourths of the seats in the Georgia state legislature, six of Georgia's ten U.S. congressmen.

Corporate power still dominated the political structure, but the Alliance was spreading new ideas and a new spirit. Now, as a political party, it became the People's party (or Populist party), and met in convention in 1890 in Topeka, Kansas. The great Populist orator from that state, Mary Ellen Lease, told an enthusiastic crowd:

> Wall Street owns the country. It is no longer a government of the people, by the people, and for the people, but a government of Wall Street, by Wall Street and for Wall Street.... We want the power to make loans direct from the government. We want the accursed foreclosure system wiped out.... We will stand by our homes and stay by our firesides by force if necessary, and we will not pay our debts to the loan-shark companies until the Government pays its debts to us. The people are at bay, let the bloodhounds of money who have dogged us thus far beware.

At the People's party national convention in 1892 in St. Louis, a platform was drawn up. The preamble was written by, and read to the assemblage by, another of the great orators of the movement, Ignatius Donnelly:

> We meet in the midst of a nation brought to the verge of moral, political and material ruin. Corruption dominates the ballot box, the legislatures, the Congress, and touches even the ermine of the bench. The people are demoralized.... The newspapers are subsidized or muzzled; public opinion silenced; business prostrate, our homes covered with mortgages, labor impoverished, and the land concentrating in the hands of capitalists.

A People's party nominating convention in Omaha in July of 1892 nominated James Weaver, an Iowa Populist and former general in the Union army, for president. The Populist movement was now tied to the voting system. Weaver got over a million votes, but lost.

The People's Party had the job of uniting diverse groups—northern Republicans and southern Democrats, urban workers and country farmers, black and white. A Colored Farmers National Alliance grew in the South and had perhaps a million members, but it was organized and led by whites. There were also black organizers, but it was not easy for them to persuade black farmers that, even if economic reforms were won, blacks would have equal access to them. Blacks had tied themselves to the Republican party, the party of Lincoln and civil rights laws.

There were whites who saw the need for racial unity. One Alabama newspaper wrote: "The white and colored Alliance are united in their war against trusts...."

Some Alliance blacks made similar calls for unity. A leader of the Florida Colored Alliance said: "We are aware of the fact that the laboring colored man's interests and the laboring white man's interest are one and the same."

When the Texas People's party was founded in Dallas in the summer of 1891, it was interracial, and radical. There was blunt and vigorous debate among whites and blacks. A black delegate, active in the Knights of Labor, dissatisfied with vague statements about "equality," said:

> If we are equal, why does not the sheriff summon Negroes on juries? And why hang up the sign "Negro," in passenger cars. I want to tell my people what the People's Party is going to do. I want to tell them if it is going to work a black and white horse in the same field.

A white leader responded by urging there be a black delegate from every district in the state. "They are in the ditch just like we are."

Blacks and whites were in different situations. The blacks were mostly field hands, hired laborers; most white Alliance people were farm owners. When the Colored Alliance declared a strike in the cotton fields in 1891 for a dollar a day wages for cotton pickers, Leonidas Polk, head of the white Alliance, denounced it as hurting the Alliance farmer who would have to pay that wage.

There was some black-white unity at the ballot box in the South— resulting in a few blacks elected in North Carolina local elections. An Alabama white farmer wrote to a newspaper in 1892: "I wish to God that Uncle Sam could put bayonets around the ballot box in the black belt on the first Monday in August so that the Negro could get a fair vote." There were black delegates to third-party conventions in Georgia: two in 1892, twenty-four in 1894. The Arkansas People's party platform spoke for the "downtrodden, regardless of race."

Still, racism was strong, and the Democratic party played on this, winning many farmers from the Populist party. When white tenants, failing in the crop-lien system, were evicted from their land and replaced by blacks, race hatred intensified. Southern states were drawing up new constitutions, starting with Mississippi in 1890, to prevent blacks from voting by various devices, and to maintain ironclad segregation in every aspect of life.

The laws that took the vote away from blacks—poll taxes, literacy tests, property qualifications—also often ensured that poor whites would not vote. And the political leaders of the South knew this. At the constitutional convention in Alabama, one of the leaders said he wanted to take away the vote from "all those who are unfit and unqualified, and if the rule strikes a white man as well as a negro let him go."

Tom Watson, the Populist leader of Georgia, pleaded for racial unity: "You are kept apart that you may be separately fleeced of your earnings. You are made to hate each other because upon that hatred is rested the keystone of the arch of financial despotism which enslaves you both." Watson wanted black support for a white man's party, and later, when Watson found this support embarrassing and no longer useful, he became as eloquent in affirming racism as he had been in opposing it.

It was a time that illustrated the complexities of class and race conflict. Fifteen blacks were lynched during Watson's election campaign. And in Georgia after 1891 the Alliance-controlled legislature, Allen points out, "passed the largest number of anti-black bills ever enacted in a single year in Georgia history." And yet, in 1896, the Georgia state platform of the People's party denounced lynch law and terrorism, and asked for the abolition of the convict lease system.

C. Vann Woodward points to the unique quality of the Populist experience in the South: "Never before or since have the two races in the South come so close together as they did during the Populist struggles."

The Populist movement also made a remarkable attempt to create a new and independent culture for the country's farmers. The Alliance Lecture Bureau reached all over the country; it had 35,000 lecturers. The Populists poured out books and pamphlets from their printing presses. Their aim was to educate farmers, revising the orthodox history, economics, and political theory.

The *National Economist*, a Populist magazine, had 100,000 readers. There were over a thousand Populist journals in the 1890s. Books written by Populist leaders, such as Henry Demarest Lloyd's *Wealth Against Commonwealth* and William Harvey Coin's *Financial School*, were widely read. The Populist movement profoundly affected Southern life.

There were only fitful, occasional connections between the farmer and labor movements. Neither spoke eloquently enough to the other's needs. And yet, there were signs of a common consciousness that might, under different circumstances, lead to a unified, ongoing movement.

Undoubtedly, Populists, along with most white Americans, had racism and nativism in their thinking. But part of it was that they simply did not think race as important as the economic system. Thus, the *Farmers'*

Alliance said: "The people's party has sprung into existence not to make the black man free, but to emancipate all men...to gain for all industrial freedom, without which there can be no political freedom...."

The Populist movement failed, finally, to unite blacks and whites, city workers and country farmers. That, plus the lure of electoral politics, combined to destroy the Populist movement. Once allied with the Democratic party in supporting William Jennings Bryan for president in 1896, Populism would drown in a sea of Democratic politics. The pressure for electoral victory led Populism to make deals with the major parties in city after city. If the Democrats won, it would be absorbed. If the Democrats lost, it would disintegrate. Electoral politics brought into the top leadership the political brokers instead of the agrarian radicals.

There were those radical Populists who saw this. They said fusion with the Democrats to try to "win" would lose what they needed, an independent political movement. They said the much-ballyhooed free silver would not change anything fundamental in the capitalist system.

Henry Demarest Lloyd noted that the Bryan nomination was subsidized in part by Marcus Daly (of Anaconda Copper) and William Randolph Hearst (of the silver interests in the West). He saw through the rhetoric of Bryan that stirred the crowd of twenty thousand at the Democratic Convention. Lloyd wrote bitterly:

> The poor people are throwing up their hats in the air for those who promise to lead them out of the wilderness by way of the currency route.... The people are to be kept wandering forty years in the currency labyrinth, as they have for the last forty years been led up and down the tariff bill.

In the election of 1896, with the Populist movement enticed into the Democratic party, Bryan, the Democratic candidate, was defeated by William McKinley, for whom the corporations and the press mobilized, in the first massive use of money in an election campaign. Even the hint of Populism in the Democratic party, it seemed, could not be tolerated, and the big guns of the Establishment pulled out all their ammunition, to make sure.

It was a time, as election times have often been in the United States, to consolidate the system after years of protest and rebellion. The black was being kept under control in the South. The Indian was being driven off the western plains for good; on a cold winter day in 1890, U.S. army soldiers attacked Indians camped at Wounded Knee, South Dakota, and killed three hundred men, women, and children. It was the climax to four hundred years of violence that began with Columbus, establishing that this continent belonged to white men. But only to certain white men, because it was clear by 1896 that the state stood ready to crush labor strikes, by the law if possible, by force if necessary. And where a threatening mass movement developed, the two-party system stood ready to send out one of its columns to surround that movement and drain it of vitality.

And always, as a way of drowning class resentment in a flood of slogans for national unity, there was patriotism. McKinley had said, in a rare rhetorical connection between money and flag:

> ...this year is going to be a year of patriotism and devotion to country. I am glad to know that the people in every part of the country mean to be devoted to one flag, the glorious Stars and Stripes; that the people of this country mean to maintain the financial honor of the country as sacredly as they maintain the honor of the flag.

The supreme act of patriotism was war. Two years after McKinley became president, the United States declared war on Spain.

Exercises

1. What was the technology that transformed the work-place from 1865–1900? What economic and social effects did the new technology have on American society?

2. Why did it "take money to make money" during the period of rapid economic expansion after the Civil War? What are the implications of this for the potential for social mobility?

3. How many railroad workers were killed or injured in 1889? Why did so many workers die on the job?

4. How did J. P. Morgan justify his methods of doing business?

5. What methods did each of the following use to build his fortune:
    a. Morgan (banking, railroads, and steel)
    b. Rockefeller (oil)
    c. Carnegie (steel)

6. Are there any facts surrounding the presidential election of 1884 and its outcome (Cleveland defeats Blaine) that support Zinn's assertion that "Whether Democrats or Republicans won, national policy would not change in any important way." Do the policies or legislation during either of the two Cleveland administrations or Benjamin Harrison's administration support any or all parts of Zinn's statement above? How persuasive is Zinn on this point? Explain.

7. How does Zinn argue that the Supreme Court cannot possibly act in a neutral fashion? What is the argument against Zinn?

8. What definition of the "law" was Supreme Court Justice David Brewer using when he addressed the New York Sate Bar Association (all options below are quoted from Webster's New Collegiate Dictionary, 1981)?

   a. a binding custom or practice of a community

   b. a rule of conduct enforced by a controlling authority

   c. the revelation of the will of God

   d. a statement of an order or relation of phenomena that so far as is known is invariable under the given conditions

   e. the observed regularity of nature

   What point was Brewer trying to make? What point is Zinn trying to make by including this quotation?

9. What role did philanthropy play in maintaining the status quo? How does this inform your understanding of the heated debate of the last fifteen years about whether the U.S. government should give grants to artists and scientists?

10. How did the educational system function as a tool to reproduce the system? In your experience, are today's educational structure, methods, and content any different from they were in the late nineteenth century?

11. What was Henry George's solution to the unequal distribution of wealth? What was Edward Bellamy's? What evidence indicates that these ideas were popular at the time?

12. What was a primary obstacle to worker unity in the 1880s?

13. Why would employers want there to be large numbers of unemployed workers around? Why wouldn't employers want large numbers of unemployed workers?

14. What evidence exists that the Knights of Labor recruited women? Blacks?

15. Why was the IWPA a "powerful influence" within the Central Labor Union of Chicago? Why would a worker belong both to the IWPA and the CLU?

16. What was the major tactical disagreement between the AFL (American Federation of Labor) and the Knights in 1886?

17. How did business respond when the 1886 strike for the eight-hour day successfully "paralyzed most of the industries in Chicago"?

18. What is the most accurate way to refer to the events and their aftermath that occurred on the evening of May 4, 1886, at Haymarket Square in Chicago? Defend your rejections as well as your choice. Which would be the most neutral way to refer to the events and their aftermath? (You may want to refer to a dictionary to help define the terms of the selections below as well as help you be clear as to the difference between accurate and neutral.)

> a. The Haymarket Riot
>
> b. The Haymarket Affair
>
> c. The Haymarket Persecution
>
> d. The Haymarket Demonstration
>
> e. The Haymarket Tragedy
>
> f. The Haymarket Travesty
>
> g. (your choice?)

19. How do standard American history textbooks refer to the events surrounding the incident at the Haymarket Square in 1886? Is there a consensus among these standard texts? Over what do they differ?

In what do they agree? How different are they from Zinn's version? How do you explain the differences?

20. Were the executions of Spies, Parsons, Fischer, and Engel a tactic on the part of business and government to damage the effectiveness of the labor movement? If it was, did it work?

21. What successes did the labor movement score in the 1880s and 1890s?

22. Why did the Thibodaux workers go on strike? Was the strike successful? What accounts for its success or lack of success?

23. What were the demands of the Tennessee coal miners in 1891?

24. *Debate Resolution*: The labor movement was more successful in the North and West than in the South.

25. What was Frick's strategy to break the steelworkers' union at the Homestead steel plant? Did the plan work? What is the evidence to support your answer?

26. What was the effect of the mass demonstrations that immediately followed the economic collapse beginning in 1893?

27. What role did Emma Goldman play in the labor history of the late nineteenth century?

28. Why were black workers reluctant to support the Pullman strike?

29. Why did the strike at the Pullman plant in Chicago become a nationwide strike?

30. On what pretext did the federal government side with the railroad owners?

31. When did Eugene Debs become a socialist? Why?

32. Why did the number of tenant families increase steadily through-out the post–Civil War period (post-1865)? What actions did the farmers take to oppose this trend?

33. Why did the Populists believe that Macune's sub-Treasury Plan was necessary? (What economic dynamic would the sub-Treasury plan have replaced?)

34. Why were the farmers not satisfied with only establishing coopera-tives? (Why did they feel a need to take control of the local and national governments?)

35. *Debate Resolution:* In the fight against monopolies, farmers ensured their failure by engaging in electoral politics.

36. How did the Democratic party use race to defeat the Populists in the South?

37. Zinn writes: "C. Vann Woodward points to the unique quality of the Populist experience in the South: 'Never before or since have the two races in the South come so close together as they did during the Populist struggles.'" (p. 211) How "close" was that?

38. Why would creating an alternative culture be a priority for both the Alliance and Populist movements? (How did Alliance and Populist teachings differ from the official teachings in the public school system?)

39. The farmers needed an expansion of currency as a practical, short-term solution to being constantly in debt. Their preferred solution was to issue paper currency based on the amount of grain produced. The final manifestation of this solution was Macune's sub-Treasury Plan. (See Lawrence Goodwyn, *The Populist Moment*, chapter one, section five for an explanation of Alliance currency theory.) How would the Democrat's slogan of "free silver" effectively lure the Populists away from the sub-Treasury plan? What was the minority Populist opposition argument against "free silver"?

40. During the period from 1865 to 1898, how did the political/economic elite

    a. contain the demands of blacks for equal rights?

    b. contain the demands of farmers and laborers for economic justice?

    c. respond to Indians' desires to be allowed to exist?

41. *Debate Resolution:* The Populist movement failed because it did not attempt to attract labor to its cause.

Appendix A

Teaching Techniques

Kathy Emery

1. The Group Paragraph*

There are important reasons for teachers to present material in a variety of ways. To always have discussions or to always lecture eventually becomes tedious to students and to the teacher, regardless of how expertly the lecture or facilitating is done. Having students work in groups to write a paragraph not only brings variety into the classroom, but it simultaneously encourages cooperative and active learning. Yet many teachers avoid this technique or use it so sparingly that the behavior induced by the experience is never internalized by the student. I have found that, used with clearly stated goals and consistently enforced rules of behavior, the group paragraph is an invaluable tool in teaching, content, critical thinking, and cooperative learning.

Group paragraphs need to be assigned two to three times a month with the exact same rules and goals expected every time. Groups of four work best (but three and five can work too). One might alternate between allowing students to choose their own groups and assigning students to groups. Each group must have a recorder, who is assigned or volunteers to write out the group's answer to the given question. It is important to ensure that the same students are not always being recorders. Over the course of the school year the responsibility of the recorder should be

---

* The following kinds of questions are well suited for group paragraph work: those whose answers require detail from throughout a chapter; those whose answers require detail from more than one chapter; those whose answers require analysis, synthesis, or evaluation.

evenly divided among the students. The recorder writes the paragraph as it is composed verbally by the group. If someone else grabs the paragraph and writes a sentence, that is fine as long as the official recorder gets the paper back. If done on paper, the essay will be a rough draft, and hence the students should be encouraged to cross out and rearrange using stars, arrows, and the like. It is ideal if each group can compose its paragraph on a computer.

It is imperative that the teacher pose a controversial question that must be answered within a clearly defined time. I prefer to give students at least forty minutes to discuss a question that has several possible answers. The more students argue sincerely, the sharper their thinking will become. Since students must commit their answer to paper and know that their written statement will be assessed, they feel accountable, and it is accountability that creates an expectation to which students will rise. Hence, the time limit. Sometimes, students think they are finished early but they are not. I deal with early finishers by quickly reading their paragraph and making a few criticisms to get them back to work. I check whether the thesis is stated in the first sentence, whether the terms are defined, if there is detail, and if the detail is relevant to their thesis.

The choice of reading assignments in advance of the group paragraph is crucial. Students must have data with which to argue. And they need to have that data in front of them when they are collectively writing the paragraph. The question needs to involve interpreting the data. If they have just read a chapter on the first women factory workers in which the fate of single and married women was described, then one can successfully ask: "Was it better to be married or single?" This question has invariably led to wonderful arguments within a group since neither condition was attractive and there were pros and cons to each. When students ask if they have to make a definitive statement, I always insist that they do even when this is often unrealistic. Forcing them to have a clear-cut opinion clarifies their thinking. Once they have arrived at an opinion, they can then see how simplistic it is and want to go beyond it. Such a discussion is an important element of the exercise. One can't achieve more complexity without establishing a simple thesis first.

To focus the students' thinking, three rules need to be consistently enforced: (1) the paragraph (or page) must begin with a thesis statement that answers the question; (2) next, students must define the terms of the thesis. If the answer is single women had more freedom than married women, then it is crucial for the writers to define "freedom" as they argue their data; (3) students must support their general statements with detail, that is, either "facts" or quotations from the text. The concept of what a "fact" is can be avoided by focusing instead on the distinction between generalizations and detail.

Selective intervention is necessary to foster cooperative behavior. As the students work, I walk around the classroom, pausing before each group, listening not for what is being said but for tone of voice and the number of voices involved. Students should feel a supervisory but not stifling presence. As long as the tone of the conversation is one of thoughtful or excited questioning and everyone in the group is at least paying attention if not speaking, then intervention is not necessary and one can go on to the next group. If there is an argument that has taken on a hostile tone, then I will pause and listen for a while to see if it is resolved. If it isn't, I will stop the group, comment on what I have observed and get the students to agree that the argument was going nowhere. Usually, arguments develop when both sides are using the same term but, unbeknownst to either, each defines the term differently. The problem is rarely solved if I tell a student that he or she wasn't listening to another student. One must define what that means. I often find that if I lead the students through the conversation by isolating each part of the argument, they can resolve the confusion themselves. Often, just by slowing down the argument, the students themselves will become more precise and listen to each other more carefully. Below is a typical exchange of the sort that needs teacher intervention.

LIYAH: The Puritans were democrats, they elected their officials.

CESAR: Yeah? Well, they were all brainwashed.

LIYAH: Not if they choose their leaders.

CESAR: The elections were rigged.

LIYAH: They had debates.

CESAR: Yeah, some debates they were!

LIYAH: Better debates than you have!

CESAR: If you would ever do your homework you might know something!

At this point they begin to raise their voices, and I decide to intervene.

TEACHER: Have you heard what Liyah said?

CESAR: Yes.

TEACHER: Can you tell her how she defined democracy in Puritan New England?

CESAR: She said that the Puritans were democrats because they elected their leaders.

TEACHER: What is your response to that?

CESAR: But the ministers told the congregation what to think.

TEACHER: Liyah, can you respond to that?

LIYAH: How could they tell them what to think if there were debates?

CESAR: What debates?

TEACHER: Can both of you look at last night's reading and find a reference to debates in the text?

LIYAH: It says here...

TEACHER: What page? (*I motion to Cesar to look at his copy of the text.*)

LIYAH: Page 34...that when John Philips [minister of Salem] denounced the Puritan ministers of Boston, Governor Winthrop went to his church and debated with him. Then the Salem congregation voted to continue to have Philips as their minister.

TEACHER: So, Cesar, was the Salem congregation brainwashed?

CESAR: It was a setup. Philips and Winthrop put on a show!

LIYAH: No they didn't.

TEACHER: Is there anything in the text that can allow us to say one way or the other?

CESAR: Huh?

TEACHER: What other detail besides what Liyah read to us just now might indicate that Philips and Winthrop were in cahoots?

CESAR: Nothing!

LIYAH: I don't know?

TEACHER: But Philips was denouncing Winthrop, why would he denounce him to begin with?

CESAR: They fabricated it all to fool the congregation that there were debates.

Textual support may not have been there, but at least the argument of the detail that was available was developed in a more sophisticated manner than before my intervention.

I like to point out to students, at that moment, that what resolved the dispute was referring to the details of the text. That is a theme I like to repeat over and over all year so that going to the text becomes an instinctive reaction when they disagree with each other. If their instinct is to go to the text, they then must figure out what they are looking for, which in turn encourages them to define their terms. Insisting that there must be textual support for anything that is said prevents shouting matches. Of course, this technique risks stifling brainstorming, although generally there is so little discipline in the students' thinking that this is not a real danger. One can spot those students who become intimidated by the need for detail despite their superior command of it. The teacher must encourage those students to speak more freely. Once students internalize these rules, they begin to demand that other students follow them. There will be more frustration but fewer shouting matches of "I'm right," "No. I'm right!"

When I have misread the situation and intervened and the students point that out, I apologize and withdraw quickly. There is no point in intervening unless one maintains the cooperation of the students. One can't teach them not to browbeat each other in discussion by browbeating them into appropriate behavior. Modeling their behavior is crucial to the success of the process. Every intervention must be one that solicits the students' agreement with one's observations. On the other hand, one cannot allow the students to pursue tangents. Knowing when to get involved and when to back off is the art of intervention (and only learned from experience, learning from one's mistakes).

It is important to be concrete and consistent when one interrupts the group dynamic. Without clear goals and parameters the students lose respect for the process. If students understand what the limits of their freedom are they are surprisingly cooperative in tackling any task one asks of them. The rules that should be clearly stated and repeated often are: (1) that everyone must participate in the creation of the paragraph; (2) there must be respect for each other's ideas at all times; (3) while discussing what to write, the students must consistently refer to the text; and (4) the paragraph must have a thesis statement in the first sentence supported by detail that is argued in terms of the thesis.

Too often students will make a laundry list of detail instead of explaining how the detail supports the topic sentence. It is in the "arguing" that the students are being analytical. To do this, the students need to break down the terms of the topic sentences into parts small enough so the detail fits snugly. In the first paragraph below, the details are *listed*. In the second paragraph, the information is beginning to be *argued*. The term "discover" is defined by those words in italics. Defining terms is crucial to the process of analysis or, in other words, arguing the detail.

> Columbus did not discover America. He landed on Hispaniola in 1492. Arawaks greeted him. Columbus took many of them as slaves. Those that were not taken back to Spain, were made to look for gold. Every Arawak was responsible for filling a hawk's bell full of gold each month. If an Arawak failed to do so, the Spanish cut his or her hands off…

> Columbus did not discover America. Hispaniola was *already inhabited* by the Arawaks. They had been living there for centuries. Columbus *took their land away from them* by enslaving them. The Arawaks, *instead of working for themselves,* were forced to find gold for the Spanish…

If one student in the group is consistently silent or, worse, not listening, then the teacher needs to intervene. One way to involve the student is merely to pick up the paper on which the recorder is writing and give it to the uninvolved student, announcing that you have just made him or her the recorder. That will force the inattentive person to be involved. Another tactic, which depends on the nature of the group dynamic, is to sit down with the students and confront them with the fact that one member of the group is not involved and ask why. If neither tactic works, then one can sit down with the group and participate in the discussion, occasionally asking the uninvolved student to answer a question or respond to a statement. If the student begins to answer, ask for textual support if it has not been provided. The other students sometimes will leap to the defense of a student who is being "picked on" by the teacher, thus creating group unity that did not exist before.

The way most schools are structured, the teacher is in the position of adversary, especially if student work is graded. One can use that normally destructive role in a constructive way by allowing and encouraging students to unite against it. The groups hand in their paragraphs at the end of the allotted time period. I found it effective to grade the paragraphs on a point system as opposed to letter grades. I gave two points for homework assignments, so I decided to make the paragraphs worth four points, grading them (on a scale 0, 1, 2, 3, 4) according to the degree to which they support their thesis.

I have discovered that it is fairly useless to write comments on student work unless the students rewrite their work. In order to make the comments useful and to simultaneously ease the individual's responsibility to the group, I make photocopies of each paragraph for every member of the group. With his or her own copy of the group paragraph, the student can choose to rewrite the paragraph individually or with any number of members of the group. I allow them to hand in rewrites as many times as they would like. Rewriting individually is an option, since group rewriting means giving up more class time. And, insisting that students rewrite together outside of class seems to be placing an unreasonable burden on them. Unfortunately, most students have very little free time during the school day.

When I first assign a group paragraph in the beginning of the year, many of the students balk at being given a grade that is dependent on the group. They argue that it is unfair to give an individual a group grade. By allowing them to rewrite the paragraph individually, I defuse this sense of outrage that has been bred into them by their lack of experience in the benefits of cooperative learning.

One can encourage students to rewrite by increasing the point value of the paragraph. If this is done, it should be done from the very beginning of the year. It is important to keep the criteria for assessment consistent throughout the year. I have increased the weight of the group paragraph during the year, but only after explaining why. Changing the criteria without making the change explicit and giving a reasonable explanation for the change makes students see the assignment as arbitrary. This perception undermines any incentive students have for doing the work.

If one can incorporate group writing throughout the year and clearly state and consistently enforce the parameters within which students must operate, then students will learn how to work in groups on their own. Ultimately, little supervision will be needed. Students eventually exhibit a sense of purpose without supervision when they have experienced highly structured group work on a regular basis.

II. The Grading System

One's grading system has a great deal to do with how much students learn from an assignment. The most detrimental aspect of "grades" is that they act to inhibit. Students become afraid of making mistakes, even though mistakes are a fundamental part of the learning process. Many of the chapter questions in Zinn will not be fully explored by the students, will not provoke creative and critical thinking unless the teacher has a grading system that does not penalize the students for coming up with "wrong" answers. I have always found it effective to have part of the student's final grade be based on percentage of work completed, ignoring whether that work was done "correctly" or not. If and when a teacher does grade an assignment, students will learn a great deal from the opportunity to rewrite the assignment (assuming that the grading criteria is explicit, concrete, and consistently adhered to).

III. Extra Credit

I have heard teachers say: "I don't believe in extra credit." I don't think extra credit is a matter of faith, but it is a useful tool. Students do not all learn at the same rate and at the same time. There are plenty of students in tenth grade who are not ready to read about Puritans or Columbus or the New Deal. The more choices students have in what they study, the more they are likely to learn. I like to use extra credit to encourage students to read the newspaper. I give them the option of finding an article that relates to an issue in the course. They must hand in a copy of the article (or cut out the original). They also must hand in a paragraph that summarizes the article and explains the connection they see between the article and an issue that they have studied in the course. For a few students this has become an entire course in and of itself. It is part of my attempt to encourage students to see the connection between the past and the present.

If students wish to invent other kinds of extra credit assignments I encourage them to do so. As long as the assignment involves writing and making connections, I think it should be permitted. Some students need to find their own "hook" into history. By encouraging and rewarding creative extra credit assignments that are connected to the history, you are looking for that "hook." I have learned a great deal about how best to teach students from the students themselves. In a sense, I provide them with the structure that allows them to teach me how to teach them.

IV. Geography

Much has been made of students' lack of geographical knowledge and the need to remedy that. It certainly is important to know where the places are that one is reading about. But, again, what is important is only that which is relevant to the thesis. It is not particularly useful to know all the state capitals by heart. If students are asked to memorize the state capitals without being told the purpose of such work, then the lesson is meaningless to them.

Most of the chapter questions in Zinn have a geography question. Having the students actually draw freehand maps can get them into the habit of looking more closely at maps generally. Betty Edwards' *Drawing from the Right Side of the Brain* includes a chapter about how to teach yourself and others "contour drawing." As with all skills, the ability to draw a map takes practice. The first time you ask your students to draw a map, many will rebel, insisting that they can't draw. It would be a good idea to give them a lesson in contour drawing first. Or better yet, have an art teacher come into your class to give a lesson. Everyone can learn to draw. The benefits are manifold: students will have practice developing their right brain functions; they will have one more small piece of evidence that disciplines do not exist in isolation of each other; it will provide the naturally visual with some confidence building experiences; and it will provide a change of pace in what you do in the classroom every day.

In addition to having my students draw their own maps, whenever my class is in the midst of a discussion of a topic that involves geography, I will ask a student to get up from his or her seat, go to the relevant map on the wall of the classroom, and point out the places we have been discussing. It is very important for this process to be fun, even though it is serious work. If the topic were the Spanish-American War, for example, I would ask a student to point to the Philippines, Puerto Rico, Cuba, Guam, China, and Hawaii. As the student searches for Guam, say, encourage the class to help out, saying: "You are getting warmer" or "You are getting colder." That way the exercise seems less like learning geography than playing pin the tail on the donkey. Keep it light.

After the student has finished, I thank her and let her sit down. Then I call on another student (preferably one who was not paying attention) to perform the same task. I do this with several students, until they are able to find the places on the map without too much help from me or their peers. Then I explain (or better, ask a student to explain) the significance of the places. For example: "The Pacific islands were important stepping stones to China, and the United States was interested in developing coaling stations for its fleet, which would then be better able to protect U.S. trade with China." It is an informal, humorous, and painless way to learn geography, a method that allows more students to learn for a longer period of time than with traditional quizzes on paper. It eliminates that bad feeling of failing a quiz and the isolation that such activities engender. If one doesn't have a map on the wall, one can be drawn on the blackboard.

I often make the first geography "quiz" of the year into a game. I tell my students that there will be a quiz the next day on specific maps in their text. But, I don't tell them what kind of quiz. The students assume it will be like any other quiz they have ever had—a map and they must identify places on it. Instead, when they come to class the next day, I have drawn a map on the board. I explain that when I call a person's name and a geographical place, that person must go up to the board, take a piece of chalk and identify the place on the map with the chalk. Then, the student must sit down. The score will be based on how fast the student is able to get out of and return to his or her chair. I have a stopwatch and a list of names and places on my clipboard. I pretend to be serious and see for how long they will believe me. This serves two purposes. First, the students learn that teachers are capable of giving bizarre assignments and that students should regularly question the methods used by their teachers. Second, students learn that geography quizzes (and perhaps all quizzes) are a little silly.

v. Debates

I have provided at least one debate resolution per chapter, usually at the end of each chapter's questions.

I use the debate format as an additional change of pace in teaching students how to define terms and support their generalizations with detail. The structure I use is developed with this goal in mind. I divide the class in half. I usually ask the students to choose the side they wish to be on. If the students don't break themselves up evenly, I ask some students to switch sides so that the class is evenly divided. (It is always important to explain the purpose of your instructions.) Those who are asked to switch often complain. I explain to them that it is useful to have to argue a point of view that one does not hold. It helps one develop one's own argument better because then one understands the opposing argument much better. I usually give the class one night to prepare. I give them a resolution that is relevant to the previous night's reading or that night's reading. Before the debate begins, I explain the ground rules. The rules below are designed to encourage all students to speak. If they know they must participate eventually, then there is more incentive to listen and think. The rules alter the dynamic of class discussion in which a few students tend to monopolize the discussion.

1. Each student must speak once before anyone has a chance to speak twice. Those who have something to say before it is their turn need to take notes in order to remember what they want to say when it finally is their turn.

2. The two sides alternate turns. Two people on the same team may not speak sequentially.

3. Students must raise their hands if they wish to speak. I decide who speaks, giving preference to those students who do not readily participate in class discussion.

4. The only exception to rules 1 and 2 is if a student needs clarification of something that has just been said. In that case, then any student may ask for a "point of clarification." I will grant the floor to the student who asked the question. If the question and answer session turns into a cross-examination, I stop it. There is to be no cross-examination. (It takes too much time away from others who wish to speak.)

At the beginning of the year, I need to intervene in the debates frequently, by pointing out whether or not the detail is relevant or whether there is detail or not. I will even add rules to encourage the kind of quality that I want to see. For example, if the students are not using details from the reading, I might stipulate that no one may speak unless she incorporates a quotation from the text in support of what she is saying. Or, if students are consistently ignoring what the other team says, I might stipulate that no one may speak, except in response to what has already been said. If that doesn't work, I might further demand that the speaker name the student whose argument is being rebutted. I only resort to these rules, however, if there is a free flow of discussion that is devoid of analysis. As the teacher, one must always be sensitive to the fine line between inhibiting student participation and insisting that when students talk, they have something relevant and substantive to say. At times, I will even jump into the debate and help a student who is struggling with an argument and develop it for him or her. Or, I might jump into the debate and respond to an argument that needs to be challenged but is not being challenged by any student in the opposition.

The purpose of the debates is not to learn official debating skills and tactics but to create a situation in which the students must argue. Structured argument develops critical thinking. When I intervene in the debate I am doing so in order to encourage the students to define their terms and support their arguments with detail from the text. The informal debate format forces some students to speak who do not do so in a free-flowing class discussion. Of course, I don't "force" everyone to speak. If there are students who cannot, then I let them pass. Students who refuse to speak in tenth grade may end up as irrepressible orators in college. People develop at very different rates, and that needs acknowledgement in the flexibility of one's "system."

If the debate resolutions prove difficult for the students to work with, don't give up on the resolutions. Break down the process even further into smaller steps, assign one step at a time and build up their skills. The best place to start is defining the terms of the debate resolution. Then there is data collection. Depending on the skill level of your class, you might have to teach students how to find data , how to take notes, and how to skim. If individuals are having trouble, put them into groups. The important thing is to not give up. The assignment may take longer to complete than you expected, but it can be completed. In completing the assignment, students will develop crucial skills, not to mention the fact that they will actually remember the content past the next test.

VI. Class Discussion

When I first started to teach, a master teacher once advised me that to have a good class discussion, one must start off the class with a "big" question. The question was so big that one did not expect the students to have an answer for it until the end of the class period. One asked it in the beginning, so the students knew where the discussion was leading. After beginning class by asking the big question, one would immediately follow it up with sub questions that would lead students to develop different parts of an argument that would then be drawn together at the end of class to answer the big question. Any of the the debate resolutions can function as the "big question." For example, "Was Watergate the result of a flawed president?" Never expect an immediate answer to such a "big" question. Have follow-up questions prepared in advance to explore different parts of the question.

* ★ What was Watergate?
* ★ Was is it only the burglary?
* ★ How long did the cover-up last?
* ★ Was Nixon flawed?
* ★ Did he make any mistakes during his presidency?
* ★ Were those mistakes the result of character defects?
* ★ Who else made mistakes during Nixon's administration?
* ★ Can we blame only Nixon? Or is the system at fault?

After exploring these follow-up questions, then one poses the "big" question again at the end of class. This provides structure to the class discussion, which is important if one wants to encourage students to become systematic in their thinking. One doesn't always have to rigidly adhere to the "big" question, but when students go off on tangents, it is important to identify them as such and then return to the original topic of conversation. Becoming self-conscious of what is relevant and what is not is crucial to the development of critical thinking. I had one student, recently, who was so right brained that she could rarely contribute to the topic at hand. I commissioned her as the "tangent police." She was so taken with her title that she became excellent at announcing to the class every time I ever went off on a tangent.

Another technique that I have found useful in developing critical thinking is to start class by asking the students to identify (by writing them down) the two most important "facts" from the previous night's reading. After most of the students are done, I ask students to volunteer their answers, defending why they think their choices are important. This allows for a discussion as to what determines "importance" (if it supports the author's thesis or if it supports a particular interest or axe that the student wants to grind). This makes everyone more self-conscious about how subjective the selection process is. It helps students develop a sense of what is important to them. It also allows for a discussion as to what a fact is and is not. After several classes devoted to this specific exercise, I found that my tenth-grade students began to appreciate the difference between a generalization and a piece of detail. "Columbus sailed for profit" is a generalization, while "His contract was to receive 10 percent of the profits from the voyage" is detail. Most students need to be taught the distinction.

If students are particularly resistant to structured class discussion as described above, one can loosen them up in the following manner. Start a class out with what is usually the worst question you can ask: What did you think about the reading? Did you like it or not, why or why not? These questions are merely to get the students to speak. It is what you do with what they say that is crucial in getting a discussion going on the historical material.

TEACHER: How did you like the reading last night?

STUDENT: This reading sucked!

TEACHER: What does "sucked" mean?

STUDENT: It means "stinks."

TEACHER: In what way did it stink?

STUDENT: It was boring.

TEACHER: Why?

STUDENT: Because I fell asleep reading it.

TEACHER: What was it that put you to sleep?

STUDENT: Well, I didn't understand it.

TEACHER: Any of it?

STUDENT: Well, what did this guy mean when he said… [At this point you are off and running!]

VII. Using Drama in the Classroom

Gavin Bolton has written several books and offers workshops on how to use drama in the classroom. I highly recommend his techniques, since they provide one more teaching technique that contributes to variety in the classroom (as well as appealing to one of the variety of learning styles). He distinguishes between "forming" and "performing." "Forming" is for the benefit of the actors involved and not for the benefit of an audience.

Students divide up into pairs and act out just with each other conversations that might have happened between historical actors, such as between a factory girl and her foreman in 1840.

Role plays are very easy to develop on one's own. Put Columbus on trial. Have a news reporter interview, on live television, an indentured servant, a slave, a merchant, and a planter giving their opinions on the growing body of legislation governing servants and slaves in Virginia (c. 1832). Have the class turn into Congress and have them introduce bills addressing the role lobbyists play in the political process. The possibilities are endless.

VIII. Students Teaching Other Students

This is a principle I try to employ as much as possible. Students are teaching each other when they participate in group paragraphs, in dramatic exercises, debates, and class discussions. Yet they can do so in many other situations as well. I have my students actually go out and teach a class about Columbus to younger students. This gives the potentially arid assignment of creating a third-grade Columbus curriculum a tremendous amount of zip and excitement. Instead of the teacher lecturing, students individually or by groups can give oral reports. I know many teachers who don't want to do this because they feel that they can't cover enough material or that the students won't teach the material the way the teacher wants it taught. But these objections are based on the assumption that what the teacher says is what the students hear. This assumption needs to be more closely examined.

I used to lecture until I discovered that many of the students did not understand the material in the way I presented it. There were too many different learning styles among the students for me to match up with all of them. The students do not present material in the manner I would want them to, but they learn much more in the process than if I had presented the material my way. Not only do they learn content but they undergo mental and emotional development. When student teachers return to their roles as students, they have had an experience that alters the dynamic of the classroom. The ex-student teachers, because they have had to wrestle with the preparation of a lesson, with the frustration of trying to make their peers pay attention to and understand what they were presenting, begin to feel more compassionate toward or connected with the teacher. Yet, at the same time, because they were in the teacher's shoes for a moment, they often become more critical of the teacher as well. Their consciences and consciousness are raised on many levels. This helps them to become more sophisticated thinkers. One student came back to visit me after he had gone to college and told me that one of the most important and memorable days in our American history course was the day that he was responsible for telling the story of the Cuban Missile Crisis. The first time he gave the report, he was confused. I made him do it again the next day. He had to go home that night and reread the text. The next day, he delivered a clear and accurate report. He had *gained ownership* over that story in a way he never would have had he merely read it in preparation for a traditional test or listened to a teacher present it. But, he was not impressed with the content he learned. He was impressed with the lesson it taught him about the most effective way to teach himself. He felt that lesson helped him succeed in college. He also felt very good about himself because he had been able to master material he had never thought himself capable of mastering before. Most students have grown passive and given up responsibility for their own learning after sitting through years of lectures. They need to be given the responsibility of teaching themselves and others in a situation in which they know they will be supported and encouraged but not bailed out.

Appendix B

Textbook Interpretations of Bacon's Rebellion (1676)

Kathy Emery

A typical assignment that I gave my students, when I used multiple textbooks, involved a series of questions about a specific event. Below are a list of six textbooks that I have used in the classroom. You can achieve similar results with any set of textbooks. They differ inherently. The page numbers refer to those pages devoted to describing the events leading to and including Bacon's Rebellion. Also listed below are the questions I asked my students when the assigned event was Bacon's Rebellion. I have answered the first question—"What was Berkeley's Indian policy and his reasons for such a policy?"—to illustrate the degree to which the textbooks differ from one another.

Textbooks:

> BAILEY and KENNEDY, *The American Pageant,* DC Heath and Co., Lexington, Massachusetts, 1983, pp. 13–14.
>
> NASH AND JEFFREY, *The American People,* HarperCollins, N.Y., 1986, pp. 76–78.
>
> NORTON ET AL., *A People and a Nation,* Houghton Mifflin, Boston, Massachusetts, 1986, p. 49.
>
> UNGER, *These United States,* Little, Brown, Boston, Massachusetts, 1982, pp. 67–69.

WEINSTEIN AND GATTELL, *Freedom and Crisis*, Random House, N.Y., 1981, p. 49.

WILLIAMS AND FREIDEL, *American History: A Survey*, Alfred A. Knopf, N.Y., 1979, p. 43.

WILSON AND GILBERT, *The Pursuit of Liberty*, Alfred A. Knopf, N.Y., 1984, pp. 39–55.

Questions for readings on Bacon's Rebellion:

★ What was Berkeley's Indian policy and his reasons for such a policy?

★ Why did the frontiersmen attack Indians?

★ Why did the frontiersmen attack Jamestown?

★ What event led Berkeley to declare Bacon a rebel?

★ Is there a hero in the story? If so, who is it and why?

★ Why did Bacon become a leader of the frontiersmen?

★ What is the historical significance of Bacon's Rebellion?

Analysis of question: What was Berkeley's Indian policy and his reasons for such a policy?

I have retrieved information from each text that is relevant to the question of Berkeley's policy toward the Indians and his reasons behind such a policy.

★ Bailey and Kennedy: Berkeley "...allegedly involved in the fur trade with the Indians, was unwilling to antagonize them by fighting back."

★ Nash and Jeffrey: The 1646 treaty with the Powhatans forbade white settlement beyond the territory north of the York river; "...stable Indian relations suited the established planters." White settlers attacked the Susquehannocks. When the Susquehannocks attacked white encroachment on their land, Berkeley denounced the whites' subsequent retaliatory raid.

★ Norton et al.: Berkeley "...hoped to avoid setting off a major war like that raging in New England."

★ Unger: When violence broke out between Indians and white frontier settlers in 1675, Berkeley decided on defensive measures, ordering "whites to withdraw from areas near Indian land and locate behind a line of forts..." Berkeley "offered good pay to farmers to enroll as soldiers..." and he built frontier forts. But building forts meant higher taxes, and it increased the value of the wealthy estates on which they were to be built.

★ Weinstein and Gattell: "When Indian warfare broke out on the frontier," Berkeley "called for restraint."

★ Williams and Freidel: In 1644, Berkeley opened up the frontier to settlement, sending explorers and an army. The defeated Indians signed a treaty "ceding all the land between the York and James Rivers to the east of the fall line, and prohibiting white settlement to the west of that line." But, the ever increasing English population pushed into Indian territory, causing increasing number of violent clashes. "Berkeley preferred not to antagonize the Indians." He and his "associates were profiting from a large scale trade with them." Berkeley ordered the militia to guard the edge of the settlement.

★ Wilson and Gilbert: "Berkeley was outraged by the open murder of the Susquehannah chiefs." He "wanted a policy of peace and order that would protect the friendly tribes and the beaver trade. He also wanted Indian policy to rest in the hands of the government at Jamestown, not in the hands of hundreds of small planters scattered along the edges of the wilderness." Berkeley declared war on the Indians, formed a militia, and started to build forts. He ordered the militia to patrol between the forts. Any attack on the Indians needed the governor's permission. Berkeley wanted to distinguish between those Indians who were abiding by the rules of treaties and those who were not.

When one compares the different versions of Bacon's Rebellion, one is immediately struck by the difference in interpretation and kind of information provided. For example, Weinstein and Gattell define Berkeley's policy but not the reason behind it, while Norton identifies Berkeley's reasons but not his policy. Bailey and Kennedy cast doubt on Berkeley's involvement in the "fur trade," while Williams and Freidel state that Berkeley was profiting directly from such trade. Nash and Jeffrey imply that Berkeley's Indian policy of restraint was morally grounded, while Wilson and Gilbert see constitutional and practical reasons for Berkeley's policy.

Is Berkeley using his position as governor to enrich himself and his cronies at the expense of poor frontiersmen? Or is Berkeley valiantly trying to negotiate peace between greedy frontiersmen and irate Indians? Depending on which text one reads, one either cannot answer these questions, or one can have a definite opinion one way or the other. It is in reading all six versions that a more complex, less simplistic answer is available. The real lesson here is that the more detail one has, the more likely one will be close to the truth of what happened. The process of sifting through different versions of the same event is the process that develops critical thinking. An open and healthy debate over these questions allows students to discover how to think for themselves and not rely on external opinions solely.

Appendix C

Additional Resources

Kathy Emery

The criteria I used in identifying the books, articles, and videos below are as follows: smooth diction; clear thesis; lots of detailed support explained clearly in terms of the thesis; challenges mainstream traditional version of American history; good supplementary reading to Zinn. There are, of course, many other titles that are useful. I only included those that I think are of the highest quality and the most useful in supporting the curriculum I have proposed.

Books

★ VERY READABLE
★★ CHALLENGING FOR HIGH SCHOOL STUDENTS
★★★ FOR TEACHER'S USE ONLY
★★★★ EXTRAORDINARY BUT DIFFICULT TO READ
    BECAUSE OF THE COMPLEXITY OF THE THESIS
    OR THE USE OF ESOTERIC JARGON

★ BELL, DERRICK, *Faces at the Bottom of the Well*, Basic Books, New York, 1992 (a series of disparate stories, some fact, some fiction, illustrating the complexities of modern day racism; readable, challenging, and provocative).

★ Brown, Dee, *Bury My Heart at Wounded Knee*, Henry, Holt and Company, New York, 1991 (a graphic and gripping account of the brutal invasion of Europeans into Indian territory west of the Mississippi from 1860 until the final defeat in 1890).

★★ Catton, Bruce, *This Hallowed Ground*, Simon and Schuster, New York, 1961 (his abridged three-volume history of the Civil War).

★★★★ Chomsky, Noam, *Year 501: The Conquest Continues*, South End Press, Boston, 1993 (a post–World War II history of American foreign policy; an excellent companion to Ehrenreich's domestic study; makes explicit what LaFeber implies; see also Chomsky's interview with Bill Moyers, PBS video).

★ Cluster, Dick, ed., *They Should Have Served That Cup of Coffee*, South End Press, Boston, 1979 (clear and concise oral testimonies of seven radicals of the 1960s, especially good ones on the activity of the Black Panthers and the growth of the women's movement).

★★★ D'Emilio, John, *Sexual Politics, Sexual Communities*, University of Chicago Press, 1984 (comprehensive history of the gay rights movement; the transformation of homosexual behavior before World War II and the emergence of a homosexual identity after World War II).

★★ DuBois, Ellen C., and Ruiz, Vicki L., eds., *Unequal Sisters*, Routledge, New York, 1990 (sophisticated articles about specific events and issues affecting women in American history; an excellent text for a women's history elective).

★ Duiker, William J., *Introduction to Vietnam, History and Culture*, The Lessons of the Vietnam War Series, Pittsburgh Center for Social Studies Education, 1991(very readable, concise but not simplistic chronology of the war).

★★★ Ehrenreich, Barbara, *Fear of Falling*, HarperPerennial, New York, 1990 (a socioeconomic study of American history since World War II, with a particularly excellent analysis of labor and women; a provocative twist to Zinn's paradigm).

★★ Goodwyn, Lawrence, *The Populist Moment*, Oxford University Press, New York, 1978 (a detailed analysis of the growth of the Grange and Alliance movements culminating in the Democratic Convention of 1896; the story of a courageous grassroots, biracial movement whose leaders were co-opted and whose power was in the end eviscerated by the power elites).

★ GORNICK, LARRY, *The Cartoon History of the United States*, HarperPerennial, New York, 1991 (it is always good to add humor, but "to get" some of the jokes one must already be familiar with the material; having students explain what's so funny would be a legitimate test of their knowledge of the actual history).

★ GORNICK, VIVIAN, *The Romance of American Communism*, Harper-Collins, New York (unfortunately, it is out of print; it is an eloquently written book detailing why people became, remained and no longer were communists; the reasons transcend theory, worth tracking down in libraries or used book stores).

★ HEIMOWITZ AND WEISSMAN, *Women in American History*, Bantam, New York, 1990 (a popular way to introduce women's history to high school students).

★ HERTZBERG, ARTHUR, *The Jews in America*, Touchstone, New York, 1990 (a good overview; some nice detail).

★★ HOFSTADER, RICHARD, *The American Political Tradition*, Vintage, New York, 1974 (cited often by Zinn; a series of biographies of presidents who presided over watershed periods in American history; the first chapter is especially good at providing evidence that the last thing the Founding Fathers wanted to create was a democracy; compelling biographies of Andrew Jackson and the two Roosevelts).

★ KOVIC, RON, *Born on the Fourth of July*, Pocket Books, New York, 1989 (the memoir on which the Oliver Stone/Tom Cruise movie was based).

★★★★ LAFEBER, WALTER, *America, Russia and the Cold War*, McGraw - Hill, New York, 1996 (incredible detail supporting his thesis that the United States created the cold war in order to convince the American people to financially support a foreign policy that would guarantee world markets for American goods).

★★ LOEWEN, JAMES W., *Lies My Teacher Told Me: Everything Your American History Textbook Got Wrong*, The New Press, New York, 1994 (an iconoclastic look at the errors, misrepresentations, and omissions in the leading American history textbooks).

★ MARTINEZ, ELIZABETH, *500 Years of Chicano History*, Albuquerque Southwest Organizing Project, 1991 (photos and text; indispensable for filling this gap in traditional history).

★★★ MERCHANT, CAROLYN, *The Death of Nature*, HarperSanFrancisco, 1990 (an analysis of the development of a European worldview arising out the Scientific Revolution, which explains why Europeans wanted to explore the New World and could massacre its innocent and peaceful people).

★★★★ MORGAN, EDMUND, *American Slavery, American Freedom*, W. W. Norton and Company, New York, 1996 (cited by Zinn; a beautifully constructed argument with persuasive detail; an in-depth analysis of why and how indentured servants were used as labor by the Virginian Company and why indentured servants were replaced with African slaves; a close look at how class prejudice and then racism were deliberately created as a divide-and-conquer technique).

★★ MORGAN, EDMUND, *The Puritan Dilemma*, HarperCollins, New York, 1987 (biography of John Winthrop, using his life and writings as a microcosm to explore the dynamics of Puritan society and ideology; excellent chapters on Anne Hutchinson and Roger Williams; explodes the Puritan myth created by Hawthorne).

★ NASH, GARY, *Red, White, and Black*, Prentice Hall, Englewood Cliffs, New Jersey, 1991 (a look at the development of the English colonies in North America as a dynamic among Indians, Europeans, and Africans).

★★ SALE, KIRKPATRICK, *The Conquest of Paradise*, NAL/Dutton, New York, 1991 (Columbus was not the great sailor Morison has made him out to be; Spain knew exactly what they were doing in sending Columbus to the New World; interesting connections made between European conditions at the time and the voyages and experiences of Columbus as well as the English in Virginia).

★ SCHIRMER, DANIEL AND SHALOM, STEPHEN, EDS., *The Philippines Reader*, South End Press, Boston, 1987 (a compendium of original sources; useful and unusually concrete information about the Filipino experience under Spanish rule; excellent source material for studying the Spanish-American War).

★★ STAMPP, KENNETH, *The Era of Reconstruction*, Random House, New York, 1967 (explores and explodes the myths of the traditional version of Southern history from 1865 to 1877 established by William A. Dunning and D. W. Griffith).

★ TAKAKI, RONALD T., *Strangers from a Different Shore* (revised edition), Little, Brown & Company, New York, 1998 (the Asian influence and role of Asian immigrants and their progeny in American history; a story given short shrift even in Zinn's text).

★ TERKEL, STUDS, *American Dreams: Lost and Found*, The New Press, New York, 1980 (another of Terkel's oral histories; excellent evidence of all that Zinn describes; see other titles by Terkel).

★★★ WOOD, PETER, *Black Majority*, W. W. Norton and Company, New York, 1996 (the story of the creation of racism in Charleston, South Carolina; an interesting contrast to how it developed in Jamestown, Virginia; a very close study of slavery in colonial America).

Articles

★★ AJAMI, FOUAD, "The Other 1492," *The New Republic*, April 6, 1992 (connects the expulsion of the Jews from Spain with Columbus's mission).

★★ CHOMSKY, NOAM, "Media Control," *Open Magazine*, pamphlet 10 (how the media engineer public opinion).

★★★★ HAYS, SAMUEL, "The Politics of Reform in Municipal Government in the Progressive Era," In eds. Dinnerstein, Leonard, and Kenneth T. Jackson, *American Vistas*, Oxford University Press, New York, seventh edition, 1994 (detailed account, with plenty of evidence, of how the municipal reforms of the Progressives succeeded in eliminating the influence of the working class in city government; connects well with *Who Will Tell the People?* and *The Times of Harvey Milk*; at large elections versus ward representation, as well as with Chomsky's "Media Control").

★★★★ JACKSON, KENNETH T., "Race, Ethnicity, and Real Estate Appraisal," In eds. Dinnerstein, Leonard, and Kenneth T. Jackson, *American Vistas*, Oxford University Press, New York, seventh edition, 1994 (an analysis of the New Deal programs HOLC and FHA; how their policies set the stage for redlining—segregated housing according to race and ethnicity; the effects of these policies can be seen in the PBS/Frontline video *Crisis on Federal Street*; this article is also an excellent companion piece to Bell's *Faces*).

Videos: *Documentaries*

Attica (a vivid account of the 1971 prison uprising, giving a powerful picture of prison conditions in our society).

Before Stonewall (a history of the creation of the gay and lesbian community from the 1920s until 1965; John D'Emilio would call it the description of the transformation from homosexual behavior to homosexual identity).

Broken Rainbow (an exposé of the supposed border dispute between the Navajo and Hopi tribes in the 1970s; the film reveals the roles that the Peabody Coal Company and the U.S. government played in taking away the land and livelihood of the Indians).

Crisis on Federal Street (PBS/*Frontline*: a history of public housing projects and welfare in Chicago; reveals the racial politics of the projects and describes the grassroots activism that has emerged to combat the problems created by federal housing policy).

Grenada (PBS/*Frontline* investigation into the reasons for the invasion of Grenada and the results of the invasion; a microcosm of American foreign policy).

The Gulf War (a PBS/*Frontline* investigation of the causes and effects of the Persian Gulf War).

Harlan County U. S. A. (documentary of the 1977 coal miners' strike in Kentucky; reveals the complex interplay of union politics and practices, the role of women, Wall Street, and the policies and tactics of the Peabody Coal company; Peabody Coal figures prominently in *Broken Rainbow*).

Metropolitan Avenue (an oral history and documentary footage of the grassroots activism in opposing the building of the Brooklyn-Queens Expressway; the effect of the needs and power of suburbia on the culture of an urban neighborhood in Brooklyn).

Out of the Depths: A Miner's Story (a Bill Moyers/PBS oral history of the events preceding, during, and following the Ludlow Massacre).

Roger and Me and its sequel *Pets or Meat* (the complexity of class prejudice and discrimination; the damage done by the layoff of automobile workers in the late 1970s; heartbreaking story told with humor).

Rosie the Riveter (oral history of women who worked in the factories during World War II; how they were seduced and betrayed).

Seeing Red (an oral history of the American Communist movement from the 1930s through the 1950s; excellent documentary footage of the depression era and the McCarthy hearings; follow-up interviews and footage as to what these old communists are doing today; a video version of Vivian Gornick's book).

The Times of Harvey Milk (an award-winning chronicle of how the first openly gay public official in the United States got elected; an exploration of why he was shot; evidence of the power of grassroots organization and the temporary overcoming of the power elite's divide-and-conquer methods; a connection to Hays's article on municipal reform—Milk was able to be elected when elections for seats on the Board of Supervisors once again were ward-based instead of at-large).

Union Maids (several women who were labor organizers in the 1930s recall the struggle of those years).

The War at Home (a long, valuable documentary on the growth of the anti–Vietnam war movement; uses the University of Wisconsin at Madison as the microcosm of the larger movement; incredible footage of hearings, interviews, riots, and demonstrations).

Who Will Tell the People? (a PBS / *Frontline* production of William Greider's book of same title; Greider argues that politics has become less democratic in the last thirty years; embroiders on Zinn's bipartisan consensus theory; lots of compelling detail).

With Babies and Banners (the GM strike in Flint, Michigan, with attention to the crucial role played by women).

The Wrath of Grapes (the social and environmental impact of mass production of grapes; includes the successful attempts to organize workers and boycotts by the United Farm Workers and the effects of pesticides on those who live near grape farms).

Videos: *Fiction*

The Grapes of Wrath (a good accompaniment to the *Wrath of Grapes*— stars Henry Fonda).

Matewan (John Sayles's account of a 1920s strike which highlights the difficulties and successes of organizing a multiethnic workforce for the purposes of collective bargaining).

The Mission (Jeremy Irons and Robert DeNiro; post-Columbian colonial expansion by Spain in South America; conflict between Portugal and Spain over boundaries in the American colonies).

Normae Rae (a moving account of textile workers in the south).

Panther (the beginning and end of the Black Panther organization; most of the story takes place in Oakland; critical of both the Panthers and the U.S. government).

Straight Out of Brooklyn (the obstacles in trying to get out of the ghetto in the 1980s—in this instance, Red Hook, Brooklyn).

X (Spike Lee's biography of Malcolm X).

Bloom's Taxonomy

Kathy Emery

I have adapted the following from Benjamin S. Bloom's Taxonomy of Educational Objectives, a Longman publication, 1984. Bloom believes that the taxonomy defined below can help teachers teach their students the skills needed for the highest levels of thinking. He categorizes cognitive skills into six categories: knowledge, comprehension, application, analysis, synthesis, and evaluation.

The taxonomy is hierarchical; skills in one category are likely to be built on skills in preceding categories. The skill categories are arranged in order of complexity (the number of prerequisite cognitions and skills) but need not imply increasing difficulty for students. With the proper content, students at all grade levels can exhibit behaviors at all six levels. The degree of difficulty can be manipulated or determined within each category by such factors as:

★ student's readiness

★ student's ability

★ amount of data given for task

★ number of steps involved in the task

★ time constraints on the task

★ mode of presentation to the students

★ student's prior experience

★ how concrete or abstract the content is

★ student's attitude

★ quantity of work given

Level One: Knowledge

Description
Knowledge of specifics, of ways or means of dealing with specifics, of the universals and abstractions in a field; ability to remember (recognition or recall) facts, names, places, trends, methods, sequence, categories, and previously learned generalizations or theories.

Verbs for Writing Objectives
Tell, list, cite, choose, arrange, find, group, label, select, match, locate, name, offer, omit, pick, quote, repeat, reset, say, show, sort, spell, touch, write, underline, point to, tally, transfer, underline, recite, identify, hold, and check.

Level Two: Comprehension

Description
Comprehension by translation (changing information into one's own words), interpretation (reordering ideas, and establishing relationships), extrapolation (making appropriate inferences based on given data); ability to know what is being communicated.

Verbs for Writing Objectives
Translate: change, reword, construe, render, convert, expand, transform, alter, vary, retell, qualify, moderate, and restate.
Interpret: infer, define, explain, construe, spell out, outline, annotate, expound, and account for.
Extrapolate: project, propose, advance, contemplate, submit, offer, calculate, scheme, and contrive.

Level Three: Application

Description
Using general ideas, rules, procedures, or generalized methods; ability to transfer learning, to solve problems by remembering and applying concepts, generalizations, and appropriate skills with little or no direction given.

Verbs for Writing Objectives
Relate, utilize, solve, adopt, employ, use, avail, capitalize on, consume, exploit, profit by, mobilize, operate, ply, handle, manipulate, exert, exercise, try, devote, handle, wield, put in action, put to use, make use of, and take up.

Level Four: Analysis

Description
Studying of elements and their relationships or organizational principles; ability to break down an idea into its component parts and examine the relationship or organization of the parts to the whole.

Verbs for Writing Objectives
Break down, uncover, look into, dissect, examine, take apart, divide, simplify, reason, include, deduce, syllogize, check, audit, inspect, section, canvass, scrutinize, sift, assay, test for, survey, search, study, check, and screen.

Level Five: Synthesis

Description
By communicating, developing a plan, proposing a set of operations, developing a set of abstract relations; ability to put together parts to form a whole, to solve a problem using creative thinking that produces an end result not clearly there before.

Verbs for Writing Objectives
Create, combine, build, compile, make, structure, reorder, reorganize, develop, produce, compose, construct, blend, yield, breed cause, effect, generate, evolve, mature, make up, form, constitute, originate, conceive, and formulate.

Level Six: Evaluation

Description
Ability to make a judgment or assessment of good or bad, right or wrong according to external or internal standards/criteria.

Verbs for Writing Objectives
Judge, decide, rate, appraise, assay, rank, weight, accept, reject, determine, assess, reject, and criticize.

Examples of Objectives

Knowledge
Given background information, students will list the characteristics of each of the three branches of the federal government.

Comprehension
1. Translation: Students will explain the main functions of each of the three branches of the federal government.
2. Interpretation: Given a data revival chart of the characteristics of the three branches of the federal government, students will identify the similarities and differences of each.
3. Extrapolation: Given a discussion of the similarities and differences between the three branches of federal government, students will write two generalizations concerning the need for these similarities and differences.

Application
Given background information on the role of the Constitution as it relates to the government, students will develop as a group a classroom Constitution.

Analysis
Given three articles written about present presidential candidates, students will distinguish the bias of each author.

Synthesis
Students will design, prepare, organize, and conduct a survey related to the role of government in America.

Evaluation
Given background information, students will prepare a debate either pro or con concerning the amount of control the federal government should exert on the citizens of the country.

Examples of Questions

Knowledge
1. Who was the president of the United States during the Civil War?
2. List the major rivers of China.

Comprehension
1. Translation: Explain the changes that have taken place in Japan since World War II.
2. Interpretation: Compare the systems of government in the United States and the Soviet Union. How are they alike? Different?
3. Extrapolation: Given the data on immigration from 1880–1980, what trend do you see emerging? What do you predict will happen as a result of this trend?

Application

1. Using a map of the United Sates, how would you plan a car trip from Summit, New Jersey, to San Francisco? Include in your plan estimated costs and a time line.
2. How would you show that the period in U.S. history from 1855–60 is similar or dissimilar to the period from 1964–69?
3. Now that you have read about the Middle Ages, how would you develop a plan for building a model of a castle?
4. After interviewing your classmates concerning their ethnic origins, how would you illustrate your finding?

Analysis

1. Third World Countries, particularly in Africa, that cannot afford to pay for oil imports are running out of supplies of firewood. Forests, the most important source of traditional energy, are being depleted at an average of six million acres a year. This situation is especially serious in Africa where it's hastening the spread of deserts. To correct this situation these countries need money to pay for reforestation, domestic oil and gas production, and other energy resources. Is the last sentence a correct conclusion? Why?
2. What motives influenced attempts by the United States to reestablish diplomatic ties with Communist China?
3. Sally has lived in more states than Sha-Ron. Sha-Ron has lived in fewer states than Maria. Who has lived in more states?

Synthesis

1. Political violence in Central America continues to spread. In Guatemala, for example, violence on both the left and the right has polarized society. What possible plans for bringing together these groups can you propose?
2. If Thomas Jefferson could return, how would he view America today?
3. Economic development in developing nations of the world has been slow. You are a member of the United Nations General Assembly, what plan for a restructured world economy can you propose that will provide for the accelerated and sustained economic development of these countries?

Evaluation

1. The young people of Summit, New Jersey, have indicated that they would like Roosevelt School to be converted to a skating rink. How do you evaluate this proposal in terms of cost and community acceptance?
2. What characteristics do you feel a superior president should have? Have the last two presidents been superior?
3. For what reasons would you favor or disfavor an Equal Rights Amendment to the Constitution?

Bibliography

Howard Zinn

This book, written in a few years, is based on twenty years of teaching and research in American history, and as many years of involvement in social movements. But it could not have been written without the work of several generations of scholars, and especially the current generation of historians who have done important work in the history of blacks, Indians, women, and working people of all kinds. It also could not have been written without the work of many people, not professional historians, who were stimulated by the social struggles around them to put together material about the lives and activities of ordinary people trying to make a better life, or just trying to survive.

To indicate every source of information in the text would have meant a book impossibly cluttered with footnotes, and yet I know the curiosity of the reader about where a startling fact or pungent quote comes from. Therefore, as often as I can, I mention in the text authors and titles of books for which the full information is in this bibliography. Where you cannot tell the source of a quotation right from the text, you can probably figure it out by looking at the asterisked books for that chapter. The asterisked books are those I found especially useful and often indispensable.

I have gone through the following standard scholarly periodicals: *American Historical Review, Mississippi Valley Historical Review, Journal of American History, Journal of Southern History, Journal of Negro History, Labor History, William and Mary Quarterly, Phylon, The Crisis, American Political Science Review, Journal of Social History.*

Also, some less orthodox but important periodicals for a work like this: *Monthly Review, Science and Society, Radical America, Akwesasne Notes, Signs: Journal of Women in Culture and Society, The Black Scholar, Bulletin of Concerned Asian Scholars, The Review of Radical Political Economics, Socialist Revolution, Radical History Review.*

Chapter 1
Columbus, the Indians, and Human Progress

BRANDON, WILLIAM. *The Last Americans: The Indian in American Culture.* New York: McGraw-Hill, 1974.

*COLLIER, JOHN. *Indians of the Americas.* New York: W. W. Norton, 1947.

*DE LAS CASAS, BARTOLOMÉ. *History of the Indies.* New York: Harper & Row, 1971.

*JENNINGS, FRANCIS. *The Invasion of America: Indians, Colonialism, and the Cant of Conquest.* Chapel Hill: University of North Carolina Press, 1975.

*KONING, HANS. *Columbus: His Enterprise.* New York: Monthly Review Press, 1976.

*MORGAN, EDMUND S. *American Slavery, American Freedom: The Ordeal of Colonial Virginia.* New York: W. W. Norton, 1975.

MORISON, SAMUEL ELIOT. *Admiral of the Ocean Sea.* Boston: Little, Brown, 1942.

————. *Christopher Columbus, Mariner.* Boston: Little, Brown, 1955.

*NASH, GARY B. *Red, White and Black: The Peoples of Early America.* Englewood Cliffs, N.J.: Prentice-Hall, 1970.

VOGEL, VIRGIL, ED. *This Country Was Ours.* New York: Harper & Row, 1971.

Chapter 2
Drawing the Color Line

*APTHEKER, HERBERT, ED. *A Documentary History of the Negro People in the United States.* New York: Citadel, 1974.

BOSKIN, JOSEPH. *Into Slavery: Radical Decisions in the Virginia Colony.* Philadelphia: Lippincott, 1966.

Bibliography

CATTERALL, HELEN. *Judicial Cases Concerning American Slavery and the Negro*, 5 vols. Washington, D.C.: Negro University Press, 1937.

DAVIDSON, BASIL. *The African Slave Trade*. Boston: Little, Brown, 1961.

DONNAN, ELIZABETH, ED. *Documents Illustrative of the History of the Slave Trade to America*, 4 vols. New York: Octagon, 1965.

ELKINS, STANLEY. *Slavery: A Problem in American Institutional and Intellectual Life*. Chicago: University of Chicago Press, 1976.

FEDERAL WRITERS PROJECT. *The Negro in Virginia*. New York: Arno, 1969.

FRANKLIN, JOHN HOPE. *From Slavery to Freedom: A History of American Negroes*. New York: Knopf, 1974.

*JORDAN, WINTHROP. *White Over Black: American Attitudes Toward the Negro, 1550–1812*. Chapel Hill: University of North Carolina Press, 1968.

*MORGAN, EDMUND S. *American Slavery, American Freedom: The Ordeal of Colonial Virginia*. New York: W. W. Norton, 1975.

MULLIN, MICHAEL, ED. *American Negro Slavery: A Documentary History*. New York: Harper & Row, 1975.

PHILLIPS, ULRICH B. *American Negro Slavery: A Survey of the Supply, Employment and Control of Negro Labor as Determined by the Plantation Regime*. Baton Rouge: Louisiana State University Press, 1966.

REDDING, J. SAUNDERS. *They Came in Chains*. Philadelphia: Lippincott, 1973.

STAMPP, KENNETH M. *The Peculiar Institution*. New York: Knopf, 1956.

TANNENBAUM, FRANK. *Slave and Citizen: The Negro in the Americas*. New York: Random House, 1963.

Chapter 3
Persons of Mean and Vile Condition

ANDREWS, CHARLES, ED. *Narratives of the Insurrections 1675–1690*. New York: Barnes & Noble, 1915.

*BRIDENBAUGH, CARL. *Cities in the Wilderness: The First Century of Urban Life in America*. New York: Oxford University Press, 1971.

Bibliography

HENRETTA, JAMES. "Economic Development and Social Structure in Colonial Boston." *William and Mary Quarterly*, 3rd ser., vol. 22. January 1965.

HERRICK, CHEESMAN. *White Servitude in Pennsylvania: Indentured and Redemption Labor in Colony and Commonwealth*. Washington, D.C.: Negro University Press, 1926.

HOFSTADTER, RICHARD. *America at 1750: A Social History*. New York: Knopf, 1971.

HOFSTADTER, RICHARD, AND MICHAEL WALLACE, EDS. *American Violence: A Documentary History*. New York: Knopf, 1970.

MOHL, RAYMOND. *Poverty in New York, 1783–1825*. New York: Oxford University Press, 1971.

*MORGAN, EDWARD S. *American Slavery, American Freedom: The Ordeal of Colonial Virginia*. New York: W. W. Norton, 1975.

*MORRIS, RICHARD B. *Government and Labor in Early America*. New York: Harper & Row, 1965.

*NASH, GARY B., ED. *Class and Society in Early America*. Englewood Cliffs, N.J.: Prentice-Hall, 1970.

*———. *Red, White, and Black: The Peoples of Early America*. Englewood Cliffs, N.J.: Prentice-Hall, 1974.

*———. "Social Change and the Growth of Prerevolutionary Urban Radicalism." In *The American Revolution*, ed. Alfred Young. DeKalb: Northern Illinois University Press, 1976.

*SMITH, ABBOT E. *Colonists in Bondage: White Servitude and Convict Labor in America*. New York: W. W. Norton, 1971.

*WASHBURN, WILCOMB E. *The Governor and the Rebel: A History of Bacon's Rebellion in Virginia*. New York: W. W. Norton, 1972.

Chapter 4
Tyranny Is Tyranny

BAILYN, BERNARD, AND N. GARRETT, EDS. *Pamphlets of the American Revolution*. Cambridge, Mass.: Harvard University Press, 1965.

BECKER, CARL. *The Declaration of Independence: A Study in the History of the Political Ideas*. New York: Random House, 1958.

BROWN, RICHARD MAXWELL. "Violence and the American Revolution." In *Essays on the American Revolution*, ed. Stephen G. Kurtz and James H. Hutson. Chapel Hill: University of North Carolina Press, 1973.

COUNTRYMAN, EDWARD. "'Out of the Bounds of the Law': Northern Land Rioters in the Eighteenth Century." In *The American Revolution: Explorations in the History of American Radicalism*, ed. Alfred F. Young. DeKalb: Northern Illinois University Press, 1976.

ERNST, JOSEPH. "'Ideology' and an Economic Interpretation of the Revolution." In *The American Revolution: Explorations in the History of American Radicalism*, ed. Alfred F. Young. DeKalb: Northern Illinois University Press, 1976.

FONER, ERIC. "Tom Paine's Republic: Radical Ideology and Social Change." In *The American Revolution: Explorations in the History of American Radicalism*, ed. Alfred F. Young. DeKalb: Northern Illinois University Press, 1976.

FOX-BOURNE, H. R. *The Life of John Locke*, 2 vols. New York: King, 1876.

GREENE, JACK P. "An Uneasy Connection: An Analysis of the Preconditions of the American Revolution." *Essays on the American Revolution*, ed. Stephen G. Kurtz and James H. Hutson. Chapel Hill: University of North Carolina Press, 1973.

HILL, CHRISTOPHER. *Puritanism and Revolution*. New York: Schocken, 1964.

*HOERDER, DIRK. "Boston Leaders and Boston Crowds, 1765–1776." In *The American Revolution: Explorations in the History of American Radicalism*, ed. Alfred F. Young. DeKalb: Northern Illinois University Press, 1976.

LEMISCH, JESSE. "Jack Tar in the Streets: Merchant Seamen in the Politics of Revolutionary America." *William and Mary Quarterly*. July 1968.

MAIER, PAULINE. *From Resistance to Revolution: Colonial Radicals and the Development of American Opposition to Britain, 1765–1776*. New York: Knopf, 1972.

Chapter 5
A Kind of Revolution

APTHEKER, HERBERT, ED. *A Documentary History of the Negro People in the United States*. New York: Citadel, 1974.

BAILYN, BERNARD. "Central Themes of the Revolution." In *Essays on the American Revolution*, ed. Stephen G. Kurtz and James H. Hutson. Chapel Hill: University of North Carolina Press, 1973.

————. *The Ideological Origins of the American Revolution*. Cambridge, Mass.: Harvard University Press, 1967.

*BEARD, CHARLES. *An Economic Interpretation of the Constitution of the United States*. New York: Macmillan, 1935.

BERLIN, IRA. "The Negro in the American Revolution." In *The American Revolution: Explorations in the History of American Radicalism*, ed. Alfred F. Young. DeKalb: Northern Illinois University Press, 1976.

BERTHOFF, ROWLAND, AND JOHN MURRIN. "Feudalism, Communalism, and the Yeoman Freeholder." In *Essays on the American Revolution*, ed. Stephen G. Kurtz and James H. Hutson. Chapel Hill: University of North Carolina Press, 1973.

BROWN, ROBERT E. *Charles Beard and the Constitution*. New York: W. W. Norton, 1965.

DEGLER, CARL. *Out of Our Past*. New York: Harper & Row, 1970.

HENDERSON, H. JAMES. "The Structure of Politics in the Continental Congress." In *Essays on the American Revolution*, ed. Stephen G. Kurtz and James H. Hutson. Chapel Hill: University of North Carolina Press, 1973.

*HOFFMAN, RONALD. "The 'Disaffected' in the Revolutionary South." In *The American Revolution: Explorations in the History of American Radicalism*, ed. Alfred F. Young. DeKalb: Northern Illinois University Press, 1976.

JENNINGS, FRANCIS. "The Indians' Revolution." In *The American Revolution: Explorations in the History of American Radicalism*, ed. Alfred F. Young. DeKalb: Northern Illinois University Press, 1976.

LEVY, LEONARD W. *Freedom of Speech and Press in Early American History*. New York: Harper & Row, 1962.

*LYND, STAUGHTON. *Anti-Federalism in Dutchess County, New York*. Chicago: Loyola University Press, 1963.

————. *Class Conflict, Slavery, and the Constitution*. Indianapolis: Bobbs-Merrill, 1967.

————. "Freedom Now: The Intellectual Origins of American Radicalism." In *The American Revolution: Explorations in the History of American Radicalism*, ed. Alfred F. Young. DeKalb: Northern Illinois University Press, 1976.

McLOUGHLIN, WILLIAM G. "The Role of Religion in the Revolution." In *Essays on the American Revolution*, ed. Stephen G. Kurtz and James H. Hutson. Chapel Hill: University of North Carolina Press, 1973.

MORGAN, EDMUND S. "Conflict and Consensus in Revolution." In *Essays on the American Revolution*, ed. Stephen G. Kurtz and James H. Hutson. Chapel Hill: University of North Carolina Press, 1973.

MORRIS, RICHARD B. "We the People of the United States." Presidential address, American Historical Association, 1976.

*SHY, JOHN. *A People Numerous and Armed: Reflections on the Military Struggle for American Independence.* New York: Oxford University Press, 1976.

SMITH, PAGE. *A New Age Now Begins: A People's History of the American Revolution.* New York: McGraw-Hill, 1976.

STARKEY, MARION. *A Little Rebellion.* New York: Knopf, 1949.

VAN DOREN, CARL. *Mutiny in January.* New York: Viking, 1943.

*YOUNG, ALFRED F., ED. *The American Revolution: Explorations in the History of American Radicalism.* DeKalb: Northern Illinois University Press, 1976.

Chapter 6
The Intimately Oppressed

BARKER-BENFIELD, G. J. *The Horrors of the Half-Known Life.* New York: Harper & Row, 1976.

*BAXANDALL, ROSALYN, LINDA GORDON, AND SUSAN REVERBY, EDS. *America's Working Women.* New York: Random House, 1976.

*COTT, NANCY. *The Bonds of Womanhood.* New Haven, Conn.: Yale University Press, 1977.

————, ED. *Root of Bitterness.* New York: Dutton, 1972.

FARB, PETER. "The Pueblos of the Southwest." In *Women in American Life*, ed. Anne Scott. Boston: Houghton Mifflin, 1970.

*FLEXNER, ELEANOR. *A Century of Struggle.* Cambridge, Mass.: Harvard University Press, 1975.

GORDON, ANN, AND MARY JO BUHLE. "Sex and Class in Colonial and Nineteenth-Century America." In *Liberating Women's History*, ed. Berenice Carroll. Urbana: University of Illinois Press, 1975.

*LERNER, GERDA, ED. *The Female Experience: An American Documentary.* Indianapolis: Bobbs-Merrill, 1977.

SANDOZ, MARI. "These Were the Sioux." In *Women in American Life*, ed. Anne Scott. Boston: Houghton Mifflin, 1970.

SPRUILL, JULIA CHERRY. *Women's Life and Work in the Southern Colonies.* Chapel Hill: University of North Carolina, 1938.

TYLER, ALICE FELT. *Freedom's Ferment.* Minneapolis: University of Minnesota Press, 1944.

VOGEL, LISE. "Factory Tracts." *Signs: Journal of Women in Culture and Society.* Spring 1976.

WELTER, BARBARA. *Dimity Convictions: The American Woman in the Nineteenth Century.* Athens: Ohio University Press, 1976.

WILSON, JOAN HOFF. "The Illusion of Change: Women in the American Revolution." In *The American Revolution: Explorations in the History of American Radicalism,* ed. Alfred F. Young. DeKalb: Northern Illinois University Press, 1976.

Chapter 7
As Long as Grass Grows or Water Runs

DRINNON, RICHARD. *Violence in the American Experience: Winning the West.* New York: New American Library, 1979.

FILLER, LOUIS E., AND ALLEN GUTTMANN, EDS. *The Removal of the Cherokee Nation.* Huntington, N.Y.: R. E. Krieger, 1977.

FOREMAN, GRANT. *Indian Removal.* Norman: University of Oklahoma Press, 1972.

*MCLUHAN, T. C., ED. *Touch the Earth: A Self-Portrait of Indian Existence.* New York: Simon & Schuster, 1976.

*ROGIN, MICHAEL. *Fathers and Children: Andrew Jackson and the Subjugation of the American Indian.* New York: Knopf, 1975.

*VAN EVERY, DALE. *The Disinherited: The Lost Birthright of the American Indian.* New York: William Morrow, 1976.

VOGEL, VIRGIL, ED. *This Country Was Ours.* New York: Harper & Row, 1972.

Chapter 8
We Take Nothing by Conquest, Thank God

*FONER, PHILIP. *A History of the Labor Movement in the United States,* 4 vols. New York: International Publishers, 1947–1965.

Bibliography

GRAEBNER, NORMAN A. "Empire in the Pacific: A Study in American Continental Expansion." In *The Mexican War: Crisis for American Democracy*, ed. Archie P. McDonald. Lexington, Mass.: D. C. Heath, 1969.

————, ED. *Manifest Destiny*. Indianapolis: Bobbs-Merrill, 1968.

JAY, WILLIAM. *A Review of the Causes and Consequences of the Mexican War*. Boston: B. B. Mussey & Co., 1849.

MCDONALD, ARCHIE P., ED. *The Mexican War: Crisis for American Democracy*. Lexington, Mass.: D. C. Heath, 1969.

MORISON, SAMUEL ELIOT, FREDERICK MERK, AND FRANK FRIEDEL. *Dissent in Three American Wars*. Cambridge, Mass.: Harvard University Press, 1970.

O'SULLIVAN, JOHN, AND ALAN MECKLER. *The Draft and Its Enemies: A Documentary History*. Urbana: University of Illinois Press, 1974.

PERRY, BLISS, ED. *Lincoln: Speeches and Letters*. New York: Doubleday, 1923.

*SCHROEDER, JOHN H. *Mr. Polk's War: American Opposition and Dissent 1846–1848*. Madison: University of Wisconsin Press, 1973.

*SMITH, GEORGE WINSTON, AND CHARLES JUDAH, EDS. *Chronicles of the Gringos: The U.S. Army in the Mexican War 1846–1848*. Albuquerque: University of New Mexico Press, 1966.

*SMITH, JUSTIN. *The War with Mexico*, 2 vols. New York: Macmillan, 1919.

*WEEMS, JOHN EDWARD. *To Conquer a Peace*. New York: Doubleday, 1974.

WEINBERG, ALBERT K. *Manifest Destiny: A Study of Nationalist Expansion in American History*. Baltimore: Johns Hopkins Press, 1935.

Chapter 9
Slavery Without Submission, Emancipation Without Freedom

ALLEN, ROBERT. *The Reluctant Reformers*. New York: Anchor, 1975.

*APTHEKER, HERBERT. *American Negro Slave Revolts*. New York: International Publishers, 1969.

*————, ED. *A Documentary History of the Negro People in the United States*. New York: Citadel, 1974.

————. *Nat Turner's Slave Rebellion*. New York: Grove Press, 1968.

BOND, HORACE MANN. "Social and Economic Forces in Alabama Reconstruction." *Journal of Negro History.* July 1938.

CONRAD, EARL. *Harriet Tubman.* Middlebury, Vt.: Eriksson, 1970.

COX, LAWANDA AND JOHN, EDS. *Reconstruction, the Negro, and the Old South.* New York: Harper & Row, 1973.

DOUGLASS, FREDERICK. *Narrative of the Life of Frederick Douglass,* ed. Benjamin Quarles. Cambridge, Mass.: Harvard University Press, 1960.

DU BOIS, W. E. B. *John Brown.* New York: International Publishers, 1962.

FOGEL, ROBERT, AND STANLEY ENGERMAN. *Time on the Cross: The Economics of American Negro Slavery.* Boston: Little, Brown, 1974.

FONER, PHILIP, ED. *The Life and Writings of Frederick Douglass.* 5 vols. New York: International Publishers, 1975.

*FRANKLIN, JOHN HOPE. *From Slavery to Freedom.* New York: Knopf, 1974.

*GENOVESE, EUGENE. *Roll, Jordan, Roll: The World the Slaves Made.* New York: Pantheon, 1974.

*GUTMAN, HERBERT. *The Black Family in Slavery and Freedom, 1750–1925.* New York: Pantheon, 1976.

———. *Slavery and the Numbers Game: A Critique of "Time on the Cross."* Urbana: University of Illinois Press, 1975.

HERSCHFIELD, MARILYN. "Women in the Civil War." Unpublished paper, 1977.

*HOFSTADTER, RICHARD. *The American Political Tradition.* New York: Knopf, 1973.

KILLENS, JOHN O., ED. *The Trial Record of Denmark Vesey.* Boston: Beacon Press, 1970.

KOLCHIN, PETER. *First Freedom: The Response of Alabama's Blacks to Emancipation and Reconstruction.* New York: Greenwood, 1972.

*LERNER, GERDA, ED. *Black Women in White America: A Documentary History.* New York: Random House, 1973.

LESTER, JULIUS, ED. *To Be a Slave.* New York: Dial Press, 1968.

*LEVINE, LAWRENCE J. *Black Culture and Black Consciousness: Afro-American Folk Thought from Slavery to Freedom.* New York: Oxford University Press, 1977.

*LOGAN, RAYFORD. *The Betrayal of the Negro: From Rutherford B. Hayes to Woodrow Wilson.* New York: Macmillan, 1965.

*MACPHERSON, JAMES. *The Negro's Civil War.* New York: Pantheon, 1965.

*———. *The Struggle for Equality.* Princeton, N.J.: Princeton University Press, 1964.

Bibliography

*MELTZER, MILTON, ED. *In Their Own Words: A History of the American Negro.* New York: T. Y. Crowell, 1964–1967.

MULLIN, MICHAEL, ED. *American Negro Slavery: A Documentary History.* New York: Harper & Row, 1975.

OSOFSKY, GILBERT. *Puttin' On Ole Massa.* New York: Harper & Row, 1969.

PAINTER, NELL IRVIN. *Exodusters: Black Migration to Kansas After Reconstruction.* New York: Knopf, 1977.

PHILLIPS, ULRICH B. *American Negro Slavery: A Survey of the Supply, Employment and Control of Negro Labor as Determined by the Plantation Regime.* Baton Rouge: Louisiana State University Press, 1966.

RAWICK, GEORGE P. *From Sundown to Sunup: The Making of the Black Community.* Westport, Conn.: Greenwood Press, 1972.

*ROSENGARTEN, THEODORE. *All God's Dangers: The Life of Nate Shaw.* New York: Knopf, 1974.

STAROBIN, ROBERT S., ED. *Blacks in Bondage: Letters of American Slaves.* New York: Franklin Watts, 1974.

TRAGLE, HENRY I. *The Southmapton Slave Revolt of 1831.* Amherst: University of Massachusetts Press, 1971.

WILTSE, CHARLES M., ED. *David Walker's Appeal.* New York: Hill & Wang, 1965.

*WOODWARD, C. VANN. *Reunion and Reaction: The Compromise of 1877 and the End of Reconstruction.* Boston: Little, Brown, 1966.

WORKS PROGRESS ADMINISTRATION. *The Negro in Virginia.* New York: Arno Press, 1969.

Chapter 10
The Other Civil War

BIMBA, ANTHONY. *The Molly Maguires.* New York: International Publishers, 1970.

BRECHER, JEREMY. *Strike!* Boston: South End Press, 1979.

*BRUCE, ROBERT V. *1877: Year of Violence.* New York: Franklin Watts, 1959.

BURBANK, DAVID. *Reign of Rabble: The St. Louis General Strike of 1877.* Fairfield, N.J.: Augustus Kelley, 1966.

*CHRISTMAN, HENRY. *Tin Horns and Calico.* New York: Holt, Rinehart & Winston, 1945.

*Cochran, Thomas, and William Miller. *The Age of Enterprise.* New York: Macmillan, 1942.

Coulter, E. Merton. *The Confederate States of America 1861–1865.* Baton Rouge: Louisiana State University Press, 1950.

Dacus, Joseph A. "Annals of the Great Strikes of the United States." In *Except to Walk Free: Documents and Notes in the History of American Labor,* ed. Albert Fried. New York: Anchor, 1974.

*Dawley, Alan. *Class and Community: The Industrial Revolution in Lynn.* Cambridge, Mass.: Harvard University Press, 1976.

*Feldstein, Stanley, and Lawrence Costello, eds. *The Ordeal of Assimilation: A Documentary History of the White Working Class, 1830's to the 1970's.* New York: Anchor, 1974.

Fite, Emerson. *Social and Industrial Conditions in the North During the Civil War.* New York: Macmillan, 1910.

*Foner, Philip. *A History of the Labor Movement in the United States,* 4 vols. New York: International Publishers, 1947–1964.

*———, ed. *We, the Other People.* Urbana: University of Illinois Press, 1976.

Fried, Albert, ed. *Except to Walk Free: Documents and Notes in the History of American Labor.* New York: Anchor, 1974.

*Gettleman, Marvin. *The Dorr Rebellion.* New York: Random House, 1973.

Gutman, Herbert. "The Buena Vista Affair, 1874–1875. In *Workers in the Industrial Revolution: Recent Studies of Labor in the United States and Europe,* ed. Peter N. Stearns and Daniel Walkowitz. New Brunswick, N.J.: Transaction, 1974.

———. *Work, Culture and Society in Industrializing America.* New York: Random House, 1977.

———. "Work, Culture and Society in Industrializing America, 1815–1919." *American Historical Review.* June 1973.

Headley, Joel Tyler. *The Great Riots of New York, 1712–1873.* Indianapolis: Bobbs-Merrill, 1970.

*Hofstadter, Richard, and Michael Wallace, eds. *American Violence: A Documentary History.* New York: Knopf, 1970.

*Horwitz, Morton. *The Transformation of American Law, 1780–1860.* Cambridge, Mass.: Harvard University Press, 1977.

Knights, Peter R. *The Plain People of Boston 1830–1860: A Study in City Growth.* New York: Oxford University Press, 1973.

Meyer, Marvin. *The Jacksonian Persuasion.* New York: Vintage, 1960.

Miller, Douglas T. *The Birth of Modern America.* Indianapolis: Bobbs-Merrill, 1970.

Bibliography

MONTGOMERY, DAVID. "The Shuttle and the Cross: Weavers and Artisans in the Kensington Riots of 1844." *Journal of Social History.* Summer 1972.

*MYERS, GUSTAVUS. *History of the Great American Fortunes.* New York: Modern Library, 1936.

PESSEN, EDWARD. *Jacksonian America.* Homewood, Ill.: Dorsey, 1969.

———. *Most Uncommon Jacksonians.* Albany: State University of New York Press, 1967.

REMINI, ROBERT V. *The Age of Jackson.* New York: Harper & Row, 1972.

SCHLESINGER, ARTHUR M., JR. *The Age of Jackson.* Boston: Little, Brown, 1945.

STEARNS, PETER N., AND DANIEL WALKOWITZ, EDS. *Workers in the Industrial Revolution: Recent Studies of Labor in the United States and Europe.* New Brunswick, N.J.: Transaction, 1974.

TATUM, GEORGIA LEE. *Disloyalty in the Confederacy.* New York: A.M.S. Press, 1970.

*WERTHEIMER, BARBARA. *We Were There: The Story of Working Women in America.* New York: Pantheon, 1977.

WILSON, EDMUND. *Patriotic Gore: Studies in the Literature of the American Civil War.* New York: Oxford University Press, 1962.

YELLEN, SAMUEL. *American Labor Struggles.* New York: Pathfinder, 1974.

ZINN, HOWARD. "The Conspiracy of Law." In *The Rule of Law*, ed. Robert Paul Wolff. New York: Simon & Schuster, 1971.

Chapter 11
Robber Barons and Rebels

ALLEN, ROBERT. *Reluctant Reformers: Racism and Social Reform Movements in the United States.* New York: Anchor, 1975.

BELLAMY, EDWARD. *Looking Backward.* Cambridge, Mass.: Harvard University Press, 1967.

BOWLES, SAMUEL, AND HERBERT GINTIS. *Schooling in Capitalist America.* New York: Basic Books, 1976.

BRANDEIS, LOUIS. *Other People's Money.* New York: Frederick Stokes, 1914.

BRECHER, JEREMY. *Strike!* Boston: South End Press, 1979.

Bibliography

CARWARDINE, WILLIAM. *The Pullman Strike*. Chicago: Charles Kerr, 1973.

*COCHRAN, THOMAS, AND WILLIAM MILLER. *The Age of Enterprise*. New York: Macmillan, 1942.

CONWELL, RUSSELL H. *Acres of Diamonds*. New York: Harper & Row, 1915.

CROWE, CHARLES. "Tom Watson, Populists, and Blacks Reconsidered." *Journal of Negro History*. April 1970.

DAVID, HENRY. *A History of the Haymarket Affair*. New York: Collier, 1963.

FELDSTEIN, STANLEY, AND LAWRENCE COSTELLO, EDS. *The Ordeal of Assimilation: A Documentary History of the White Working Class, 1830's to the 1970's*. New York: Anchor, 1974.

*FONER, PHILIP. *A History of the Labor Movement in the United States*, 4 vols. New York: International Publishers, 1947–1964.

————. *Organized Labor and the Black Worker 1619–1973*. New York: International Publishers, 1974.

GEORGE, HENRY. *Progress and Poverty*. New York: Robert Scholkenbach Foundation, 1937.

GINGER, RAY, *The Age of Excess: The U.S. from 1877 to 1914*. New York: Macmillan, 1975.

*————. *The Bending Cross: A Biography of Eugene Victor Debs*. New Brunswick, N.J.: Rutgers University Press, 1949.

*GOODWYN, LAWRENCE. *Democratic Promise: The Populist Movement in America*. New York: Oxford University Press, 1976.

HAIR, WILLIAM IVY. *Bourbonism and Agrarian Protest: Louisiana Politics, 1877–1900*. Baton Rouge: Louisiana State University Press, 1969.

HEILBRONER, ROBERT, AND AARON SINGER. *The Economic Transformation of America*. New York: Harcourt Brace Jovanovich, 1977.

HOFSTADTER, RICHARD, AND MICHAEL WALLACE, EDS. *American Violence: A Documentary History*. New York: Knopf, 1970.

*JOSEPHSON, MATTHEW. *The Politicos*. New York: Harcourt Brace Jovanovich, 1963.

*————. *The Robber Barons*. New York: Harcourt Brace Jovanovich, 1962.

MASON, ALPHEUS T., AND WILLIAM M. BEANEY. *American Constitutional Law*. Englewood Cliffs, N.J.: Prentice-Hall, 1972.

*MYERS, GUSTAVUS. *History of the Great American Fortunes*. New York: Modern Library, 1936.

PIERCE, BESSIE L. *Public Opinion and the Teaching of History in the United States.* New York: DaCapo, 1970.

POLLACK, NORMAN. *The Populist Response to Industrial America.* Cambridge, Mass.: Harvard University Press, 1976.

SMITH, HENRY NASH. *Virgin Land.* Cambridge, Mass.: Harvard University Press, 1970.

SPRING, JOEL H. *Education and the Rise of the Corporate State.* Boston: Beacon Press, 1973.

WASSERMAN, HARVEY. *Harvey Wasserman's History of the United States.* New York: Harper & Row, 1972.

*WERTHEIMER, BARBARA. *We Were There: The Story of Working Women in America.* New York: Pantheon, 1977.

*WOODWARD, C. VANN. *Origins of the New South.* Baton Rouge: Louisiana State University Press, 1972.

*———. *Tom Watson, Agrarian Rebel.* New York: Oxford University Press, 1963.

*YELLEN, SAMUEL. *American Labor Struggles.* New York: Pathfinder, 1974.

Index

Books of related interest
from The New Press

MALAIKA ADERO
Up South: Stories, Studies, and Letters
of This Century's African American Migrations
(PB, $12.95, 1-56584-168-9, 240 PP.)
Primary sources from the greatest migration in American history.

IRA BERLIN AND LESLIE S. ROWLAND, EDITORS
Families and Freedom: A Documentary History
of African American Kinship in the Civil War Era
(PB, $16.95, 1-56584-440-8, 304 PP.)
A sequel to the award-winning *Free at Last*, moving letters from freed
slaves to their families.

IRA BERLIN AND BARBARA J. FIELDS, ET AL.
Free at Last: A Documentary History
of Slavery, Freedom, and the Civil War
(PB, $16.95, 1-56584-120-4, 608 PP.)
A winner of the 1994 Lincoln Prize, some of the most remarkable and
moving letters ever written by Americans, depicting the drama of
Emancipation in the midst of the nation's bloodiest conflict.

AMERICAN SOCIAL HISTORY PROJECT
Freedom's Unfinished Revolution:
An Inquiry into the Civil War and Reconstruction
(PB, $19.95, 1-56584-198-0, 320 PP.)
From the award-winning authors of *Who Built America?*,
a groundbreaking high school level presentation of the Civil War and
Reconstruction.

IRA BERLIN
Slaves Without Masters: The Free Negro in the Antebellum South
(PB, $16.95, 1-56584-028-3, 448 PP.)
A vivid and moving history of the quarter of a million free blacks who
lived in the South before the Civil War.

JAMES W. LOEWEN
Lies My Teacher Told Me:
Everything Your American History Textbook Got Wrong
(HC, $24.95, 1-56584-100-X, 384 PP.)
The best-selling, award-winning, iconoclastic look at the errors, misrepresentations, and omissions in the leading American history textbooks.

JAMES W. LOEWEN
The Truth About Columbus: A Subversively True Poster Book
for a Dubiously Celebratory Occasion
(PB WITH POSTER, $14.95, 1-56584-008-9, 48 PP.)
A provocative educational poster and booklet that draws on recent scholarship to debunk the myths and discover the man.

STEPHEN J. ROSE
Social Stratification in the United States 2000:
The New American Profile Poster
(PB WITH POSTER, $18.95, 1-56584-550-1, 48 PP.)
A graphic presentation of the distribution of wealth in America.

VIRGINIA YANS-MCLAUGHLIN, MARJORIE LIGHTMAN,
AND THE STATUE OF LIBERTY-ELLIS ISLAND FOUNDATION
Ellis Island and the Peopling of America: The Official Guide
(PB, $19.95, 1-56584-364-9, 224 PP.)
A primary source reader and resource guide to Ellis Island and issues of immigration.

HOWARD ZINN AND GEORGE KIRSCHNER
A People's History of the United States: The Wall Charts
(PORTFOLIO, $25.00, 1-56584-171-9, 48-PAGE BOOKLET
WITH TWO POSTERS)
Two oversized posters based on Zinn's best-selling social history.

To Order, call 1-800-233-4830
www.thenewpress.com